SOUTH UIST

ARCHAEOLOGY AND HISTORY OF
A HEBRIDEAN ISLAND

D1556560

SOUTH UIST

ARCHAEOLOGY AND HISTORY OF
A HEBRIDEAN ISLAND

MIKE PARKER PEARSON,
NIALL SHARPLES AND JIM SYMONDS

with contributions by
Jacqui Mulville, John Raven, Helen Smith and Alex Woolf

TEMPUS

First published 2004

Tempus Publishing Ltd
The Mill, Brimscombe Port
Stroud, Gloucestershire GL5 2QG
www.tempus-publishing.com

British Library Cataloguing in Publication Data.
A catalogue record for this book is available from the British Library.

ISBN 0 7524 2905 1
Typesetting and origination by Tempus Publishing.
Printed and bound in Great Britain.

CONTENTS

CHAPTER 1

INTRODUCTION
An Island Archaeology

A small Scottish island with few claims to fame, South Uist has no whisky, no tweed, no impressive mountains and no world-famous megalithic monuments, and yet it has its place in history. Its most celebrated inhabitant was Flora Macdonald, the Scottish heroine who delivered Bonny Prince Charlie from the redcoats and over the sea to Skye after the failure of the 45.

Most people have also heard the story of the SS *Politician* which went aground in 1941 in the narrow strait between South Uist and the little island of Eriskay which lies off its south-eastern tip. The tale of how the islanders salvaged and secreted the ship's cargo of whisky bound for America was retold in the film based on Compton Mackenzie's book *Whisky Galore*, but the reality of the punishment inflicted on the island's men is rarely mentioned. Several spent a short spell in a mainland prison for their unwillingness to deliver up the cargo. Other readers may know of the Eriskay ponies, one of Britain's miniature breeds, sturdy little creatures adapted like Shetland ponies to the harsh environment of these northern islands. Werner Kissling's famous film *A Poem of Remote Lives* shows us life on Eriskay in 1934, and his many photographs of South Uist preserve the memory of a way of life now vanished and a landscape that has changed very little.

South Uist was also the setting for a second, less well-known book by Mackenzie, *Rockets Galore*, about the building of a rocket range at the north end of the island in 1957. Initial hostility to the building of the range and to the construction of an army base on the adjacent island of Benbecula soon faded and today, in these times of cuts in defence spending, South Uist struggles to retain the much-needed jobs on the rocket range. There are few ways to make a livelihood here, with fishing, crofting, salmon farming and a small tourist industry being the sources of income for many islanders.

Most recently, South Uist hit the headlines with its hedgehog crisis – the ground-nesting birds of the Uists are being decimated by the multitudinous offspring of two hedgehogs introduced in 1974 and plans to exterminate or expel the prickly aliens have led to protests from across the rest of Britain.

South Uist is one of Britain's smaller islands. It lies off the north-west coast of mainland Scotland, towards the southern end of the island chain of the Western Isles (known to geographers as the Outer Hebrides). At the north end of the Western Isles are Lewis and Harris. South of them are the Uists – North Uist, Benbecula in the middle and then South Uist. South of South Uist lie Barra and several now uninhabited islets. The island chain is separated from the islands of the Inner Hebrides and the Scottish mainland by the Minch, a channel of deep water 14 miles wide. South Uist can be seen from Skye, from the top of the Cuillins, but most tourists never make the short ferry crossing from Skye to these seemingly remote islands.

As we shall see, the Uists were once a single island and, even after their separation by the force of the sea, were still considered in the historical period to be a single entity, called Vyist by Donald Munroe, High Dean of the Isles, in 1549. The dangerous tidal crossings and fords between North Uist, Benbecula and South Uist were replaced by concrete causeways many years ago, and today new causeways join the Uists to the outlying islands of Eriskay in the south and Berneray in the north.

Geologically, the islands consist of a bedrock of Lewisian gneiss (pronounced 'nice'), one of the oldest rocks in the world, and its glaciated surface gives them a harsh appearance *(1)* which is very different to the rolling landscape of Orkney, off the northern tip of Scotland. Here, as in Orkney, ample supplies of stone within an increasingly treeless landscape provided the materials for building prehistoric tombs, stone circles and the great round

1 The gneiss bedrock is a metamorphic granite and is one of the oldest of the earth's rocks

2 Setting off to survey around the edges of a freshwater loch in the early days of the SEARCH project

towers known as brochs, but the gneiss is a difficult rock to cleave and work, unlike the sandstones of Orkney and Shetland, and the monuments of the Western Isles often appear less well made than their counterparts in the Northern Isles.

South Uist is 22 miles long and 10 miles wide. The west coast is relatively straight, with three major promontories and a single island. The east coast is steep and rocky, cut by fjord-like sea lochs, with a fringe of many small islands and islets. Anyone looking at an Ordnance Survey map of South Uist for the first time will be astounded by the number of small freshwater lochs *(2)* that cover the island and give it the appearance of being made up as much by water as by dry land. The land surface is mostly rock and bog, with grassland along the west coast.

The island's physical character, like an easy geography lesson, is divided longitudinally into three. On the east coast are the mountains and hills, covered in blanket bog, which sweep down to a deep-water coastline. The waters of the west coast are very shallow and fetch up against a 1km-wide stretch of sandy plain and dunes *(3)* whose springy grassland is known as machair *(colour plate 1)*. This sand has formed largely from crushed seashells and is alkaline, unlike the quartz sands found in the rest of the British Isles. Between mountains and machair are the 'blacklands'. These have thin and acidic soil, formed from peat. At the interface between the machair and the peat, the acid black soil mixes with the alkaline shell sand, forming a fertile strip of land.

3 The shell sand beaches of South Uist

Today, one can walk a long way to find a tree on South Uist. There are a handful of very small conifer plantations on the Uists but otherwise one sees only a few pockets of small trees and shrubs growing on small islets within freshwater lochs, out of reach of the sheep, or in certain secluded spots on the east side. One of these is Loch Druidibeg in the middle of the island, where rhododendrons grow together with native species around the loch's edge. Heather and similar species are the ubiquitous plants of the hills and mountains and of much of the peatlands as well.

The wildlife is one of the great draws for visitors. Puffins no longer nest on the island but South Uist is still a birdwatchers' paradise, with an array of other sea birds and rare species such as corncrakes and golden eagles. Seals, dolphins and – on the east coast – killer whales are the most abundant sea mammals today but there are occasional strandings of even bigger cetaceans. Red deer roam the hillsides and mountain moorlands. Otters hunt both in the sea and in fresh water, and can be seen running across the machair from the lochs to the seashore. Mink that have escaped into the wild and polecats feed off the growing legions of rabbits that live in burrows on the machair. The creature that can have people running and screaming throughout the Scottish highlands and islands is the midge, which in summer swarms the length of the east side of the island. Here the sheep tick also lies in wait in the heather, where it will attach itself to the legs of passing walkers. Fortunately, there is no habitat for ticks on the west coast, and for most of the summer there are no midges on the dry machair.

The usual weather warnings for Scottish islands apply. High winds and heavy rain can make this a challenging environment in which to work or travel. The warming effect of the Gulf Stream, however, keeps winter temperatures at reasonable levels and snow is never deep or long-lasting. Summer days can be outstanding – serious sunburn and even sunstroke can afflict the unwary. The changeable quality of the weather is, of course, a feature of daily life: 'if there's any weather to be had, we'll be bound to get it'. Within hours a heavenly summer's day of white beaches, aquamarine seas and purple-headed mountains shimmering with heat haze can be transformed to the back end of hell in the form of pouring rain, low clouds and greyness all around.

ISLAND ARCHAEOLOGY

The great thing about islands is that they have nice sharp edges *(4)*. There is absolutely no doubt as to where their boundaries are and so the researcher can confidently define a study area that leaves no ambiguities. Islands are self-defined regions and have often been considered as 'laboratories of culture change', the nearest the archaeologist can get to putting a human community into an isolated setting in order to see what they do over several thousand years.

Yet there are problems with such assumptions. Island landforms can change dramatically through time. As noted above, South Uist was part of a much bigger island for much of human prehistory. Even when it did become separated from Benbecula and North Uist, it was still considered conceptually, at least by some people, as part of that composite known as Uist. Just as no man is an island so, in a metaphorical way, no island is an island. South Uist's past is intricately bound up with the rest of the Uists, with the Western Isles as a whole, with western and northern Scotland, with the Northern Isles and the north Atlantic, with Scandinavia, Ireland and England.

This may cause no small concern for keen researchers who see the boundaries of their study area disappearing off in all directions over the horizon. How can one maintain the integrity of an island study area when its inhabitants are bound by invisible chains into a dense network of social and economic relationships that stretch around the globe? Of course, the answer is simple. The island and its people can only be studied in relation to that outside world. Moving between the local scale and the global, between the specific and the general, between institutions and individual acts, is at the heart of the enterprise.

Islands can be paradoxical places. On the one hand they are out-of-the-way backwaters where people lead remote lives. On the other they are the nodes through which seafaring communities come together and communicate. How can these two aspects be reconciled?

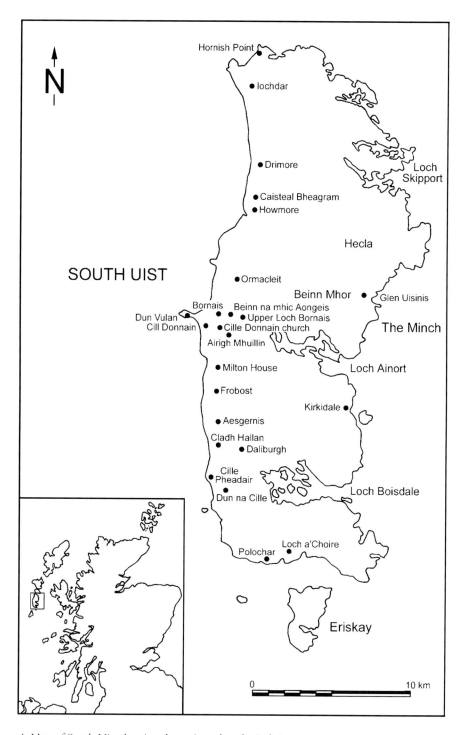

Hornish Point

●Iochdar

Loch
Skipport

●Drimore

●Caisteal Bheagram
●Howmore

Hecla

SOUTH UIST

●Ormacleit

Beinn Mhor ● Glen Uisinis

Bornais Beinn na mhic Aongeis
Dun Vulan ●Upper Loch Bornais
Cill Donnain ●Cille Donnain church

The Minch

Airigh Mhuillin

●Milton House

Loch Ainort

●Frobost

Kirkidale ●

●Aesgernis

Cladh Hallan
●Daliburgh

Cille
●Pheadair
●Dun na Cille

Loch Boisdale

Loch a'Choire
●Polochar

Eriskay

0   10 km

4 Map of South Uist showing the main archaeological sites

The modern-day perspective is generally that of the landlubber. Motorways and fast roads (not to mention aeroplanes) let us travel far more quickly than is possible by boat or ship. The sea, for us, is a barrier to be crossed and yet it is not so very long ago, just a couple of centuries, that water offered the fastest means of travelling any great distance. To go from London to Edinburgh by boat was quicker and more comfortable than riding or by coach. For those without horse transport, there was simply no contest. It is an interesting exercise to imagine a travel time-map comparing, say, walking time with sailing time. Distances across land increase whilst those across sea shrink: places that seemed far away across the sea become closer.

If South Uist is placed at the centre of that map based on journey times, then travelling to Ireland is a matter of just a few days' sail. Likewise, the Northern Isles of Orkney and Shetland are only a few more days away. To travel to even the English coast or the Isle of Man involves no insuperable voyage. The west coast of Scotland has been one of the principal thorough-fares of the north Atlantic ever since reasonably seaworthy craft were in use – probably from the Neolithic onwards. Within such a setting, the most important links for South Uist and the Western Isles in prehistory and early historic times were more probably made up and down this sea road rather than laterally, deep into mainland Scotland.

This high degree of connection to the greater world across the sea permits islands to develop long-distance trading networks, together with the flip side of commerce – raiding and feuding. Island alliances have formed powerful confederations in many times and many places, from the Mediterranean world of the Athenian empire in the later centuries BC, to the Pacific Ocean and the Lapita culture whose remains are found throughout much of Polynesia, and the Lordship of the Isles in the medieval period. Even very small islands can support the development of great states, as happened in the Greek islands known as the Cyclades during the Bronze Age, but only if the technology of sea travel can reduce sailing times and as long as the islands' landmass can provide sufficient food and wealth to maintain suitably large populations. Islands may be places of innovation – as we see on the tiny islands of Orkney during the Neolithic period – from which new ways of living, and new archi-tectural and artefactual forms, eventually reach the mainland.

Yet other, more bizarre social practices can be fostered in island settings. The Easter Island syndrome is a good way of describing the excessive building schemes that can take over an island population's self-identity. The large, elaborate Neolithic tombs in Orkney and on Arran, churches on the mid-Atlantic islands of the Azores and perhaps brochs in Atlantic Scotland can all be considered in such terms. Isolation is generally not something imposed from outside but comes from within, fostered by an island community's sense of identity. In the case of Easter Island, extreme isolation stemmed from the inhabitants' impact on their fragile environ-ment: felling of all the trees prevented the islanders from ever building boats again.

Islands are also settings for fatal encounters with the outside world. The diseases brought by European sailors decimated Easter Island's population. The chiefdoms of Hawaii collapsed after European arrival. In his influential book *Islands in History*, the anthropologist Marshall Sahlins describes the extraordinary cultural misunderstanding behind Captain Cook's death. Cook arrived in Hawaii in 1779 during the annual four-month Makahiki festival when the chiefs and their god Ku went into hiding. This fortuitous timing led to his being identified as the god Lono, and he was greeted rapturously by 10,000 people. At the end of Makahiki, Lono is symbolically driven off by Ku and the rule of the chiefs is restored for the next eight months. Lono should not be seen again until the following year. Cook left Hawaii shortly after the festival ended but came back seven days later with a broken mast. After three days of rumbling conflict, Cook came ashore with armed marines to take the king hostage and was killed on the beach.

There is no doubt that island communities develop a strong sense of common identity in opposition to the outside world, an identity which is created not just out of close personal contacts on a daily basis but is also reinforced by voyaging away from home, in circumstances where that identity and sense of difference may be brought into sharp focus. Island identities can also provide strength to resist nation-state ideologies, as generations of Scottish kings found when trying to bend the Lordship of the Isles to their way of thinking.

Island living sometimes creates 'island mentalities', when islands really are islands. The outside world can be perceived as something to be resisted, and collective solace can be sought in maintaining traditions in contrast to a greater world which embraces change. Communities that perceive themselves under threat from outside often drop their heaviest cultural anchors, as anthropologist Anthony Cohen puts it. Retreat into the traditions of the past may seem to be the best strategy when the uncertainty of the world around becomes too great. And yet there are also moments of change, as well as acceptance of the novelties and innovations that the outside world has to offer. The two aspects may run hand in hand: we can consider the religious community of the Amish of North America as an 'island culture' in that they reject many aspects of the outside world, and yet their traditional avoidance of mechanical forms of power sits side by side with young Amish men taking to rollerblading.

All in all, islands raise interesting issues about identity, isolation, connectivity, power and resources. It is wrong to see them as 'laboratories of culture change' but comparison between their indigenous developments and those of the outside, mainland communities is worthwhile and revealing. Islands are fascinating places.

ARCHAEOLOGICAL RESEARCH ON SOUTH UIST

The first archaeological surveying on South Uist was conducted in the mid-nineteenth century by Captain Frederick Thomas, a naval officer who carried out the hydrographic survey of the Western Isles with a colleague named Captain Otter. In 1870 and 1890 Captain Thomas published descriptions of some of the archaeological monuments of South Uist, with plans of sites such as the Iron Age wheelhouse (roundhouse) and its souterrain (underground passage) in Glen Usinis and the large Iron Age broch of Dun Mhor in Geirinis.★

By the turn of the century a gentleman archaeologist, Erskine Beveridge, was conducting a single-handed excavation programme and survey of North Uist, and his results have recently been reprinted. The Ordnance Survey's first map of 1881 includes a number of archaeological sites but otherwise South Uist received no further coverage until the visit of a Mr J. Wedderspoon, who communicated his findings of sites and artefacts along the machair to the Inverness Scientific Society and Field Club in 1912. Amongst other things, he had observed crofters demolishing what seems to have been a complete Iron Age wheelhouse, missing only its roof, and a number of roundhouses in order to build the walls of Cladh Hallan (Hallan cemetery on Dalabrog machair).

The Royal Commission on Ancient and Historical Monuments for Scotland has the duty of compiling inventories of archaeological sites throughout the nation and, during the First World War, a survey team had the lucky task of working in the Outer Hebrides rather than facing possible death in Flanders. Based in Lochboisdale (Lochbaghasadal), the men spent many weeks trekking the hills with local guides to observe and record the antiquities. One can picture them dressed in their ties and Norfolk jackets, struggling through bogs and deep heather to distant cairns or wading out to crannogs and duns in shallow lochs. On their longer forays they must have stayed in Hebridean 'blackhouses' (the traditional houses built following an architectural style which had changed little for several hundred years) and thus have come to learn much about the island way of life.

By all accounts the Royal Commission survey team had an enjoyable time fishing as well as walking. Perhaps rather too much time was spent fishing – when the results of their work were published in 1928, the volume was a little thin on detail and vast sections of the island, particularly the machair, were largely ignored. We must not judge them too harshly though: it was a very difficult landscape in which to work without motor transport or any of the facilities that archaeologists today take for granted. And, of course, had their job been done too well, what would have been left for others to discover later?

★Today's place names are almost entirely in Gaelic, even though many are actually Norse in origin. We have tended to follow the Gaelic spelling, with a few exceptions. A glossary at the end of this book gives English-language equivalents of the Gaelic names.

5 Werner Kissling on his yacht off Eriskay

After the Second World War, a charismatic German named Werner Kissling captivated the people of South Uist. He had been a diplomat based in London but, not liking the mood of German politics with the rise of the Nazis, changed sides in 1931. He became an avid folklorist and ethnographer of life in the Western Isles and his remarkable story is told in two recent books by Michael Russell, *A Poem of Remote Lives* and *A Different Country*. After Kissling had been interned on the Isle of Man with other Germans during the war, he spent many summers on South Uist *(5)* and is fondly remembered today for teaching the children to swim, encouraging sports and athletics, and bringing his boundless energy and enthusiasm to all.

Kissling had struck up an acquaintance with a Cambridge archaeologist, Tom Lethbridge and his wife, who spent holidays sailing around South Uist on their yacht. Lethbridge and Kissling installed themselves in the Lochboisdale Hotel and set out to find archaeological sites on the machair to the west of Lochboisdale. In 1950 Kissling and Lethbridge carried out the first archaeological excavation on the island. They wanted to dig into a sand dune on the machair at Cille Pheadair which they believed was not a natural feature created by the wind, but a man-made mound covering the traces of an ancient settlement. The crofter was naturally concerned that such an excavation could result in a disastrous sand blow-out once the turf was cut away. He refused them permission but, undismayed, they asked his neighbour, who was happy for them to dig into a smaller mound. Like many other machair mounds, this was known in tales as a place of the fairies (*sithean*) and, in the very dry early summer, the parching of the grass on the surface of the mound indicated the presence beneath of three circular buildings.

Kissling and Lethbridge recruited a supervisor from Skye, John Robertson, and hired a gang of local labourers. Driving out each morning from Lochboisdale in their large car, they supervised the shovelling-out of one of the three circular buildings within the mound *(6)* . It was a wheelhouse, only the second ever to have been found and recorded on South Uist and, amazingly, it was also completely intact apart from its roof. Wheelhouses had previously been excavated by Beveridge on North Uist and so this was no surprise to Kissling and Lethbridge.

Circular stone buildings which look like a spoked wheel in plan, wheelhouses have six or more stone piers which project from the walls towards the centre of the house, leaving an open area around a central hearth. Wheelhouses are a Western Isles tradition, found nowhere else except Shetland, and were built during the Iron Age, about 2,000 years ago. In sandy sites, such as the

6 The Cille Pheadair (Kilpheder) wheelhouse under excavation in 1950

South Uist machair, the wheelhouses were constructed with most of their structure below ground – a large circular pit dug into the sand was lined with thick drystone walls revetted into the soil.

Kissling and Lethbridge's team found a small passage leading off from the southwest side of the Cille Pheadair wheelhouse and, the next summer, they returned to dig out the small circular back room at the end of the passage. This was a magnificent example of an Iron Age house and it was left open for people to see. Plans to point the stonework with mortar were scuppered when the Ministry of Public Buildings and Works declared that this drystone structure should not receive this kind of unsympathetic treatment, out of character with its original mode of construction. The piers eventually fell down and the structure now lies in ruins.

In the late 1950s South Uist was the scene of the biggest archaeological project ever mounted in Scotland. Archaeologists were recruited from across the nation to rescue a section of machair landscape that was about to be buried beneath the proposed rocket range. A survey identified a dozen sites at risk and the more impressive of these settlement mounds were selected for excavation. Horace Fairhurst excavated one wheelhouse – A'Cheardach Bheag ('the little smithy') – and Alison Young dug another, A'Cheardach Mhor ('the big smithy'). Alastair MacLaren excavated a large Viking Age longhouse at Drimore whilst, to the south of him, Jack Scott investigated some hut circles. Further away, on North Uist, Richard Atkinson – later famous for his excavations at Stonehenge and Silbury Hill – excavated a pair of wheelhouses at Sollas.

The project promised so much – a combined landscape investigation on the machair – but in the end each site was published separately, with no overview or integrated research strategy. Nonetheless, it was a major undertaking and provided a firm basis for further research. The archaeologists were required by the Ministry of Defence to tear down any standing structures, so all the stone walls of the prehistoric houses that they had found were destroyed. Ironically, the MoD then changed its plans and decided that it would construct the range and its buildings slightly further to the north, at Geirinis.

During the 1960s a freelance archaeologist, Iain Crawford, began an extra-ordinary project. He started to excavate a complete sequence of North Uist's ancient past, preserved within three settlement mounds at the Udal on the northern tip of that island. The first mound that he tackled was a township (village or *baile*) which had been abandoned in the great storm of 1697. The mound was 8m high, and beneath the seventeenth-century remains were layers of medieval, Viking, Pictish and Iron Age occupation. The adjacent mound then picked up the story from the Middle Iron Age and a third, much smaller mound, being washed away by the sea, contained Early Bronze Age and Neolithic remains.

At the end of the 1980s the project came to an end – the excavations halted on the second mound and few of the results have yet been published. Over the

7 Members of the South Uist Historical Society (CEUD) attend an open day at Cladh Hallan in 2001

years, the Udal attracted many young volunteers from all over Britain and its fame spread far and wide. What it showed the outside world was that the machair of the Uists covers archaeological remains on a scale seen nowhere else in the British Isles: the machair sand has preserved the most impressive sequences of buildings and other signs of human occupation, with the earliest sites dating back over 5,000 years.

The force of the wind and tide on the Uists is breathtaking and archaeological sites on the west coast in particular are very vulnerable to erosion. In 1984, John Barber of the Scottish Development Department (SDD, whose Ancient Monuments Division was later to become Historic Scotland) carried out a series of excavations on the most endangered machair sites within the Uists, at Baleshare and Balelone on North Uist, and Hornish Point and Gortan on South Uist. The sites were of the Bronze Age and Iron Age and formed a coherent research project into prehistoric farm mounds which has recently been published.

Our own work began as part of the SEARCH project: in 1987 Sheffield University launched 'Sheffield Environmental and Archaeological Research Campaign in the Hebrides', and the southern islands, south of Benbecula and North Uist, were selected as the study area. Our colleagues were keen to carry out an integrated investigation of environment and landscape in an area where little or no modern archaeological research had been done before. At that time there were well-established and long-running projects on Lewis and on North Uist but South Uist and especially Barra had not been host to much work in recent years. The story of how the project has operated appears in the appendix to this book and in the introduction to *Barra and the Bishop's Isles* by our colleagues Keith Branigan and Patrick Foster. Over the years there has been much involvement from the local community *(7)* as well as students and volunteers from all over Britain and many other parts of the world.

CHAPTER 2

CLEARING
THE FOREST

Stand in a glen or on a hillside anywhere in South Uist and try and picture in the mind's eye a tree-filled wilderness of hazel, birch, elm, oak and willow. It is hard to believe that the majestic but bleak uplands of heather, blanket bog and bare rock were ever forested, yet that was how they appeared 8,000 years ago. This wooded landscape had developed since 14000 BC, with trees slowly covering the denuded massif left behind by the glaciers that once enveloped the Western Isles as well as most of the Scottish mainland. The forests grew and filled the islands at an infinitesimally slow pace during these eight millennia and then, in the much shorter period of time between 6000 BC and 2500 BC, they disappeared almost entirely.

For several thousands of years after the end of that last glaciation, Britain and Ireland were connected to the rest of Europe by land bridges, across which people and animals could travel and plants and trees could propagate. There was still so much water locked up as ice in this early post-glacial period that the English Channel was only a river and vast expanses of the North Sea were dry land.

The deep channel of the Minch, separating the Western Isles from Skye and the mainland, was never dry and always provided a watery barrier to people, animals and plants. Trees and other plants could only colonize the islands by being carried as seeds on the waves and winds or in the beaks of birds. For certain animals, particularly terrestrial mammals and reptiles, the Minch was an insuperable divide. Red deer may be capable of swimming the 14 miles but badgers, hedgehogs, polecats, hares, rats, mice and voles were not to reach these shores until they were brought by people in the ensuing millennia.

The first trees to take root in these islands were birch, followed by hazel. Their appearance is no later than in other parts of the Scottish mainland and their arrival, around 8000 BC, marks the end of the Ice Age (the Pleistocene) and the beginning of the Holocene, the geological period that continues to this day. Within two millennia the woodland had become extensive and diverse. We know of the growth, extent and composition of the forests thanks to two sources of evidence: pollen and the remains of the trees themselves. At the bottom of many peat cuttings there are branches and even tree boles *(8)*. These prove that, before the peat began to develop, there were areas of woodland. More extraordinary (and generally older) are the remains seen at low tide out among the rocks off the west coast. Here are filled-in freshwater lochs and lagoons which filled with peat, reeds and trees before being buried beneath the sand by the encroaching sea *(9)*. These remains of ancient wood and peat are found at various spots along the west coast of the Western Isles. On South Uist, they can be seen at Hornish Point, Cille Pheadair and Smercleit.

Some of the existing freshwater lochs of South Uist preserve the history of the island's plant life in deep layers of mud which have built up during the thousands of years since the end of the Ice Age. Within this mud, pollen grains have been preserved. Geologists and archaeologists use a technique called 'coring' to take samples when they want to examine thick deposits of soil which has built up in layers. A hollow metal tube is hammered into the mud and the core of soil that it removes can be examined layer by layer. A series of radiocarbon-dated time slices can be used to build up a clear picture of changes in vegetation.

8 Tree roots in a peat bog

9 Freshwater peat deposits exposed on the beach at Polochar

One of the first steps for recovering and interpreting those changes is to map the current distributions of plant species, to use as a comparison. The second is to compare pollen cores from a variety of different locations to see how vegetational conditions varied across the island. Pollen from different species has different quantities and ranges – pollen of some species travels much further than pollen from other species. How pollen grains reach the bottom of a loch is by no means straightforward – the wind may carry these grains many miles, or streams may wash them some distance, before they sink to the bottom of that loch. On South Uist the predominant westerly winds and the narrow width of the island east–west provide ideal circumstances for working out the pollen 'catchment area' of a loch's sediments. Not only were the density and composition of the ancient forest variable across the island but the catchments of the pollen 'rain' must also be carefully evaluated.

Another useful means of reconstructing past environment is to analyse the remains of beetles which are found in peat bogs and loch sediments. Beetles are as useful as pollen for finding out about past landscapes because many of them are highly selective about where they live. Some species prefer open ground or meadows and others are restricted to woodlands of particular types. Some are found in and among decaying trees and others are dung-feeders. The variation and percentage of beetle species from any location can provide a reliable picture of the extent of open country or of woodland conditions. Whereas pollen provides a broad-brush picture of conditions deriving from several or more square miles, the beetle evidence is much more specific to the particular patch of ground around the bog or the margins of the loch from which the sample is taken.

Thanks to studies of pollen and beetles, we now know that most of South Uist's trees disappeared by 2500 BC, leaving only small pockets of woodland which had mostly gone 3,000 years later. This deforestation was the result of Neolithic farmers clearing the land and grazing their animals. Once the trees had gone, continuous browsing by cattle and sheep prevented regeneration of this woodland.

BEFORE THE MACHAIR

Today the west coast of the Western Isles, and particularly South Uist, is covered by shell sand which forms the plain of grassland known as machair. Its unique vegetation is a mass of colour in the summer months, full of orchids, wild pansies, buttercups and daisies. In places along the west coast the machair is more than a kilometre wide. In areas such as Iochdar, at the north end of the island, or Bornais in the middle of South Uist *(colour plate 1)*, it is a flat plain fronted by a coastal dune ridge. In other parts such as Dalabrog, it is an uncultivable moonscape of grassed-over dunes, hummocks and low but steep hills of sand.

The machair sand is formed from the crushed shells of millions of marine molluscs mixed with quartz sand. It seems to have formed as a series of wellings-up out of the ocean in which great dunes of sand gradually moved inland across the flat ground of the west coast. Just when the process of machair sand formation began is not known, but it probably took place during the 2,000 years before the third millennium BC, perhaps after 5000 BC. The machair plain was largely in place by about 2500 BC – when it became a place on which people chose to build their houses – although sand dunes continued to move across the land until just over a century ago.

As people gazed westwards from the wooded hillsides of South Uist around 8,000 years ago, then, they would have looked out over a very different coastline, devoid of sand. Instead they would have seen a patchwork of freshwater lochs in a lightly wooded, flat plain which extended much further west than it does today. The trees along that west coast were probably less numerous than further inland and would have been bent by the strong westerly winds. Today all that survives of the plain is the shallow continental shelf that lies under the sea. The sand on the sea bottom covers all but the rock outcrops and the basal layers of peat, the last remnants of the freshwater lochs that formerly dotted this landscape. Nearer the higher ground inland, that plain survives untouched by the sea but it is buried many metres beneath the machair sand.

SEA LEVELS

The Uists formed a single landmass over 46 miles long with a steep east coast and extensive low plains to the west. Those plains are now under water as a result of the post-glacial rise in sea level. Although this rise was intially fairly rapid, it was not great enough in the Mesolithic or Neolithic periods to separate the land into the three islands that exist today. The Uists probably divided into three main islands at some time after 2000 BC.

The process of sea-level change was a complex one. The release of the weight of the glaciers caused the land to rise upwards, a process known as isostatic readjustment. At the same time, sea levels rose as the ice melted. By 6000 BC some parts of the Scottish mainland and islands of the Inner Hebrides had beaches which today are still visible to geologists, raised several metres above the current sea level. In the Western Isles, conversely, the land sank relative to the sea and continued to do so until after 3000 BC. At Sig More, on the north end of South Uist, there is a Neolithic tomb, built around 3500-3000 BC, which is now partially below the high–water mark. Another such tomb of the same period at Ceann nan Clachan on North Uist bears similar witness to rising sea levels.

CLIMATE CHANGE

After the melting of the glaciers, the climate warmed up rapidly from around 8000 BC. A thousand years later, temperatures were equivalent to today and, by 6000 BC, Scotland was drier and warmer in summer than it is now, although Scotland's winters were colder than they are today. Since then there has been a sequence of short-term fluctuations in climate, with higher rainfall in the periods 3000-2300 BC and from about AD 600 to 700. Studies of dune formation on the machair suggest periods of greater storminess during 3800-2200 BC, 1800-1300 BC, AD 300-700, AD 1400-1800 and from 1900 to the present day.

Even with the multitude of sources of climate evidence – deep-sea cores, ice cores, speliotherms (from cores taken in cave deposits), machair dune instability, pollen, beetles and tree-rings – there is no agreement among specialists about the precise causes, fluctuations and impacts of climate change, although broad trends are generally recognized. One of the main problems is that certain indicators, such as sand movement, can be as much the result of human activities – causing erosion by removing protective turf, for example – as reflections of climatic change.

THE DECLINE OF THE FOREST AND THE ARRIVAL OF PEOPLE

By 6000 BC there were people living on the islands of the Inner Hebrides, such as Rhum, Islay and Oronsay. People had also crossed the sea from the very north of the Scottish mainland to Orkney, making the short boat crossing between Thurso and the islands. These Mesolithic (Middle Stone Age) people fished, hunted deer and gathered shellfish and a variety of fruits, nuts, stems and roots; there was no farming (its development marks the Neolithic period) in Britain for at least another 1,000 years.

The remains of Mesolithic camps have been found on the raised beaches and moorlands of these islands, detected by the telltale presence of stone tools, made principally of beach flint, pitchstone (a rock which crops out on the Isle of Arran) and bloodstone (from Rhum). These flaked stone tools are of a particular type known as microliths. These tiny worked flakes, of a style found throughout the British Isles in the sixth and fifth millennia BC, were used to make composite tips of arrows and other tools.

Did these hunter-gatherer-fishers actually reach the Western Isles around this time? The islands were in sight from Skye and these people clearly had boats capable of short sea crossings. Yet not a single microlith has been found in the Western Isles, suggesting at first glance that the islands remained uninhabited. There is, however, other evidence which makes it extremely likely that South Uist was not only being visited but that people also lived there.

The pollen cores from South Uist tell us that, between about 6500 and 6000 BC, the tree cover in the glen at Reineval (south of Cill Donnain glen) and just to the southwest of it around Loch an-T'sil on the coastal plain, began slowly to diminish. These changes are associated with the appearance of substantial quantities of tiny fragments of charcoal in the mud and peat layers. Anywhere else on the Scottish mainland and inner islands, this kind of pattern at this date is interpreted as firm evidence of the arrival of people, burning trees to create clearings in which red deer may graze.

These prehistoric hunters managed the wild herds: game needed to be encouraged to multiply and also to congregate in open locations where the animals could be hunted. Yet red deer were not indigenous to the islands. There is always the possibility that one or two individuals had swum the Minch but it is more likely that the deer were introduced by the hunters themselves, bringing over a breeding stock and then leaving them to multiply. An alternative explanation for the charcoal and the forest clearance must also be considered: they might have been the result of forest fires caused by lightning strikes. The mild climate was slightly warmer than today and summer droughts could have been followed by thunder storms in which the canopy was set ablaze and small areas devastated.

The lack of other hard evidence – microliths and remains of camp sites – prevents us from reaching a definite conclusion about Mesolithic occupation. On South Uist we have searched for over ten years to find such traces but without success. The overriding difficulty is that there are unlikely to *be* any such surface traces – the landscape has changed too much. The ancient coastal plain is now either underwater or buried deep below the machair. The uplands are covered in blanket bog which grew long after the end of the Mesolithic period and, despite peat digging, the lowest layers often remain un-dug. There are few clues as to where specific habitations or hunting sites might have been located, since South Uist has no upland caves or rock shelters which could have been used. This is a needle in a haystack. There is no simple, systematic method of looking for such remains and, if they exist, they will most likely be found by chance, by someone out walking in the hills finding a handful of flints in a layer eroding out of the base of the peat.

At Reineval the clearance of trees which began during the Mesolithic intensified during the Neolithic, after farming had begun, in the period between 4000 BC and 2500 BC. However, another pollen core from the west side of South Uist shows a very different pattern. A mile or so north of Cill Donnain glen there was uninterrupted tree cover until much later – here the large-scale disappearance of the trees occurred around 2500 BC, the end of the Neolithic. Over on the east side of the island the pollen cores show sequences similar to that in Cill Donnain. At Loch Hellisdale, the project's researchers found sufficient quantities of tree pollen to indicate that woodland survived here until around 1000 BC.

But not all the woodland was cleared during the Neolithic period and the Bronze Age. Small pockets of woodland – no doubt carefully managed – survived even longer, until around AD 200: our excavations found wood grown from local trees in deposits outside the Iron Age broch of Dun Vulan. Finally, in 1549 a visiting cleric, Donald Munroe, noted that there was still forest on the east coast of South Uist.

The Neolithic was a period of profound changes, humanly and naturally induced – machair incursion, deforestation, continued sea level rise, and the growth of blanket bog. The latter affected the treeless high ground, following the erosion of the thin forest soils that had developed in such places. In the main, the bogs seem to have developed from the Neolithic period onwards. Until covered by blanket bog, the peaty forest soils were fertile and cultivable, providing a wide range of potential settlement areas in the sheltered glens and small valleys throughout the Uists.

CHAPTER 3

ANCESTRAL MONUMENTS

The Neolithic Period, c.4500-2500 BC

One evening in the bar of the Borrodale Hotel in Dalabrog, a tourist was enquiring how many people there were on South Uist. He was taken aback when the barman asked if he wanted to include the dead as well as the living. For the outsider such concerns may seem a little strange but the dead do have a prominent place in people's minds, although their burial places today lie as far from the living as possible, out on the edge of the uninhabited machair. Just where the first islanders were buried is something of a mystery, but the bones of some of these people of the Neolithic (4500-2500 BC) were kept in stone-walled chambers within large cairns of rocks. These impressive monuments, known as chambered tombs, are the largest, most visible and most enduring remains of those Neolithic lives and convey some idea of how important the dead were for the living.

In the Uists, Neolithic chambered tombs are often called *bharpa* (pronounced 'varpa') in Gaelic. The tomb at Loch a'Bharp *(10)* is the basis of the place names of both the township (Dalabrog), and of the glen close to which it lies (Borrodale). Such tombs are found in most parts of the British Isles and throughout the coastal areas of western Europe. They are one of the defining characteristics of the Neolithic period, along with pottery, stone axes, domesticated crops and animals, and a new flint-working technology which replaced the microlithic industries of the Late Mesolithic.

The term 'Neolithic' was coined originally to refer to that 'new' (neo) stone technology but it covers many more important changes in society, above all the beginnings of food production (as opposed to food collecting by hunting, fishing and gathering) and the building of monuments like the chambered tombs. This characterization of what defines the Neolithic period is by no means clear-cut and archaeologists continue to argue about whether the change was gradual and piecemeal or rapid and abrupt. Certain wild foods – nuts, berries and edible roots in particular – continued to be important during the Neolithic and the earliest monuments (of wood rather than stone) had already been constructed in Britain during the Mesolithic. Was the change

10 Loch a'Bharp Neolithic tomb

brought about by new arrivals – incoming farmers – or was it adopted by indigenous hunter-gatherer-fishers who had contacts with other cultures? Was it a purely economic transformation or did the change in lifestyle have a religious and spiritual dimension?

There are other debates about whether Neolithic communities lived in permanent villages or whether they were relatively mobile, moving their grazing herds from place to place. For those who have visited the extraordinary remains of the stone-walled Neolithic village of Skara Brae in Orkney, it may seem easy to imagine that people elsewhere in Britain must also have lived in similarly substantial and permanent houses, arranged into large hamlets or small villages. Yet Orkney appears to have been an exception: even in the relatively similar context of the Western Isles, there is no evidence at all for large settlements during this period. Elsewhere in the British Isles, the large sites of the Neolithic all appear to have been associated with activities beyond the domestic realm. We see the remains of great stone and earth structures but very few traces of houses.

During the Neolithic, the people of Britain built a variety of enclosures of great banks and ditches, earth-built tombs, and linear monuments (known as

11 Dun Trossary Neolithic tomb

cursuses), but none of these are known in the Western Isles. Instead, the chambered cairns seem to have been the only form of monument constructed in South Uist and the other islands during this period. These tombs were built in a variety of shapes and sizes but the most common are roughly circular in plan, between 20m-30m in diameter. Tombs of this type are edged by a ring of upright stones, forming a kerb known as a peristalith, and have a short stone-lined passage leading to a small stone-built, corbelled chamber, roofed with a large capstone.

This style of 'passage tomb' is referred to as the 'Hebridean round cairn' and has been identified as a regional style found largely but not exclusively in the Inner and Outer Hebrides. Other types of chambered cairn are also found in the islands. For example, there are rectangular 'long cairns' *(11)* of a type better known around the Clyde in mainland Scotland: these can be seen at Dun Trossary (South Uist) and Clettraval (North Uist) and might originally have been about 60m long with protruding 'arms' known as hornworks enclosing a forecourt area outside the chamber entrance. On the isle of Barra there are two small cairns with U-shaped ends, known as 'heeled cairns', a style found as far away as Shetland.

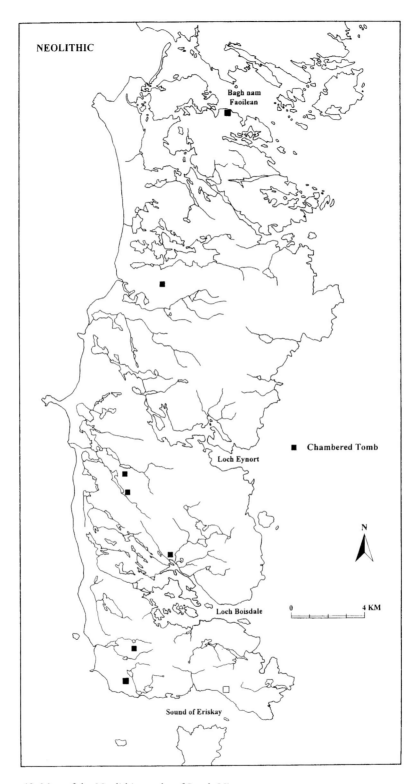

NEOLITHIC

Bagh nam
Faoilean

Loch Eynort

■ Chambered Tomb

N

Loch Boisdale

0   4 KM

Sound of Eriskay

12 Map of the Neolithic tombs of South Uist

Just what these different architectural styles represented is an unanswered question. Were certain styles (the long cairns) built before the others? Or were the different styles constructed by groups with origins in geographically different regions? Or was the choice of tomb architecture influenced by more subtle and complex factors? The regional 'Hebridean round cairn' style does suggest a developing identity for the Western Isles and Inner Hebrides which contrasts markedly with the extraordinary stalled cairns and cellular chambered tombs of Orkney.

Most of these chambered tombs have been dismantled over the millennia, since they provide valuable sources of stones which have been reused to build field walls, houses and animal pens. As a result, despite having been such large and obvious monuments, the total number of Neolithic tombs that once existed is not known precisely, either for South Uist or for the Western Isles generally. There are seven certain tombs on South Uist at Sig More, Glac Hukarvat, Reineval, Barp Frobost, Loch a'Bharp, Dun Trossary and Leaval *(12)*. Large circular cairns which also may be Neolithic tombs but show no evidence for an interior passage and chamber are found at Tigh Cloiche and at Tobhta Mhor na Leaccaich. A stone structure on the Ardvule promontory is just possibly the damaged remains of a long cairn.

The only tomb in South Uist to have been excavated is at Leaval *(13)*, towards the southern end of the island. This survives as a box-like arrangement of four upright stones, forming the chamber walls within a cairn whose stones have been largely removed ('robbed' in archaeologists' terminology!) over the centuries. The only objects found were pieces of worked flint. More promising results were obtained from Sir Lindsay Scott's excavation of a Hebridean round

13 Leaval tomb during excavation

cairn at Rudh an Dunain on Skye. Within the tomb were human bones and fragments of Neolithic pottery.

The acidic peat soils on which virtually all the Hebridean tombs are located do not normally preserve bones and this lucky circumstance contrasts with all other excavations of Neolithic tombs on the islands – no other bones have ever been found, except in the case of Clettraval where Scott found cremated bones whose altered composition makes them resistant to acidic environments. Elsewhere in Britain, particularly on the chalk soils of the south, bones survive very well, so we know that Neolithic tombs were not built for single individuals but as communal burial places. At West Kennet long barrow in Wiltshire, for example, the tomb contained the bones of over 30 people whilst the tombs of Isbister and Quanterness in Orkney each held the remains of more than 300.

Within the Western Isles the geographical distribution of chambered tombs is variable. It is possible that what was originally a more even pattern is now disguised by the survival of some monuments and the destruction of others, but this is not entirely likely – a few have probably gone completely but the remains of most are likely to have survived. The highest density of tombs – more than 20 of them – can be found at the northern end of the long island of Uist in North Uist, which was still joined to Benbecula and South Uist during the Neolithic. Much smaller groupings are found on Barra and at the south end of South Uist, on Benbecula and Harris and in the Callanish (Calanais) and Stornoway areas of Lewis.

The extraordinary density of North Uist tombs is likely to be more than the result of fortuitous preservation and may indicate that this part of the former 'long island' of Uist had a special religious or political significance during the Neolithic. An attractive theory that Neolithic tombs formed the centres of small political territories controlling the more fertile strips of land was developed for Orkney and Arran. Tombs appear to have been equally spaced with regard to fertile land but the theory has its problems because not all areas with evidence of Neolithic settlements seem to have been provided with tombs.

When we turn to the more intimate local scale and consider the settings, prospects and orientations of the South Uist tombs, it becomes clear that there is more to learn. Tombs seem to have been constructed throughout the earlier part of the Neolithic, so there was no 'pioneer' phase, as far as we can tell, when the minds of the island's early inhabitants were focused solely on wresting a living from the earth. At Reineval the pollen core indicates a major transformation during the period when the tomb was constructed from woodland to heathland, together with burning: this human alteration of the landscape perhaps initiated a period when the area was managed for grazing.

New work by young researchers Vicki Cummings and Cole Henley of Cardiff University has shown that the location of the Reineval tomb is similar to that of four of the other six, set high up on the west-facing slope of the high

14 Sig More Neolithic tomb

ground that runs the length of the island. Like three of the other four tombs on the western slopes, Reineval sits below a pass which links the east and west sides of South Uist *(colour plate 2)*. The two tombs with rather different locations are Loch a'Bharp and Sig More, the former within the Lochboisdale-Dalabrog glen which crosses the island and the latter in the former valley (now open sea) that divides South Uist from Benbecula *(14)*.

The tombs appear to mark east–west passage across the island, perhaps guarding the routeways for herds and flocks or signposting the seasonal movements of animals and people between the two coasts. Dun Trossary is an exception: although it sits on a west-facing slope like Reineval, its location and orientation are different. It appears to stress the north–south axis of movement up and down the island, perhaps playing more of a community-wide role for this southern part of the long island. An alternative but possibly complementary explanation for the locations along east–west valleys running across the island is that the Neolithic tombs were placed in relation to more ancient, Mesolithic settlements which were positioned to monitor the movement of red deer herds across the island. Unfortunately there have been no excavations of layers underneath any of the chambered tombs; the few flints recovered from excavations around the Leaval tomb did not include Mesolithic microliths.

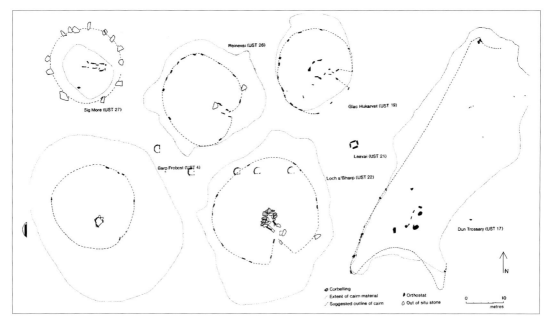

15 Plans of South Uist's Neolithic tombs

Views from the tombs are generally unusual or even spectacular. One can see distant horizons such as the mountains of Barra or the nearer peaks of Stulaval, Eaval and Hekla. St Kilda is visible from Glac Hukarvat near Howmore. Yet the tombs were mostly placed so as to ensure that there are certain locations below them that are *not* visible. In other words, they were not located so as to maximize the panoramic view: low hills or hillsides in their immediate vicinity often obscure the view of some of the surrounding land. The tombs are also generally not intervisible.

This mysterious arrangement may be comprehensible when we consider the topography between the Neolithic settlement of Alt Chrisal on Barra and its nearest tomb, just 100 metres or so further up the valley side. The settlement and the tomb are of the same date and yet, despite their proximity to each other, the tomb was located precisely so that it could *not* be seen from the dwellings. Perhaps this principle of separating the living from the dead was widespread throughout the Uists but only future investigation will reveal the locations of most settlement remains.

The passage tombs uniformly have east- or southeast-facing entrances, regardless of location: for many, the entrance opens onto the featureless hillside rather than facing the prominent mountain tops *(15)*. Only the Dun Trossary long cairn is different, with an entrance that faces south, mimicking the north–south lie of the land. The southeast and east entrances of the passage tombs can be best explained by comparison with the few Neolithic houses found in the Uists, at Eilean Domhnuill, an islet settlement in North Uist.

Where identifiable, three of the houses on this site have doorways which face southeast and the entrance to the whole complex is from the south.

This link is somewhat tenuous since so few house sites are known, but it helps us to reflect on the relationships between house and tomb. In Orkney, for example, it is clear that the interior architecture of Neolithic tombs echoes that of dwellings. The 'stalled' tombs of Orkney are so-called because internal stone walls divide the tomb's chamber into separate stalls like those in a stable. This arrangement of space mirrors very closely the layout of the rectangular houses, where vertical stone partitions subdivide the dwelling space into two or three units, as can be seen at the site of Knap of Howar. Similarly, 'cellular' tombs such as Maes Howe imitate the use of space within Skara Brae-type houses, in which a central area is surrounded by recesses.

The layout of the houses found at Eilean Domhnuill and the plans of the less well-defined structures at Alt Chrisal indicate that houses in the Western Isles were probably far more simple internally – echoing the simple single-cellular forms of the islands' tomb chambers. Although entrance orientations might have been shared between house and tomb, the ground plans do not always correspond. The Eilean Domhnuill houses are rectangular, as are most tomb chambers, but some tomb chambers are square rather than rectangular, or even circular. The houses at Alt Chrisal survive only as arrangements of postholes – all that is left after a wooden structure has rotted away, or a stone structure has been dismantled. The postholes at Alt Chrisal suggest a circular or sub-circular structure stood here during its earliest period of use and it is possible that such forms were used for the abodes of the living as well as the dead.

The long cairns such as Dun Trossary have rectangular chambers placed next to each other, forming several separate 'cells'. The construction of these segmented rows of rectangular cells in the long cairns is interesting because each cell could signify a social group, hinting at a more communal, community-wide role for these particular monuments in comparison to the round cairns with their undivided chambers.

The distribution of known and possible chambered tombs is very uneven across South Uist and throughout the Western Isles more generally. As places for the collective burial of human remains, it is very tempting to perceive them as equivalents to the medieval and modern church, serving as religious centres for Neolithic equivalents of the parish or township. Interestingly, the linear distribution of five of the seven certain tombs on South Uist is matched by the distribution of historical church sites. The two exceptions are Reineval and Barp Frobost which are close together and in an area two miles from the nearest known church site at Cill Donnain. The mismatch is compounded by two further church sites which have no tomb in their vicinity.

It is clear from excavations in many parts of the British Isles that even those few Neolithic tombs that contained bones from hundreds of people could not possibly have housed the corpses and charnel of entire communities over the thousand years or so during which they were in use. In most tombs just a handful of skeletons and body parts are ever recovered. So what happened to everyone else? In some respects, archaeologists' insistence on calling these monuments 'tombs' has misled us: most contain deposits of human bones that are more like token burials than the remains of the population at large.

Even if the tombs were reserved for a special few – the leaders, healers, magicians, prophets, seers or whatever – they were still important ancestral monuments that represented the achievements of their communities. Certain places, such as North Uist, might have gained a reputation and history throughout the islands as the place where many people's ancestors hailed from and thus the places where their ancestral dead resided.

PLACES OF THE LIVING

There is a sad lack of settlement evidence to go with the tombs of the Western Isles in this period, especially when compared with Orkney and Shetland. On South Uist the only known sites are a light scatter of flints and sherds of pottery found on an islet within Loch a'Choire near the south coast *(16)*, and a single find of a Neolithic sherd which turned up during the excavation of a post-medieval settlement at Kirkidale on the east coast of the island.

Neolithic settlements, of minor and more substantial proportions, have been excavated in North Uist on an islet at Eilean Domhnuill, in the peat at Bharpa Cairinis and Screvan, and within the machair at the Udal. There is a Neolithic settlement in the peatlands at Alt Chrisal on Barra and another below the machair at Northton on Harris. The complex and long-lived settlement on Eilean Domhnuill – 11 phases were detected during excavation – produced a number of houses which survive as low stone-walled buildings with central hearths. None of the other sites have produced anything but the scantest traces of structures, except for Alt Chrisal, where the precise plans of the houses are difficult to reconstruct. If house walls were built of turf with only a foundation course, if any, of stone, then they are particularly difficult to spot during excavation, particularly on long-lived sites in peat where earlier phases are often disturbed by later activity.

The major questions about these settlements concern their size and their permanence. Opinion is divided as to whether there is a Skara Brae awaiting discovery somewhere in the Western Isles. Eilean Domhnuill is much smaller than Skara Brae and, in our view, is likely to be at the upper end in terms of settlement size. For all periods up to the present day, Orkney's settlements have a more 'nucleated' character than those of the Western Isles. This is probably also the case for the Neolithic so we must expect South Uist's Neolithic landscape to have been composed not of big villages like Skara Brae but of small and scattered dwellings.

16 The Neolithic site at Loch a'Choire

Once archaeologists accepted that they were not going to find large villages of substantially built houses anywhere in the British Isles except Orkney, they began to debate whether the Neolithic was in fact a period of temporary and short-term settlement, with the population remaining highly mobile. Were people living in 'benders', insubstantial tents made of animal skins and light wooden stakes, or even in the roofed-over holes left when people uprooted the vast trees which grew in the great forests? Archaeologists have located a few substantial but isolated timber buildings, but did these actually derive from special or even ceremonial activities rather than from daily use?

This idea of a highly mobile Neolithic population moving across the landscape with their herds of animals may have some validity for southern Britain, but it is roundly refuted for Ireland and also does not square with the Orcadian evidence. What was the situation in South Uist and the Western Isles? Like Orkney, the relatively small landmass of the Uists does not provide much scope for lengthy transhumance or long-distance treks with the herds and flocks. The long-term and complex sequences at Eilean Domhnuill and Alt Chrisal also suggest that life was rather more rooted and sedentary.

DAILY LIFE

With the north Atlantic full of fish and shellfish, it would seem likely that Neolithic farmers augmented their diets with the harvest of the sea, following the traditions of their Mesolithic forebears. There are pieces of worked pumice from Alt Chrisal which could have been used as floats for fishing nets but the acidic soils on this site prevented the survival of bone so there is no way of knowing whether fish were caught. Because of these acidic soils most of the settlements of the Western Isles have produced no remains of the bones of animals consumed.

An analysis of the animal bones from Neolithic settlements in Orkney such as Skara Brae indicates that fish were caught, but in very low numbers. Furthermore, Skara Brae is a coastal site and yet most of the fish eaten here were actually freshwater trout. It is difficult to know whether the Neolithic people of the Western Isles were the exception to this pattern but it should be remembered that farming communities do not need to place much reliance on the sea other than for getting from one place to another and for the smallest of dietary supplements.

Analysis of human bones includes looking at chemical signatures called isotopes. Evidence of everything we ingest – food and water – is preserved forever in our bones and can reveal to archaeologists where people came from and what they ate at different stages in their lives. Carbon and nitrogen isotopes in the bones of prehistoric coastal populations, in Britain and from Portugal to Scandinavia, reveal that Mesolithic hunter-gatherers tended to derive much of their animal protein from seafood whereas Neolithic farmers were largely reliant on terrestrial-derived protein.

Cattle, sheep and, to a lesser extent, pigs were the mammalian mainstay of the Neolithic economy and their presence in the islands at this time is accepted rather than demonstrated. Wild foods were certainly collected throughout Neolithic Britain and red deer might also have been significant. However, the special circumstances in which complete or partial skeletons of deer have been found in Neolithic Orkney suggests that these animals were treated in special ways after death, so we need to exercise caution in considering deer to have been a standard, no frills source of meat. Barley and wheat were the two important crops in the Neolithic of the Western Isles. Eilean Domhnuill in particular contained large quantities of the burnt and waterlogged remains of these cereals. Their association with huge quantities of pottery and readily available fresh water at this site raises the possibility that beer or mead were brewed here.

Neolithic pottery is normally fairly scarce in Scotland but it was made and used in huge quantities in the Western Isles. From Eilean Domhnuill alone there are over 20,000 sherds and only slightly smaller amounts have come from Alt Chrisal and the Udal. It varies enormously in size, shape, quality and decoration, even on the same site. Three basic styles have been identified: plain pots (bowls and often large storage vessels, some with suspension lugs around their waists); Unstan Ware (carinated [ridged] bowls with highly decorated upper sides, in the same style as a pottery type first identified in Orkney); and Hebridean Ware (incision-decorated jars sometimes with multiple carinations and occasional lugs).

The sequence at Eilean Domhnuill demonstrates that all three styles were in use together over many centuries. This is particularly unusual because Unstan Ware in Orkney appears to have gone out of use by about 2800 BC (before the Late Neolithic) and, throughout the British Isles, plain bowls are generally also a feature of the Early Neolithic period (4500-3000 BC). In the Western Isles, both pottery styles remained in use for much longer.

It is as if the Hebridean potters found the styles that they liked and stuck to them, regardless of innovations and changes in ceramic fashions elsewhere in the British Isles. The creation of a Hebridean style not found outside western Scotland hints at a strong sense of regional identity. Most intriguing is the rarity of a style of pottery that was a 'hit' everywhere else in Britain and in eastern Ireland. Around 3000 BC people in Orkney began to produce a repertoire of pots decorated with applied and incised motifs, known as Grooved Ware. Within a couple of centuries it was in use throughout Britain and yet, in the Western Isles, it has been found only at Callanish on Lewis and at Uneaval chambered cairn on North Uist. Intriguingly, it is not present among the 20,000 Neolithic sherds at Eilean Domhnuill, even though the site was still occupied when Grooved Ware was in use everywhere else. In one sense, it was unnecessary here because the Hebridean Ware has many of the same qualities of size, shape and decoration. In fact, examples from both styles look like skeuomorphs (copies) of containers made from basketry. In other words, it appears that basketry was the inspiration behind some of their shapes.

So far, no one has found in the Western Isles any traces of the Later Neolithic 'super' tombs of Orkney or the henge enclosures that are often associated with Grooved Ware elsewhere in Britain. Instead, it seems as if the Neolithic Hebrideans chose to maintain the ways of their ancestors in the face of changes all around them in the third millennium BC. They built no new-style monuments and continued to make the same pottery. Yet they were not entirely isolated from the outside world. The Shetland-linked heeled tombs and finds in the Western Isles of polished stone axe-heads from Rathlin Island in Northern Ireland point to some influx of ideas and products. But very soon, around or just after 2500 BC, the Western Isles rejoined that wider world and produced some of the greatest achievements of the new era.

CHAPTER 4

A NEW WORLD

The Earlier Bronze Age, c.2500-1200 BC

South Uist's machair is covered in ancient settlements. There are over 200 of them now recorded and most are visible as low, grassy mounds. Prehistoric settlements have become mounds because the everyday rubbish scattered outside the houses helped to trap windblown sand and gradually, over the years of occupation, the ground surface rose to form a low hillock. In some cases the settlement mounds are between 4m and 8m high, the result of millennia of living in the same place. Of course, there are thousands of grassy mounds on the machair but only those 200 or so have produced the telltale traces of human occupation – sea shells, animal bones and pottery sherds – which reveal that people once lived on these spots. In most parts of the machair, it is thanks to the rabbits that archaeological sites have been recognized, since they deposit the finds outside their burrows as they dig into the sand.

The style of pottery from a mound is a good guide to the date or period when it was inhabited, and the earliest settlements on the machair of South Uist date to 2500-1700 BC, sharing a type of pottery known as Beaker pottery. Settlement mounds of this period are much lower than those of later date, being scarcely knee-high. There is one small cluster of these Beaker period mounds on the rocket range at Iochdar at the north end of the island, covering an area 200m across either side of a small stream immediately to the south of the rifle range.

In one of the mounds there lived an industrious rabbit whom we came to call 'Beaker bunny'. We never laid eyes on Beaker bunny but he/she became a favourite of the archaeologists because out of one burrow came pieces of a beautiful Beaker, decorated with fine lines and feather-like incisions *(17)*. Each year we would go back to the same spot and collect a few more sherds of this fine vessel until, one summer, there was no more. We didn't get all the pieces of the pot but it had clearly been complete or nearly so when it was left by its owners 4,000 years ago. Beaker bunny has moved on or died, so the rest of that pretty pot lies there for future archaeologists to find.

Beakers are the most amazing prehistoric pots. They are often exquisitely made, with their outside surface decorated from head to foot with all manner

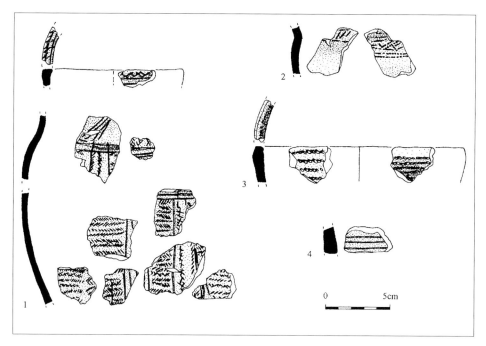

17 Beaker pottery from the rocket range at Iochdar, including Beaker bunny's discovery (1)

of chevron, zigzag and banded patterns, impressed and incised with twisted cord, comb teeth, fingernails and other instruments. Very often their fabric is exceptionally fine, the clay having been carefully prepared to make these high-quality pots. For the British Isles in general and the Hebrides in particular, such vessels are a beacon of technical excellence in pottery-making, in striking comparison to periods before and after, for which the pottery tends to look a bit rough – made with two left hands by people who took no pride in their work! Most intriguingly, the Hebridean Beakers are among the most beautifully decorated of all Beaker pottery. The fineness of their incised lines and feather-like decoration is virtually unmatched.

The second startling thing about Beakers is their huge geographical range. After two millennia of adherence to insular and regional ceramic styles, the Neolithic people of the British Isles chose to adopt a pan-European fashion. Beakers have been found from Britain to the Danube, as far south as Portugal and Algeria and as far north as Norway, and are part of a wider tradition of pottery known generally as Corded Ware which is found throughout eastern and central Europe. This pottery was once thought to be the 'trademark' of an ethnic group, the Beaker people, who had migrated across Europe propagating their broad-headed (brachycephalic) offspring at the expense of the local narrow-heads and bringing a proto-Indo-European language.

This ethnic interpretation does not match the archaeological or genetic evidence very well and has long gone out of fashion in archaeological circles.

It now seems that there was a complex intermixing of indigenous and immigrant populations in which Beakers were adopted into existing local contexts of use as well as being the trappings of an invading people who brought this new culture from Europe.

Beakers are often described as coming to the British Isles in a 'package', together with copper and gold metallurgy, new styles of archery and new forms of alcoholic drink. The earliest wholly convincing evidence for an alcoholic drink in prehistoric Britain comes from the pollen preserved within a Beaker found in a grave at Ashgrove in Fife. The contents appear to have been some form of mead and it seems that the smaller Beakers were handheld drinking vessels. Some archaeologists think that there was no alcohol until Beakers were adopted, which is why their spread was so successful. Others have suggested that their alcoholic contents were supplemented in some cases by infusions of cannabis.

Given the strong regional identity of the Hebrides in the Later Neolithic, one may expect that the inhabitants would have been slow to catch on – or even resistant – to this new fashion for Beakers. Yet this seems not to have been the case. The earliest Beakers in the British Isles date to 2500-2200 BC, and one of the Beaker settlements in Uist, at Cladh Hallan, dates to this period before 2000 BC. There are at least 15 known or likely settlements of the Beaker period in the Western Isles and this ceramic style was clearly very popular here *(18)*.

There is as yet no Beaker metalwork – copper or bronze daggers, flat axes and awls, and gold basket-shaped earrings – from South Uist or from the Western Isles, but the distinctive barbed and tanged flint arrowheads of this period have been found on many Beaker settlements, including those in South Uist at Cladh Hallan and Cill Donnain. Other diagnostic flint tools of the period are thumbnail scrapers and very finely flaked points and awls. At about 2200 BC, bronze (eight parts copper to one part tin) replaced copper throughout the British Isles. Another wide-ranging innovation at this time was the development of a new form of decorated pottery, used alongside Beakers, known as Food Vessels (though this old-fashioned name is not particularly accurate, since these pots were used for a whole variety of storage, cooking, eating and drinking purposes).

Neolithic houses are rare in the British Isles but not nearly as rare as those of the Beaker period. Oddly enough, the best place in Europe to find out about Beaker houses is in the Western Isles *(19)*. These buildings seem to have been so ephemeral that their remains have survived the following four millennia only in the most exceptional circumstances. The machair offers such conditions, although it is only a matter of time until Beaker bunny's friends and family systematically destroy them with their burrowing.

The Beaker period houses are about the same size as their Neolithic prede-cessors, with floor areas of 15-20sq. m, but their shapes are very different. Some

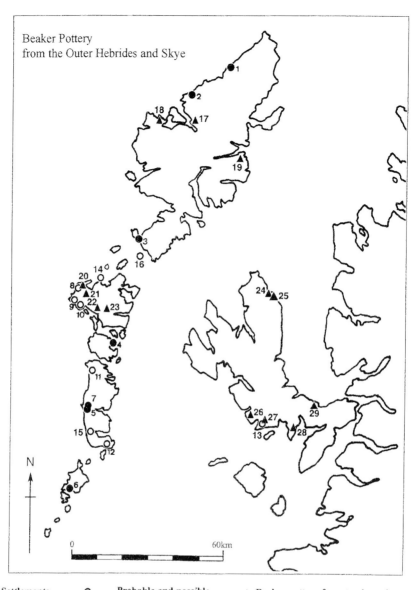

Beaker Pottery
from the Outer Hebrides and Skye

N

0   60km

	Settlements		Probable and possible settlements		Beaker pottery from tombs, cairns and burials

●	Settlements	○	Probable and possible settlements	▲	Beaker pottery from tombs, cairns and burials
1	Barvas	8	Scalpaig	17	Callanish
2	Dalmore	9	An Dige, Paiblesgarry	18	Cnip
3	Northton	10	Balronald	19	Lochs
4	Rosinish	11	Machair Mheadhanach	20	Geirisclett
5	Cill Donnain 1	12	Gortan	21	South Clettraval
6	Allt Chrisal	13	Rudh an Dunain Cave	22	Unival
7	Sligeanach	14	Udal	23	Barpa Langass
		15	Cladh Hallan	24	Garrafad
		16	Ensay	25	Elishader
				26	Kraiknish, Loch Eynort
				27	Rudh an Dunain
				28	Cnocan Nan Gobhar
				29	Liveras (wristguards)

18 Map of Beaker settlements in the Western Isles

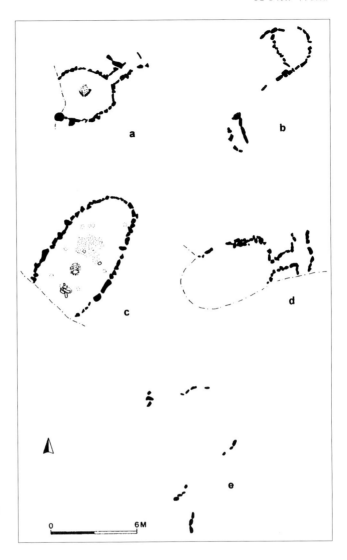

19 Plans of Beaker period
houses in the Western Isles
a) Dalmore; b) Northton 1;
c) Northton 2; d) Barvas;
e) Cill Donnain

are boat-shaped or U-shaped, such as one found at Northton on Harris, and
others are oval or irregular, like those at Dalmore and Barvas on Lewis *(20)*. The
only house plan recovered from South Uist is from the southern mound of a
site on Cill Donnain machair and, since excavations were only exploratory, it is
not a complete plan. This building lies largely unexcavated with only a few of
its wall stones poking out as upright slabs. These once formed the interior wall
of a house which was oval in shape and about 5m across.

In these Beaker period houses, the hearth appears to have been roughly in
the middle of the floor but there is no indication of where people slept or
whether there were distinct activity areas within the house. Orientations of
doorways are highly variable and show no consistent patterns. Like the
Neolithic houses at Eilean Domhnuill, the walls were low but, because they
were on the machair, they were often revetted into the sand so that the floor

was sunk slightly below ground level. Sadly, almost all of these houses were excavated prior to modern methods of sampling floor deposits, techniques that could tell us about how their interior spaces were organized. For the future, the Beaker period and other Early Bronze Age houses on the machair of the Western Isles offer the best circumstances anywhere in western and northern Europe for finding out about domestic life in detail – but the thousands of rabbits means that time is running out!

There are three complexes of Beaker period settlement mounds along the west coast of South Uist and another, smaller one – excavated before it was destroyed by erosion – in a pocket of machair on the southeast coast at Gortan. The site on the rocket range at Iochdar (also known as Machair Mheadhanach) is the largest. At the mid-point of the island is the Cill Donnain complex, consisting of two mound groups about 200m apart *(21)*. On the west coast, the most southerly group of mounds is at Cladh Hallan, in Dalabrog township. The only occupation site off the machair that may date to this period was revealed by a handful of worked flints eroding out of the peat in Cill Donnain glen. There may be more such sites in the peatlands but they are hard to find. In any case, the increased growth of blanket bog during the Bronze Age must have made these areas less attractive for settlement than before.

Elsewhere in the Western Isles, Beaker period settlement remains have been excavated at Alt Chrisal, at Rosinish on Benbecula and the Udal on North Uist. On Harris, the Northton settlement, like Alt Chrisal, is directly on top

20 Excavation in progress on the Beaker house at Dalmore, Lewis

21 Sligeanach Beaker settlement, Cill Donnain, South Uist

of its Neolithic predecessor. On Lewis there are sites at Barvas, Callanish, Cnip and Dalmore. Paible on North Uist is one of several sites of this period which await investigation. For Early Bronze Age sites – the period after Beakers, 1800-1400 BC – there are no settlement sites excavated at all. Two have been located at Cladh Hallan and Cill Donnain but the former has already been almost entirely destroyed by quarrying for sand.

One of the major questions is whether the machair settlements represent just one small part of the total number of settlements, the remainder being hidden under the peat. On South Uist, the locations of the three main settlement complexes are well arranged so as to give each an equal share of the island and so that each is served by a major loch with access to the east coast. Cladh Hallan is a short distance from the Lochboisdale sea loch whilst Cill Donnain is close to the head of the Loch Ainort sea loch. In the north, Iochdar is adjacent to Loch Bee, formerly a freshwater loch, which could be traversed by boat leaving just a short hop to the east coast.

These are optimum settlement locations which continued to be chosen as the sites for subsequent villages for the next two millennia. This makes it likely that they were the largest Early Bronze Age settlements on the island, but the find of flints in Cill Donnain glen hints that there were probably many smaller and perhaps more temporary residences in other parts of the island, off the machair.

FARMING AND MAKING A LIVING

The people of the Early Bronze Age were farmers like their Neolithic predecessors. We have better evidence of their farming practices because their fields
have been preserved within the machair. They can be identified from the
presence of thin, dark layers of organic soil, at the base of which are criss-cross
marks made by ards. The ard is a basic form of plough that has no ploughshare
but ends in a simple wooden tip. Here on the machair, ards could have been
pulled by human force rather than by draught animals since the sandy soil is so
soft. In the Beaker period it was the practice to plough in one direction
east–west and then again north–south, as well as diagonally to these alignments.
In the Western Isles examples of such fields have been excavated at Sligeanach
in Cill Donnain and at Cladh Hallan *(22; 23)*. Another set is known from
Rosinish on Benbecula. At Sligeanach we found traces of shallow gullies that
formed the boundaries between different plots.

The ploughsoils are very interesting because they contain many tiny pieces
of pottery and flaked tools of flint and quartz. These come from the ground-
down debris of domestic rubbish which has been added to the soil to make it
more fertile. Machair sand is capable of producing good cereal crops but it
needs constant nourishment. Today and in recent times, seaweed is spread on
the fields as a fertilizer and the fields also need long fallow periods. The

22 Ploughmarks of the Beaker period at Sligeanach

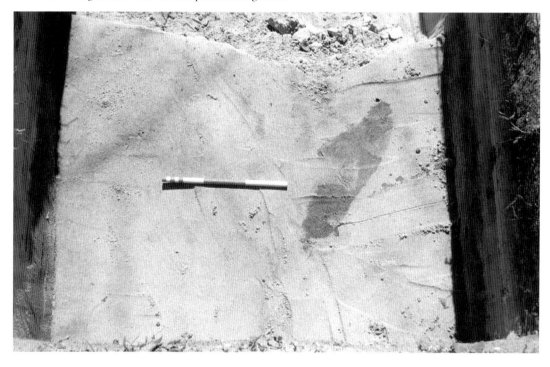

ploughsoil at Cladh Hallan is highly alkaline but little bone or shell has survived in it, having broken up in the continuously tilled soil. The soil was largely an artificial creation and it can be seen to have been replenished. As one layer was eroded by the wind, so another was manufactured and spread over the field's surface.

This type of field indicates a very intensive, infield or garden-plot kind of agriculture practised not far from the settlement itself. We do not know if there were more distant arable outfields at this time but it seems to have been the one period in prehistory when domestic rubbish was spread on the fields as fertilizer. In the Late Bronze Age and afterwards, this useful fertilizer was left to accumulate on the settlement rather than being put to good use. This practice may explain why the settlement mounds of the Early Bronze Age are so low compared to those of later periods – domestic debris was spread out, rather than mounded up around the inhabitants' houses.

The Early Bronze Age islanders grew barley and wheat in these fields and reared the same animals as their Neolithic predecessors – cattle, sheep and pigs. Analysis of the isotopic values for human bones from three people living in South Uist around 1500 BC and buried at Cladh Hallan indicates that, as suspected for the Neolithic population before them, their diet was largely derived from terrestrial sources. High levels of nitrogen isotopes indicate a major reliance on animal protein and the carbon isotopes indicate that very

23 Beaker period ploughmarks at Cladh Hallan

little of this, less than 10 per cent, came from fish or shellfish, even though the settlements are littered with the shells of limpets, cockles and winkles. This does seem surprising since it was not as if they were incapable of fishing – Mesolithic populations long before had developed effective methods of harvesting the sea.

One of the individuals analysed was a girl who had died in her mid-teens. Her skeleton gave no indication of how she died but her shoulder blades and torso were small and undeveloped for her age, and her femurs (thigh bones) were curved instead of straight. This is likely to have been the result of rickets, a disease brought on by lack of Vitamin D (found in fish oil). Even with such a dietary deficiency, exposure to sunlight should prevent rickets from developing. Contrary to some tourists' expectations, South Uist does have perfectly adequate amounts of sunshine – in fact some of the highest levels in Britain – and perhaps the unfortunate girl spent much of her life sequestered indoors.

BURIAL PRACTICES

A few of the chambered tombs in the islands have produced sherds of Beakers from the soils which fill their interior, notably the fine tomb of Barpa Langass, the tomb at Clettraval and the unusual small tomb within the stone circle at Callanish. But this pottery seems not to have been directly associated with burials and it is more likely that the Beakers were deposited here during the closing-up of these Neolithic tombs in the same way as is found in other parts of Britain during the Early Bronze Age.

Burials with Beakers are relatively rare in the Western Isles but a number of Early Bronze Age burials have been discovered, some without any pottery and others with different types of pot, from sites such as Cnip in Lewis, the Udal and Sithean an Altair (also in North Uist). Most of these have been found beneath cairns, and a few burials are of cremated bones: cremation was a common funerary ritual in Britain during the Early Bronze Age, and burials of this period can be either whole skeletons or deposits of burnt bone. These cairns are considerably smaller than those of Neolithic date and cover the graves of single individuals. Probably starting after 1800 BC, a new style of cairn appeared – the kerbed cairn – which contained single cremation burials, some of them with occasional grave goods of ornaments or tools (see chapter 5 for more detail).

One of the few cemeteries known from this date in the Western Isles was located at Cladh Hallan. The archaeological site is named after the nearby modern cemetery ('cladh' is graveyard and 'Hallan' may refer to a Father Allan who founded the graveyard here several hundred years ago). None of these Early Bronze Age burials were excavated archaeologically and many have certainly been lost during quarrying. Nevertheless, chance recording and salvaging of a few finds has enabled us to work out that there were cremations, with the burnt remains being buried in pots, and ordinary burials as well. It seems that they were placed in the vicinity of, or even within, a settlement of the same period.

The pots in these burials are the same as those found in the settlements. Until about 1700 BC, Beakers and Food Vessels were the main styles. From about 1800 to 1500 BC unusual jars known as Cordoned Urns were in use: these have wide, applied bands of clay around their waists and cord impressions around their necks. They are normally known only from cremation burials in other parts of Scotland and northern England but have been recovered from settlements at Cladh Hallan and Cill Donnain. After 1700 BC undecorated pots (aptly named the Plain Style) appeared and, after 1500 BC, this was the only style of pottery remaining in use for many centuries thereafter.

By the end of the Early Bronze Age the people of South Uist were performing an extraordinary funerary rite which has not so far been recognized anywhere else in Europe during the Bronze Age; they were able to mummify their dead. We know this because of a find from the Late Bronze Age settlement at Cladh Hallan (see chapter 5) where we discovered the skeleton of a man buried beneath a house: such burials of people, animals or valuable objects beneath buildings occur in many times and places and are known as foundation deposits.

The man's 'skeleton' actually belonged to three different people: it had been put together by amalgamating the head of one man with the jaw of another and the torso of a third *(colour plate 6)*. Radiocarbon dating indicated that the owner of the torso died at some time around 1500 BC whilst the head and jaw belonged to two men who had been alive probably a century later, dying in about 1400 BC.

Just how the body lost its skull, and how it came to be given someone else's head and someone else's jaw, is not known but we do know that someone kept the body for some 400-500 years before it was finally buried at Cladh Hallan. The position of the bones in any burial tells an archaeologist if a body was buried intact, held together by the muscles and soft tissue, or if it had rotted or been cut up into pieces before burial. The body found at Cladh Hallan had been buried with its soft tissue intact – with the exception of the head (which belonged to someone else), the bones still articulated with each other. And yet this body had been dead for over 400 years when it went into the ground.

Scientific analysis of the skeleton has identified some of the processes that brought about a type of mummification which preserved this body's soft tissue for centuries before it was buried under the house at Cladh Hallan. At his death, the man's body was left for a short while to begin the natural process of decay but this was halted abruptly when the corpse was placed in an acidic environment, presumably in peat, for just long enough that the surfaces of his bones became demineralized. This would not have taken very long, probably less than a year, and then his corpse, tanned by the action of the peat, was preserved for almost half a millennium.

As far as we know, Egypt and South America were the only other parts of the world where corpses were mummified at this period. It may be tempting to speculate that there was some kind of contact or exchange of knowledge between ancient Scotland and ancient Egypt. Yet this seems highly unlikely. Firstly, immersion in peat is very much a local recipe that owes nothing to ancient Egypt! This seems to be a case of independent invention.

Secondly, the South Uist body was not laid flat on its back, as in the Egyptian way, but was bent double in a tightly crouched position with its knees under its chin, no doubt held in place by bindings or tight wrappings. A second skeleton from Cladh Hallan, dating to just a little later around 1300 BC (discussed in chapter 5), was similarly treated. A tightly crouched skeleton, found in a pit dug into a Beaker 'midden' (rubbish heap) at Barvas on Lewis, may be the remains of a third mummified body but it has not yet been dated or analysed.

The significance of finding evidence for mummification in the Early Bronze Age – albeit as a fairly simple technological process – is that it shows that the dead need not all be summarily disposed of by burial or cremation. This individual's remains were kept somewhere where the preserved body did not deteriorate in the cold and wet of successive Hebridean winters. He might have been kept in someone's roof space or in a special ancestral house.

An interesting type of burial chamber from this period in the islands is the corbelled cist, a drystone-walled beehive-shaped chamber, buried below ground surface. Examples have been excavated at Rosinish in Benbecula and at Northton in Harris. Were the skeletons in these the last remains of bodies which were once mummified? We do not know as yet. In any case, would a buried stone chamber, entirely unheated, be sufficient to keep the preserved skin and ligaments from decaying if left there for centuries? We suspect not.

Evidence from societies around the world that have practised mummification shows that preserved bodies may be regarded as 'living' entities which are brought out at particular times of celebration and ceremony, such as a coronation or an initiation. They may even be regarded as having the power of decision-making, communicating to a seer about events affecting the living. Most importantly, this mummified individual from Cladh Hallan would surely have been someone whose name and deeds were recalled long after his death – he was history personified. We don't know what he did that merited this post-mortem special treatment but he must have been an illustrious citizen of South Uist three-and-a-half millennia ago.

The men represented by the skull and the torso were in their forties or older when they died and they might well have had many offspring. They can almost certainly be considered as ancestors of the later generations who guarded their desiccated corpses. People might well have calculated their kinship connections with each other through their genealogical distance to these men. If the Neolithic had been a time of commemorating the ancestors as an anonymous collectivity who dwelt in their cold abodes of stone, then the people of the

Early Bronze Age preferred their ancestors to have an individuality after death, exhibited in the practice of single burial (or cremation) and given fullest expression towards the end of this period through the use of mummification to preserve individual bodies.

STONE CIRCLES AND STANDING STONES

The shift from collective burials to an emphasis on single ancestors and the individual dead which occurred at the very end of the Neolithic and in the Early Bronze Age is a cultural change which can also be perceived in the stone monuments. The communal ancestors of the Neolithic were embodied in stone in the form of the multitude of rocks massed together to form the chambers, passages and cairns of chambered tombs. In contrast, the people of the Early Bronze Age marked the transcendental permanence of their ancestors not with rocks gathered together but with single upright stones, set in the landscape either in isolation or as members of a circle or similar arrangement.

Prehistoric stone circles might have been ceremonial centres or demonstrations of astronomical ability but we should also be aware of the need to commemorate the ancestral dead. The best-known standing stones in the Western Isles are, of course, those at Callanish (Calanais) on the Isle of Lewis, well to the north of South Uist *(colour plate 4)*.

Sometimes called the 'Stonehenge of the north', the stone circle at Callanish is eloquent testimony to the stone-moving skills and astronomical knowledge of the people of the Hebrides. It was built around 3000 BC, when this particular part of Lewis became the ceremonial and religious centre of the islands. Callanish was not built in isolation: it is one of five stone circles in this area of Lewis. Four more stone circles, equally spaced across Lewis, hint at a geographical apportioning of other ceremonial centres in addition to the focus at Callanish. This spectacular concentration of monuments suggests that the islands' power base, expressed in the building of great stone monuments, shifted away from North Uist, where it seems to have been centred in the earlier part of the Neolithic.

North Uist may have been the centre of power no longer, yet it certainly retained some of its former importance, with three stone circles being constructed at its north end during this period, a further three at its south end, and numerous standing stones marking the landscape in between. The southern three circles are close to two on the north coast of Benbecula and possibly formed a larger complex located around the sea channel between the two islands. This suggests that Benbecula and North Uist were perhaps still one landmass, with what is now a sea channel being a freshwater loch at this period.

At the southern end of the island chain, there was another monument complex on Barra, focused on the Brevig area of its southeast coast. A total of seven stone circles have been found there, together with numerous standing stones. The more southerly small islands of Mingulay and Vatersay have also yielded three very small circles.

South Uist was thought to be without a large stone circle until a few years ago when Mary Harman, a biologist working for Scottish Natural Heritage, chanced across the low stones of one hidden in the heather in the hills east of Aesgernis (Askernish), revealed in the aftermath of a moorland fire which had burnt off the vegetation. Arrangements of stones located in Cill Donnain glen are thought to be the remains of another two small circles.

South Uist's standing stones are easier to locate. Their distribution is focused on this central area of the island, with the tall stone of An'chara up on the hillside above Stoneybridge, the standing stone at Cnoc a'Breac on a small headland in the same township, and the Cill Donnain standing stone just a few hundred metres southeast of Sligeanach. This stone is now entirely buried beneath machair sand and is marked today only by a small, flat stone on the surface of the dune.

There are other former standing stones in South Uist that are no longer in their original locations. Drinkers at the Polochar Inn can sit out on fine evenings and admire the Polochar stone, said to have been re-erected where it now stands on the shore close to the pub *(colour plate 3)*. At Aesgernis a 2m-long stone lies just north of the road that leads to the golf course *(24)*. It is the only South Uist stone to have been worked and has a pecked line around one end. According to local legend, its removal from its original setting to be used as a lintel in one of the barns at Aesgernis brought bad luck and it was finally taken out of the building and left in the field.

The focus of the stone monuments on the Cill Donnain area is very interesting for two reasons. Firstly, this part of the island was still largely undisturbed forest at the end of the Neolithic – it was a wild place, left untamed by the inhabitants. Secondly, the presence of the monuments here towards the centre of South Uist suggests that links to the northern islands were no longer maintained. South Uist had become a separate entity in ceremonial and religious terms – perhaps it was now separated from Benbecula by the sea.

It seems remarkable that such a major monument as a stone circle lay undiscovered until very recently. Of course, the stones of the Aesgernis circle are very short, nothing like the heights of the Callanish stones (and we should remember that those great stones were themselves largely buried under peat for many centuries). Are there more stone circles still to be discovered on South Uist? Perhaps. A recent airborne, heat-sensing survey has detected a circular arrangement on Cill Donnain machair, close to the standing stone and settlements. Could this be another lost stone circle, covered by the sand?

So much more remains to be discovered on South Uist. We still know almost nothing about the life and times of the man mummified around 1500 BC. What kind of house did he and his kin live in? What happened to the remains of most of the dead? Were the stone circles still being built or were ceremonies still being performed at them? Although Callanish was built in the Neolithic period, some of the smaller stone circles may well have been erected in the Early Bronze Age. There are many, many questions to ask of this dimly understood period at the end of the Early Bronze Age. What makes South Uist and the Western Isles important for studying this elusive period is that, under the sands of the machair, there lie the preserved remains of people's houses and settlements, as well as their burials.

24 The fallen standing stone at Aesgernis

CHAPTER 5

ROUNDHOUSES

The Later Bronze Age and Early Iron Age,
c.1200-200 BC

The great monuments of the Iron Age in northern and western Scotland are the enormous stone towers known as brochs. Unlike the Neolithic chambered tombs and Bronze Age burial cairns, these were monuments constructed for the living rather than the dead. They are properly the subject of our next chapter but must be introduced at this point because they help to highlight one of the most remarkable transitions in British and European prehistory – the shift in social and symbolic emphasis from ancestors and tombs to hearths and homes.

We know quite a lot about the people who built and lived in brochs but, until very recently, nothing was known about the houses and daily life of the inhabitants of the Western Isles in the centuries before their construction. All of this has now changed. The gap in our knowledge has been filled by the results of our excavation of a Late Bronze Age and Early Iron Age settlement at Cladh Hallan. By extraordinary luck, that excavation also shed unexpected light on the tomb-to-house transition.

For many years the only find of Late Bronze Age date from South Uist was a pair of bronze swords, now in the National Museum in Edinburgh. They were found in Iochdar, at the north end of the island, in the late nineteenth century, presumably while digging peats. There have been very few other archaeological finds from peat digging. Carved stone balls of the Neolithic period were found in Dalabrog and Bornais townships and there is a wooden bowl, possibly from the Viking Age, found in a peat bog at Loch Ainort in the 1980s.

Elsewhere in the Western Isles the picture for the Late Bronze Age is not much different. Everywhere, finds have been very sparse: there is another bronze sword from Aird in Lewis and an important hoard of bronze artefacts, deposited at the beginning of the Iron Age around 700 BC, from Adabrock at the Butt of Lewis. Add to them the Sheshader 'thing' found in a bog on Lewis – an unidentified artefact of compressed cow hair and cords of wool and horsehair – and that is about it.

Another find from the peat came up in 1976. Iain Morrison was out at his peat cutting in Carinis, North Uist, when he noticed four green circles in the peatface. As he dug them out he realized that they were the bases of four bronze spearheads which had no doubt been deposited as a bundle. They were not wrapped in anything, and digging out the peat around them failed to reveal any more finds. Why had they been left there? It is possible that they had merely been lost, put down in a careless moment. But it is more likely that they were deliberately placed or buried in the peat. Were they hidden by an anxious Late Bronze Age warrior, hoping to retrieve them if he returned from afar? Or were they offerings, left here with no intention of ever retrieving them? This last explanation is the most likely because of the unusual location, far from the settlements of the period which are all on the machair. The spot is also a special one, close to the edge of the loch which is ringed by five stone circles.

Across Europe and the British Isles thousands of Late Bronze Age weapons have been found in peat and other watery places and most archaeologists accept that these objects were deliberately left as offerings. The peat bogs of Skye have produced an impressive number of bronze weapons over the years. So why have so few been recovered from the Western Isles, especially when peat digging by hand has continued up to the present day? It may simply be because such things were ignored when they were found in the past, or that no-one chose to make a record of them. Happily we can be confident that any future finds will be recognized for what they are and saved for posterity.

SETTLEMENTS

Late Bronze Age and Early Iron Age pottery is undecorated – the Plain Style discussed in chapter 4 – and this has made identification of the settlements of this period slightly difficult. Iain Crawford's excavation at the Udal provided information on later periods but the Udal project ended before the Late Bronze Age and Early Iron Age layers were fully investigated. The lack of Late Bronze Age metalwork recovered from peat digging also led some archaeologists to suspect that few people had lived in the Western Isles during this period.

There was certainly a downturn in climatic conditions at this time and some indications that the climate change could have been catastrophic. Fluctuations in climate can be traced through dendrochronology – the study of tree rings – and the narrow growth rings in Irish trees in the 18 years after 1159 BC show clearly that growing cycles were inhibited. Was the poor weather which affected these trees bad enough to have caused crop failure across western Scotland in these years? Did this – or some other – climatic disaster result in the abandonment of much of the region until many centuries later in the Iron Age? The answer seems to be no – the islands were not abandoned. We have located 11 settlements of this Late Bronze Age period on South Uist's machair and the excavated site of Cladh Hallan shows a sequence of activity all the way through.

The Late Bronze Age settlements are located, by and large, close to their Early Bronze Age predecessors. At Cladh Hallan, in the south, the settlement was built on top of earlier, long-abandoned fields and also on top of the post-Beaker settlement. At the north end of the island, in Iochdar, the settlement mounds are several hundred metres east and inland from the previous settlement. There is less certainty about the location of Late Bronze Age settlement mounds on the Cill Donnain machair. A small mound at Ormacleit, further north, is of this general date but the sites with Plain Style pottery – under the Dun Vulan broch, on Upper Loch Bornish, and at Sligeanach – have radiocarbon dates which place them in the Early Iron Age. It is possible that one very large mound with Middle Iron Age remains in its upper levels began life in the Late Bronze Age. It lies on Bornais machair south of the Ardvule headland and is identifiable by the flagpole on its summit.

The Iochdar machair settlement is the most impressive of the lot, comprising five very large and high mounds. There are only three or four mounds at Cladh Hallan, although one of the two excavated mounds there is 80m across. If Iochdar housed the densest population in any one place on the machair, then it could very well have been the centre of power and authority. Situated at the northern end of South Uist, it lies at the midpoint of the Uists, a suitable location for a regional 'capital'. To date there has been no large-scale excavation of these mounds but investigation of this Iochdar settlement is a priority for the future. In the meantime, our knowledge of village life in the Late Bronze Age and Early Iron Age is based largely on the results of the Cladh Hallan excavations.

THE LAST BURIAL CAIRNS

The Late Bronze Age marks a watershed in funerary monumentality. After millennia of burying the remains of the dead (or at least some of the dead) communally in chambered cairns during the Neolithic and singly in smaller cairns during the Bronze Age, this tradition of providing substantial and permanently marked resting places was coming to an end. From about 1000 BC the investment of labour into stone masonry was transferred to the construction of the abodes of the living.

The Bronze Age cairns in the Western Isles are generally less than 6m in diameter and have a border or kerb of stones around them. Their distribution in the islands is puzzling. Only five have been recorded on South Uist, with others on the offshore islands of Eriskay and Fuday. There are 14 on Barra but a staggering 75 on the small islands south of Barra. The majority probably date to the Early Bronze Age but some were erected in the Late Bronze Age. Most of them seem to have covered a cremation burial within a small pit or in a short cist (a 'box' made of stone slabs). This form of burial in a pit or cist without a cairn or a mound was also being practised but, because these graves are unmarked, finding these flat graves is much harder. The absence of cairns on the larger islands may be because flat graves were more popular in these areas. Another possibility is that the outlying islands were specially selected as burial places for many of the people who lived on these larger islands.

Curiously enough, the Late Bronze Age village at Cladh Hallan began with a cemetery *(colour plate 5)*. There had once been an Early Bronze Age settlement here, with fields and a cemetery, but these had disappeared beneath a deep layer of windblown sand. Around 1500 BC, long after the Early Bronze Age village had been covered up by the action of the wind, a group of five or more cremations were placed on the surface of the sand. Most were simple heaps of cremated bone and pyre ash, but two of them were treated differently.

One set of cremated remains was laid on a surface of burnt stones brought from the pyre and was covered over with a capping of peat. Around it was arranged a circle of stones, rough rocks on the inland side of the circle and smooth beach pebbles on the side towards the sea, with a small entrance at the northeast. Another set of remains was placed in a shallow hollow scooped out of the sand and was similarly capped with peat. A few sherds from a broken pot were mixed with these ashes and a ring of stones, smaller than the other, ran all the way around it.

These are the first steps to take when building a Bronze Age burial cairn. The next is to create a kerb of upright slabs and then to fill in the whole area with stones to form a small stone monument which stands knee-high. Examples of the process have been excavated on Vatersay (south of Barra) and near Callanish on Lewis. The dates of construction of these cairns indicate that this style of mini-monument building continued from the Early Bronze Age until well into the Later Bronze Age. Examples from the Scottish mainland also fall within this date range.

A bronze cloak-fastener was found in one of the Vatersay burials, and a pot in the Callanish cairn, but these cairn burials never contain much in the way of grave goods. Were the sherds from the Cladh Hallan grave all that the mourners could scrape together to acknowledge the status of the deceased? The answer is almost certainly no. From slightly later levels on the site we have finds of bronze tools, together with clay moulds for making a wide variety of bronze weapons and ornaments. It seems that the inhabitants' wealth in metal was mostly reserved for other purposes and they chose not to leave gifts to accompany the dead.

The individual whose cremated remains were buried within the smaller of the stone rings at Cladh Hallan was more important than his/her modest accoutrement of a few sherds may have us believe. A house was built on top

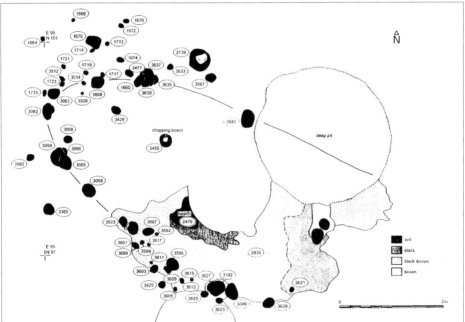

25 Excavation of the house built over the cremation burials at Cladh Hallan

26 Plan of the house built over the cremation burials at Cladh Hallan

of this grave while it was still visible above ground, around 1400 BC *(25; 26)*. The builders of the house set their fireplace directly on top of the cremated ashes: the dead person's remains lay beneath the source of the household's warmth and – through cooking – nourishment.

27 The pit dug through the Cladh Hallan
house floor into the cremation burial

In the course of time this house on top of the grave was abandoned and largely dismantled. What was left standing – notably one of the door posts – was then burnt. Sand blown by the wind settled in a thin layer on top of the ruins and, later in time, the whole area was ploughed. And then something very surprising happened. Someone came to this place and dug a large pit just to the north of the hearth of the old, abandoned house. Having located the hearth, they then dug a small tunnel beneath it, leading into the base of the cremation burial *(27)*. We know that they removed some of the cremated bones because the soil which refilled their pit contained fragments of bone from the burial beneath.

It is difficult to know whether this strange activity took place years, decades or even a century or so later but, together with the positioning of the hearth, it does tell us that there was something very important about the person whose remains were buried here. The last vestiges and last resting place of this individual were something to be remembered and passed on to future generations. In a way, the transformation of a burial into the site of a house's fireplace is an eloquent statement of the cultural change under which the people of the Late Bronze Age turned from memorializing the dead to exalting the living.

CHANGING STYLES OF HOUSE ARCHITECTURE

The house which was built on top of the burial was about 6.2m long and 3m wide *(26)*. The doorway faced southeast and the hearth was placed slightly off-centre in the middle of the building. The house's rear end tapered to a narrow point and an arc of posts, placed outside it, might have served as a windbreak. The entrance was marked by a large threshold stone (which was removed when the inhabitants abandoned their house), and the doorway was composed of two upright posts set slightly in from the threshold.

Tiny broken sherds concentrated in the doorway indicate that people sat here in the entrance area while cooking food on the hearth. Unfortunately the north and west sides of the house were badly disturbed by later activity and it is not possible to be sure where the occupants slept, although the most likely places are around the westward side of the hearth.

The house itself was rather flimsy by our standards. Like most prehistoric houses in Britain, it had an earth floor. This simple layer of beaten sand and peat had been laid directly on the bare soil of the cremation cemetery. Its walls were constructed using small wooden posts with additional, smaller stakes, presumably forming a wattle wall that carried the weight of the roof. Some of the wall posts were replaced up to three times, so this house must have been occupied for some years.

The house is similar in size and shape to the boat-shaped house at Northton on Harris which was built in the Beaker period about six hundred years earlier. Another, slightly larger structure at Rosinish on Benbecula is also similar in shape and, although not securely dated, is thought by the excavators to also belong to the Early Bronze Age, around 2000 BC. This likely continuity in domestic architecture is striking and the Cladh Hallan house marks the end of an era. What was to follow, almost directly on top of it, was a revolutionary building programme on a scale hitherto undreamed of.

After this house at Cladh Hallan was abandoned – and before any further houses were built – a line of holes was dug in the area around it, heading northeast and aligned with the summit of Ben Mhor, South Uist's highest mountain. The pit which was dug into the north side of the house's hearth, in search of the cremation burial, was just one of this line of pits, some of them very deep. The pits were filled in with the sandy soil which had been dug out and very little was added, other than some human skull fragments and a handful of cremated bones in one pit and a complete pot in another. Rather oddly, some of the pits were then dug out again, and refilled again.

What was the purpose of digging these pits? Did they serve some practical purpose for the builders of the roundhouses that were soon to be erected here? Perhaps they were trying to find the level of the groundwater before building here. If so, why dig so many holes, to different depths? Were all the pits like the one from which someone reached the cremation burial – were the builders trying to locate the ancient remains beneath the sand? The deepest pits reached the level of the Beaker cultivation soil and stopped there.

Our own excavations at Cladh Hallan were limited by the extent of the modern sand quarry: the southern half of this ancient village is protected beneath a mound of sand 2m high and we have been able to explore only the northern part of the settlement where the mound has been quarried away. Here in the northern half we excavated nine of the Bronze Age pits but the alignment of pits disappears beneath the mound to the south so we cannot know its full length.

Having filled in the pits, the builders next constructed a tiny building at the mid-point of what was to become the new settlement *(28)*. It was very different to the previous house. Instead of having its floor at ground level, it was sunk slightly into the ground and had a low wall of stones around its edge. These were revetted into a sand wall which originally came up to knee-height on the outside and formed a thick wall for the house. Its entrance faced east but it lacked one essential feature of any house – it had no hearth. The floor was a very thin layer of soil and contained little debris, just a couple of bone tools dropped on its surface. Measuring about 2.5m by 2m, there was scarcely room inside to swing a cat (not that domestic cats reached the islands until 1,000 years later). This oval house was not big enough to have been a proper dwelling. One possibility is that it was a 'test run' or builders' model for what they were about to build.

The next step was a bold and sweeping architectural project. The builders constructed a long terrace of roundhouses, running north–south right across the top of this tiny house. We were able to excavate three of these houses and find the northern edge of a fourth *(29; colour plate 7)*. The size of the settlement mound provides room for another three houses in its unexcavated southern half and we detected part of one of these at the southernmost end of the mound. This was a built-to-order community, probably consisting of seven houses all sharing party walls. It has been dubbed 'Scotland's first terraced row' and seems to have been one of the few such terraces anywhere in Scotland or the British Isles.

At that time, almost all buildings in Britain were round or approximately round – even though contemporary societies on the Continent built rectangular houses, they are extremely unusual in Britain until after the arrival of the Romans, at the end of the Iron Age. These roundhouses were usually built singly or sometimes in groups of two or three, but very rarely as a chain of linked dwellings. A number of similar roundhouse terraces have been recognised in Perthshire but little is known of their date and use.

The floor areas of these houses were much larger than those of earlier dwellings. Of the three excavated roundhouses, the middle house was the largest with a floor area of about 60sq.m – as much living space as in a modern-day two-storey terraced house. We found the edge of another, equally large house at the south end of the excavated area; this house lies protected beneath the settlement mound and has therefore not been excavated.

This increase in house size might have been linked to a growth in the size of the household, or to the range of activities undertaken within the house, or both. There was certainly more room for a bigger household. The sleeping

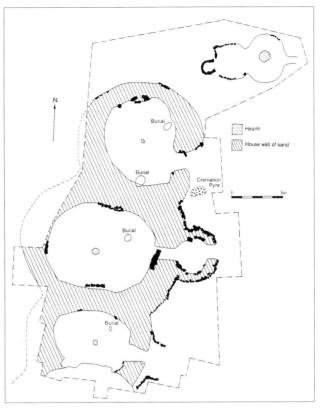

28 The mini-roundhouse under the south roundhouse at Cladh Hallan

29 Plan of the three roundhouses at the north end of the terraced row at Cladh Hallan

area alone was as large as the entire interior space of previous house forms. These dwellings could house extended families rather than the nuclear unit of parents and offspring. Alternatively, interior space became a measure of familial status and pride. Whatever the reason, for the first time in Hebridean prehistory it would be possible to talk of families and lineages as 'houses'. This was the beginning of a 'house-society' in which one's residence became a defining element of individual and corporate identity.

The profound nature of the change was also expressed in the architectural massiveness of the buildings. Each was dug into the sand so that the floor could be laid on the flat bottom of the large circular pit that formed the house interior. The upcast sand was treated, probably by mixing it with peat, to give it some firmness and then banked up into a thick but low wall, 1-2m wide, around the sunken-floored house. This sand bank was held in place by revetted stone walls on each face, inside and out.

Each house could be entered only through a single doorway, which faced east, leading into a small passageway that sloped down into the sunken gloom of the house. The roof rested partly on the thick, stubby walls and partly on timber posts arranged around the interior. Even with a low angle of pitch, at about 35°, the roof would have provided head room of up to 5m in the larger houses and 4m in the smaller ones.

30 A whale bone lamp
from Cladh Hallan

We can only guess at the roofing materials but, by looking at the materials used in traditional Western Isles 'blackhouses', we can presume the Bronze Age builders used a layer of reeds laid over the roof timbers, with a final outer covering of large blocks of turf. The turf would probably have continued to grow, so the village would have appeared in the landscape as a row of green, grassy cones entered through small porch arrangements on their east sides. Since the walls were so low there would have been no windows: experiments have shown that smoke-holes in the roofs of roundhouses are unnecessary and even dangerous, creating a vortex of wind which scatters burning embers everywhere.

The dark gloom of the interior was thus illuminated only by the small central fireplace and by the light that came in through the doorway. After some years of use, the middle house was remodelled and at this time its occupants added a small, circular reception room on its east side, thereby extending the entrance and passageway into the house and further reducing the amount of natural light coming into the building. We have found one lamp, made from a block of whale bone but, even if fuelled by bird or seal oil, it would have provided only a little light *(30)*.

Such ways of living and working in near-complete gloom disappeared with the blackhouses nearly a century ago in the Western Isles and many readers may find it hard to credit that anyone could live without our creature comforts such as lighting and chairs! And it was not as if people did their craftworking outside, sitting on the threshold step or in the doorway. The telltale micro-debris left behind on the spots where people once worked skins or trimmed deer antlers was not found trampled into the outdoor surfaces, or on the ground around the door. Instead, it is found only *inside* the houses. Even then, these signs of craftwork are not found between the fire and the door – where there would have been most light – but towards the back of the house and to the left-hand side.

From the vantage point of our own society, it is difficult to appreciate the impact of this new form of housing. For us, it is part of the natural order of things that a house is a permanent object, with a life expectancy much longer than any of its individual inhabitants. The people of the Late Bronze Age lived in a time of revolutionary ideas: stone tombs and the cairns of the dead were once the pinnacle of permanence but now houses became the vehicle for expressing lineage, ancestry and associations with place.

Yet there was even more to these roundhouses than size, solidity and semi-permanence. There was a symbolic dimension which linked the inhabitants and their activities into the greater cycle of life. Religious observances were no longer something separate from the daily routine, performed at other, outdoor venues such as stone circles and standing stones, but were integrated into the workings of the house itself.

ROUNDHOUSES AND THE LIFE CYCLE

Before we started excavating at Cladh Hallan, we had a strong indication that British roundhouses of the first millennium BC were organized according to certain principles which followed a sunwise (to us, clockwise) layout. As we began work at Cladh Hallan, we even drew up a series of models to see whether our expectations would be met. And they were, in more ways than we had ever anticipated.

Round domestic architecture is an odd choice of design, especially given that the rest of prehistoric Europe was building in rectangular forms. We had noticed that, throughout the British Isles in the first millennium BC, house doorways, enclosure entranceways* and burials mostly face east or southeast. There are exceptions to this rule: some houses face in exactly the opposite direction, to the west.

Given this east–west axis, some more literal-minded archaeologists in the past tried to explain the predominantly easterly direction of doorways as a practical means of avoiding westerly winds, but why should that apply to burials and the entrances to hillforts and other enclosures? In addition, of course,

---

* An 'enclosure' is a type of archaeological site identified by having a boundary of a raised bank and/or ditch. Hillforts are an elaborate type of enclosure. Neither hillforts nor enclosures are found in Uist.

houses of this period in areas which suffer from bitter east winds – such as the Fens of eastern England – still face east, straight into the coldest weather system. It was evident that the east–west axis was telling us something more important.

The breakthrough came in the early 1990s when the archaeologist Andrew Fitzpatrick was digging an Iron Age roundhouse in Thatcham, Berkshire – a very long way from South Uist! Lacking the exceptional preservation of house floors in machair sand, most roundhouses elsewhere in Britain survive only as settings of postholes and an eavesdrip gully (a shallow circular hollow created where water has run off the sloping roof of the roundhouse). There was no surviving floor, but Fitzpatrick found the postholes to be unusually full of artefacts which had fallen in after the timber posts had been removed. The doorway faced southeast and the hearth was in the centre of the house.

Broken pots in the postholes of the southeast quadrant of the house, just inside the doorway, indicated the cooking area. Tools of bone and stone in the southwest quadrant showed where daytime activities had been carried out. The lack of finds in the north suggested to him that this was the sleeping area. He realized that this interior arrangement matched the diurnal cycle of the sun's passage. As it rose in the east and moved south, so people sat in the southern half of the house and did their daily chores. As it dipped below the horizon and moved around the north, so people took to their beds in the northern part of the house.

If the roundhouse marked the daily or diurnal cycle, we also speculated that its architecture should embody other sunwise cycles of time, from the very short – actual movement around the house – to the very long – the life cycle from birth in the southeast to death in the northeast quadrant. Our guess was that the roundhouse way of life was as much about beliefs as it was about practical activities. In fact, beliefs and activities were inseparable aspects of life. We were going to find out if Fitzpatrick's daily cycle could be traced in the remains in and on the floors of the Cladh Hallan houses but how could we possibly find evidence of the directions used when people moved around inside their houses? And what traces of birth or death could we find to establish whether the life cycle was truly embodied in the house's architecture? As it turned out, we found more evidence than we expected.

In all, we have excavated 14 different floors in the roundhouses, each floor a layer of sandy soil spread over an earlier, worn-down earth floor. These floors, laid one of top of the other, give us a sequence of over 700 years of occupation at Cladh Hallan, from about 1100 BC to after 400 BC (*31; 32*). Fitzpatrick's prediction fits every one of them. And, better still, we have actually found the preserved remains of the sleeping areas that Fitzpatrick could only hypothesize.

Any reader who has visited Skara Brae on Orkney will know that the Neolithic inhabitants of that village slept in box beds with stone surrounds. At

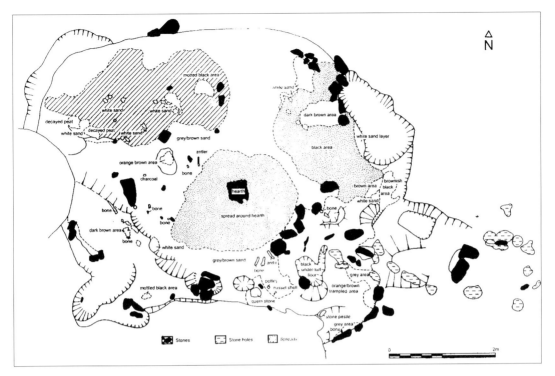

Key labels within plan:

motted black area

white sand

dark brown area

decayed peat

white sand

decayed peat

white sand

white sand layer

grey/brown sand

black area

antler

orange brown area

bone

brownish black area

charcoal

brown area

white sand

bone

bone

bone

bone

spread around hearth

hearth

bone

bone

dark brown area

bone

white sand

grey area

grey/brown sand

antler

bone

black under-turf floor

orange/brown trampled area

mottled black area

bone

potlid

mussel shell

quern stone

stone pestle

grey area

bone

◼ Stones   ▭ Stone holes   ▭ Spreads

0   2m

31 Plan of the floor of the south roundhouse

32 The middle roundhouse at Cladh Hallan with its forecourt

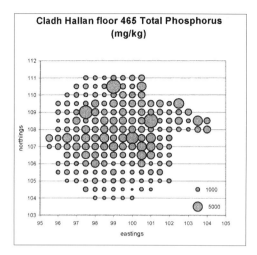
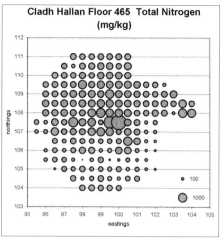

33 Graphs depicting the distribution of phosphate and nitrogen on the fourth floor of the middle roundhouse

Cladh Hallan there were no such individual beds, just a simple raised platform of turf on which the whole family slept together. The turfs were cut from the machair grass and were piled up with the grassy sides uppermost. Clean sand was also brought in to line some of the deeper sleeping hollows. Probably there was a layer of soft, springy heather on top – these were standard features of beds in Hebridean houses in later millennia and were described in 1695 as 'with the tops uppermost, [they] are almost as soft as a feather bed, and yield a pleasant scent after lying on them once.' Scientific measurement of levels of phosphorus and nitrogen across the house floors show high levels on the sleeping platform *(33),* possibly resulting from this organic matter (or from urine – babies and small children wetting the bed!). As predicted in advance of excavation, there were very few artefacts within the bed area other than the very occasional broken bone ornament or tool.

The southeast quadrant of each floor was filled with broken sherds of pottery and a variety of discarded bone and stone tools – spoons made of sheep's scapulae (shoulder blades), pounding and grinding stones, and stone 'plates' or lids. In some cases, there were 'pot boilers', stones heated in the fire and then dropped into water. This was where the cooking was done, presumably as the first task of the day. The south of the house was also the area where crops were cleaned and processed *(34).* In the first phase of the middle house, its southwest quadrant had a small cellar, presumably once covered by planks, entered down a short curving flight of stone steps.

The southwest quadrant of each house was full of small discarded tools and their broken fragments. The three items that were most common here were bone points, pumice stone and polished stones. These make up a kit for leatherworking: the pointed bone tools were used to stretch out the hide on a wooden frame, pumice was used to scrape the fat off the underside of the skin, and the leather was softened and burnished by rubbing it with the polishing stones. Judging from the animal bones littering the settlement, calfskin, lambskin, fawnskin and pigskin were the main products.

In the medieval period, calfskin was used to make vellum, a precursor of writing paper, and this beautifully soft, thin and supple material might have helped clothe the inhabitants of Cladh Hallan in high-quality stitched leather dresses, tunics and coats. On only one house's floor was there evidence for a loom – paired posts and a single loomweight – but spinning was a common enough activity, since we found many spindle whorls (the circular weight on the end of the hand-held spindle).

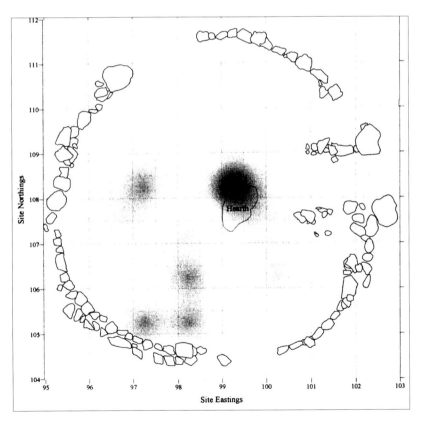

34 Plan of the distributions of plant remains (burnt weed seeds) from the fourth floor of the middle roundhouse

THE DEAD UNDER THE FLOOR

The sleeping area did not extend entirely around the northern half of the house. Not only was it set back a metre or so from the hearth but its east end terminated before the east wall, leaving a flat and bare sector in the northeast quadrant where the only trace of activity was the remains of a small fireplace set against the house wall. This northeast area was where some very special things lay waiting to be found. In each of the three houses, after the walls had been built but before the first floor surface was laid down, a human body was buried in a pit in this northeast quadrant.

The southernmost house on the excavation site was the smallest and poorest, and its foundation burial was the jumbled skeleton of a three-year-old child *(35)*. Given the tangled disorder of this skeleton, the body had probably been left to rot in a bag or sack which was then buried. Under the largest house, in the middle of the site, was the burial of a child aged 10-14, possibly

35 The disarticulated skeleton of a three-year-old buried beneath the south roundhouse

36 The skeleton of a 10 to 14-year-old child buried beneath the middle roundhouse

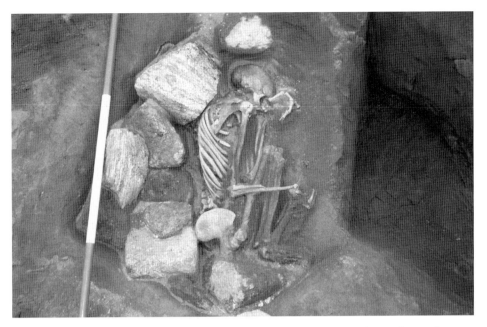

37 The skeleton of the adult woman, formerly mummified, buried under the north roundhouse

a girl, who had been buried in a crouched position, on her side with her legs tucked up towards her body *(36)*. Under the north house was the skeleton of the centuries-old mummy (which we have described in chapter 4) and another body of a woman *(37)*.

We had predicted human burials in the northeast quadrant of each house but this second skeleton was unexpected. The woman had been about 40 when she died in around 1300 BC and her body seems also to have been mummified and kept for two centuries before it was buried at the foundation of the roundhouse row in about 1100 BC, in the south area of the north house. Whilst mummified, she had had two teeth (the upper lateral incisors) removed and placed in her hands, the left tooth in the left hand and the right tooth in the right hand. Why was this done? We simply do not know. And why was she buried in the wrong part of the house? Perhaps she was thought to have died before her time, or perhaps this burial was placed here following some special and complex decision in the circumstances of the moment.

One of the hardest tasks for the archaeologist is to detect and explain anomalies. It is often not that difficult to recognise cultural patterns – the results of following social conventions – but rather harder to understand and interpret the changes and the actions that contravene the rules. Yet this is probably the most interesting aspect of archaeology because the human agency behind such changes and contraventions is what makes things happen, otherwise we'd still be putting up stone circles. For an example of an anomalous female burial from our own times, an archaeologist in the future would soon understand our era's strong conventions which permit burial only in cemeteries and churchyards and would therefore be perplexed by Princess Diana's grave, all by itself on an island. How can anyone who doesn't know the circumstances unravel why that happened?

The middle house was remodelled seven times over more than 600 years. Each rebuilding required a new wall and a new floor, formed by bringing in a layer of soil to build up the eroded surface, a make-up layer like hardcore on a worn path, followed by spreading a new floor surface on top. When the first floor of each house required this treatment, special offerings were left in the northeast quadrant to mark the end of its previous life, to 'close' the house. In the middle house these offerings were a pair of bronze woodworking chisels. In the north house someone placed a broken bronze bracelet here and in the south house all its inhabitants could afford to deposit were a pair of stone hammers. These offerings of a bracelet and stone tools are particularly interesting because these are exactly the sort of items placed in earlier Bronze Age burial cairns such as those on Vatersay. In a sense these offerings of bronze and stone were funeral offerings for the house itself.

The south house was never used again but the north house was rebuilt twice. Its third phase was preceded by the burial of a newborn child under the floor in the northeast quadrant *(38)*. In the middle house there were no further human burials but a couple of dogs, one of them headless, were buried beneath the northeast quadrant in the fourth phase *(39)*. The burial of the mummified woman in the south side of the north house was thus a complete anomaly. All the other burials were in the northeast quadrants. Why was hers different?

One possible answer may be to do with the particular role of that house and possibly its inhabitants. It lies at the north end of the row – it is technically the northeast house because the terraced row is slightly curved. Perhaps the life cycle was symbolized in the layout of the whole community as well as within each house. Might this northeast house have a special association with death? Indeed it does. Not only was the stone platform of a cremation pyre built right outside its door *(40)*, but some of the pits inside the house also contained pieces of cremated bone. Did the people who lived in this house have a special role as undertakers for the community? If this was their role, they do not seem to have been poor, or social outcasts, since someone lost a gold-plated bronze ring outside the front of the house *(41)*.

Each of the three houses was occupied by a family of differing social circumstances. As already mentioned, the occupants of the short-lived southern house seem not to have been well off. The people in the middle house, in contrast, had some connection with the metal trade. The floor of the reception room and part of the floor inside the house were covered in fragments of clay moulds used for casting bronze swords, spearheads, dress pins, razors and ornaments *(42)*. All of the metal must have come from elsewhere in the British Isles – copper from Wales and Ireland, tin from Cornwall and gold from Ireland

38 The skeleton of a baby buried in the north roundhouse

39 The decapitated dog in the middle roundhouse

40 The cremation platform outside
the north roundhouse

41 The gold-plated pennanular ring
found outside the north roundhouse

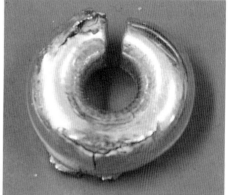

42 Fragments of clay
moulds for casting
bronze swords, found
in the forecourt of
the middle house

– indicating that these were people with connections. Even if the inhabitants of Cladh Hallan were recycling, making the objects from scrap metal, it still has to have been brought here from the Scottish or Irish mainland.

AGRICULTURE AND DAIRYING

From the lipids (fatty acids) and proteins preserved in the walls of the pots at Cladh Hallan, Oliver Craig and a team from Newcastle University have been able to identify bovine milk protein and milk fats in about two-thirds of the pots that they have analysed. Some of the remainder contained residues of vegetables and pulses. It is possible that milk was poured into the pots merely as a greasy coating to create a waterproofing layer so that they could be used to cook other things, but the accumulation of cream at the top of the pots indicates that milk was kept in them long enough for the cream to rise. It was probably cooked in combination with barley to produce that Scottish culinary contribution to the world, porridge! There was some baking, revealed by the discovery of a dismantled earth oven, but most of the meat seems to have been roasted over the fire unless it was eaten in a milky stew.

The increased use of milk at this time is borne out by the pattern of cattle culling. Examining the thousands of animal bones found on the site reveals that only a few cattle, mostly females, reached old age and most were culled very soon after birth. This pattern is not unique to Scotland. On sites where such a pattern is present in the animal bones, some archaeologists have interpreted it as evidence of a resource-poor and marginal environment in which all but a few beasts have to be killed before winter, to make sure that the limited stocks of fodder are sufficient to go round. However, our evidence indicates that the mortality pattern is the result of dairying as a specialized farming strategy. As in

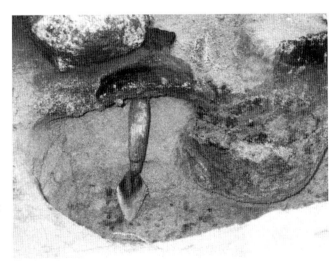

43 A complete cooking pot
buried as a foundation
offering under the wall of a
roundhouse at Cladh Hallan

earlier periods, seafood was a minor component of the diet and this suggests that conditions were never so unfavourable that these Late Bronze Age and Early Iron Age farmers were forced to diversify from their agricultural way of life.

Wheat was no longer cultivated and barley was the sole cereal crop. The weeds that were gathered, probably accidentally, with the barley harvest indicate that a wide variety of machair and peatlands were cultivated. This suggests a more extensive regime of fallowing and out-field cultivation than had been practised before. Yet these farmers were keen to make the most of the fertile middens (rubbish heaps) accumulating outside their houses, not by mixing them into the fields as the islands' inhabitants had done in the Beaker period, but by ploughing the settlement mound and planting right up to the sides of the houses. Cattle were also permitted to roam next to the houses, quite possibly to nibble at the grass growing on the roofs! Their hoof prints have survived in the sand for over 2,000 years.

The huge sizes of the settlement mounds of this period are testimony to the desire to keep these middens around the houses and also to the degree of permanence that the settlements now represented. As the centuries passed, the mounds became literally 'ancestral piles' in which the past lay directly beneath people's feet. The middle roundhouse at Cladh Hallan is a good example of this attitude, being inhabited for more than half a millennium, an extraordinary length of time for a prehistoric house! Over the years its front wall was widened to 3m thick, forming a solid structure which, although only knee-high on the outside, was not unlike the substantial walls of the brochs that people started building later in the first millennium BC.

TIME AND TRADITION

The Cladh Hallan roundhouses were far more than places to shelter from the wind and rain. They were complex metaphors for expressing and confirming a new understanding of the world, a new universal truth about the nature of time and human life. From Berkshire to Uist, and from 1100 BC until the end of the first millennium and beyond, this was a way of life that was expressed in the architecture itself. There are many aspects of the inhabitants' lives that appear irrational to us but they do serve to highlight the extent to which religion or superstition ruled people's everyday activities, a world in which religious belief was expressed on a daily basis as well as during special rituals and rites of passage enjoyed by the household as well as by the house itself.

Cladh Hallan has preserved all kinds of details about the smaller events in people's lives. A line of stones in the south house was laid to guide visitors in a southwards, sunwise direction when entering. The greater degree of wear in the floors on the south sides just inside the doorways is probably the result of wet feet coming in causing more erosion than dry feet leaving from the north side. Even the directions that the burials face conform to this sunwise principle. It seems that widdershins was not an acceptable direction of movement in the home.

If the organization of cooking, working and sleeping was fixed and inviolate over many centuries, the shape of the house itself could change with the fashions of the time. The middle roundhouse began as a very roughly circular building, almost sub-rectangular in plan, and was rebuilt as an oval on an east–west axis; it then became circular, then oval again on a north–south axis, then hexagonal, then circular and so on. Every time the middle and north houses were rebuilt, care was taken to ensure that the new build was slightly off-centre in relation to the old house. This was clearly deliberate and might have been to ensure that the living maintained their separation from the dead.

The founding of the middle house involved the construction of a stone-slabbed cist (a long stone 'box'), partly under the threshold and partly under the wall, empty apart from a piece of human scapula *(colour plate 9)*. Next to it, buried under the house wall, we found a deliberately broken quern (grinding stone) of massive proportions, together with domestic 'rubbish' which had presumably been collected and brought here from an earlier settlement. In the north house, broken querns were buried or left on the south side of the house interior, together with large spreads of broken pottery. Pots, and presumably their contents of milk, were used as special offerings in several houses, placed under the new wall of the house on the west and southwest sides *(43)*. Other offerings of antler tools were also placed against the west wall of the middle house.

The burial of the mummies under the floor of the north house marks a crucial moment in the history of South Uist. They had been kept for a very long time and so must have been figures of sacred power or ancestral authority. The decision to bury them cannot have been taken lightly and it might have been for several reasons. Either their power was lost so that they had to be got rid of, or their power had to be transferred to the new house, or their significance was obliterated by the new house and its inhabitants. A similarly dramatic change in architecture, religion and economy was to occur almost 2,000 years later with the arrival of the Vikings, but does this Bronze Age hiatus indicate a migration or a conversion? The strontium, sulphur and oxygen isotope levels of all the Cladh Hallan skeletons (under the floors and elsewhere) are consistent with their origins in the Western Isles so there is no evidence for incomers as yet.

The care with which these bodies were buried under the floors does not tally with the notion of invaders imposing their new ways on the local inhabitants by overthrowing their deities, and it is far more likely that this moment saw a conversion in local beliefs. New architecture, new religious beliefs and probably new agricultural practices were now being adopted. The ancestors were metaphorically swept under the carpet, at the same time providing the foundations on which the new order rested. The old order of sacred and religious authority, vested in the ancestors whose bodies were preserved as testimony to their continued existence, was now accommodated within the new order as the local religion came to be replaced by a set of beliefs and change in lifestyle which swept through the entire British Isles in the eleventh century BC.

CHAPTER 6

BROCHS AND WHEELHOUSES

The Middle Iron Age, c.200 BC–AD 400

Brochs have always been a 'problem' for archaeologists. For many years no one could believe that these formidable, two-storey, circular stone towers *(44)* were invented within Scotland – even though they are found only in Scotland and nowhere else! Lengthy and complex theories were developed to explain them as the innovation of Iron Age incomers from England, migrating from the south to lord it over the locals and show them a thing or two about how to build a proper house. During the 1970s and 1980s a series of excavations in Orkney revealed that the brochs had a worthy ancestry within Scotland: the towers appear to have developed from an earlier architectural style, in the form of single-storey thick-walled roundhouses, which date to the beginning of the first millennium BC.

Then there was a crisis of confidence about their name. Wasn't it better to call them 'complex Atlantic roundhouses' to differentiate them from the single-storey examples?* Throughout our own work on South Uist we have chosen to call a spade a spade and the term 'broch' is what we have stuck to. Our prejudices were reinforced when we began excavating Dun Vulan, described in early records as a 'galleried dun', and realized that it was a broch all along.

Another 'problem' was that, although many brochs had been excavated, most of the excavations were not only carried out many years ago but had also recovered relatively little evidence of refuse, the discarded rubbish that can reveal so much about prehistoric everyday life. Brochs raise many more questions. Were these structures used only as refuges in times of strife? Or were they occupied all year round? And if so, by whom – Iron Age chiefs or nobility, warrior groups, or families with a bit more wealth than their compatriots? Western Isles brochs seem to be isolated in contrast to examples in Orkney, Caithness and certain brochs in Shetland that had small villages around them –

---

* In older terminology, many brochs are called 'duns' - fortified mounds or single-storey fortified round-houses - further adding to the confusion.

44 The broch of Dun Carloway, Lewis

was this entirely the case and what did it mean in terms of social structure? Finally, were they really fortified houses or was their imposing solidity designed more to impress the neighbours than to repel enemies?

There still remained big questions of dating. The period when many brochs were in use is the Middle Iron Age (*c*.200 BC–AD 400), but were some or even all of them built much earlier, soon after 400 BC, towards the end of the Early Iron Age (*c*.750 BC–200 BC)? Were brochs in the Western Isles contemporary with another type of Middle Iron Age dwelling, the wheelhouses (like the house at Cille Pheadair excavated by Kissling and Lethbridge, described in chapter 1), or were they built before them? Were the brochs of the Western Isles contemporary with or later than their Orcadian counterparts? We have made some headway towards answering these questions about purpose and date but there is huge disagreement amongst the experts. Not so long ago a conference on brochs (appropriately entitled 'Tall Stories?') was reported by one interested but uninvolved participant as an unseemly verbal catfight and slanging match.

Wheelhouses present similar problems to be unravelled *(colour plate 11)*. If brochs were all about impressing people from the outside, wheelhouses looked modest – until one stepped through the door. Named after their resemblance to a spoked wheel in plan, wheelhouses have six or more stone piers which subdivide the concentric space around the outer part of the house, leaving an open area around the central hearth. Sometimes the piers are freestanding –

their stonework does not actually meet the stonework of the circular wall – and the resultant aisle created around the edge of the house has led to these examples being called 'aisled houses'.

It is possible that stone piers were used in these buildings' construction because there was no wood available to provide the long rafters needed to roof a large house: the piers reduced the span, requiring only the central circular area to be bridged with precious timbers. Certainly, the pollen cores tell us that South Uist had very little woodland indeed by this period, and they indicate that the hills and valleys were now covered with bog and heather. What is particularly interesting is that wheelhouses are a Western Isles tradition, found nowhere else except Shetland. If brochs are a Scottish regional form, then wheelhouses are a genuine local product of these two groups of islands, probably originating in Shetland where the oldest examples are found.

CLADH HALLAN AND THE DOUBLE ROUNDHOUSES

The wheelhouses were not the only local architectural innovation of the islands in the Iron Age. As the Cladh Hallan settlement was coming to an end around 400 BC, with most of its roundhouses now abandoned, two very unusual houses were built. One was at the northeast end of the main settlement mound *(45)* and the other is all that survives from another settlement mound 100m to

45 The double roundhouse south of the track at Cladh Hallan

the northwest, on the north side of the modern trackway *(colour plate 8)*. Both are 'double roundhouses' – a connecting doorway links two circular rooms. Only one other example has ever been found anywhere else, located on top of a Bronze Age burnt mound (a boiling trough with heaps of 'pot boiler' stones) at Ceann nan Clachan on North Uist.

As with the roundhouses, these three double roundhouses have east-facing entrances. There was a central hearth in the east room but no evidence of a sleeping area on the north side or, indeed, anywhere inside. These were special-purpose buildings whose use was bound up with very particular activities: boiling and smoking. In the double roundhouse north of the track at Cladh Hallan, the west end of the building had been destroyed by quarrying but enough remained of the west room for us to discover that a central stone-lined tank and pot boiler stones had been used for boiling. As the building came to the end of its life, its east room was used as a workshop for casting bronze artefacts.

The other double roundhouse was intact but its walls had been largely removed in the Iron Age. The southeast quadrant of its main room was littered with pot boilers and a single pot lay smashed in its southwest quadrant. Fish bones littered the south side and the floor of the north side was covered in tiny fragments of burnt pumice. The most curious feature was a large, stone-built niche at the west end in which a series of very smoky fires had scorched the

46 The double roundhouse's niche

47 The broch of Dun Vulan

rock and left thick deposits of soot *(46)*. This had been a smokery, no doubt for fish, but probably for joints of meat as well. The pot boilers might also have been used to create steam. The excavators of the Ceann nan Clachan double roundhouse have interpreted that building as a sweatlodge, a sort of sauna, and it is possible that the Cladh Hallan structures could have been used for pleasure as well as business!

THE BROCHS OF SOUTH UIST

Brochs with tall walls and intramural stairs and cells appear first in Orkney and Shetland around 400 BC. None of those in the Western Isles has been dated so early but there are impressive if smaller stone roundhouses. One of these is Dun Bharabhat at Cnip on Lewis, which was constructed some time before 200 BC. A similar islet location in Upper Loch Bornish on South Uist was used for another impressive stone building – probably a stone roundhouse – at around the same date but its ruins are badly disturbed by later Iron Age buildings and more recent structures *(cover picture)*.

Brochs in the Western Isles do, therefore, appear to be rather later than those of the Northern Isles. The pottery from a broch on the little island of

48 The buildings
outside the Dun Vulan
broch

Pabbay, now uninhabited, off Barra and from the broch of Dun Cuier on Barra dates their earliest occupation to the first and second centuries AD. The only broch on South Uist whose construction is accurately dated is Dun Vulan *(47; 48)*. Radiocarbon dates from early in the sequence of its construction indicate that it was built around 150–50 BC. Located on the coast in the same township as Upper Loch Bornish, it was probably the successor or replacement for this roundhouse on the island in the loch.

Twelve brochs have been found on South Uist *(49)*. This is slightly more than on Benbecula and on Barra and the southern isles but fewer than on North Uist and Lewis. None of the South Uist brochs are as well preserved as Dun Carloway on Lewis but several survive as high as the base of the first floor. One of the characteristic locations for brochs in the Western Isles is on islets within freshwater lochs, and this is certainly the case for all the South Uist

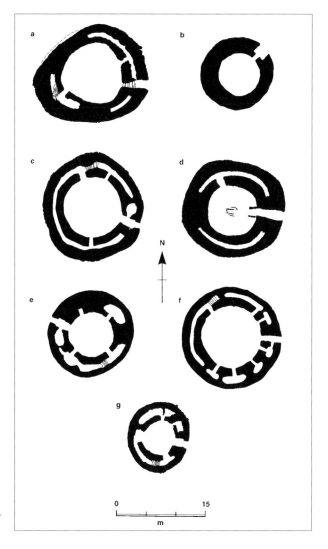

49 Plans of brochs in the
Western Isles
a) Dun Vulan; b) Dun Mhor;
c) Dun Mor Vaul, Tiree;
d) Dun Cuier, Barra; e) Dun
Carloway, Lewis; f) Loch na
Berie, Lewis; g) Dun Bharabhat,
Lewis

examples. Even Dun Vulan, now situated on a coastal promontory, was originally constructed within a freshwater loch, until the sea forced the shingle bank
forming the south side of that loch northwards on top of the broch itself.
Elsewhere in Scotland, brochs are situated in many different locations. On
Skye, for example, they tend to command the landscape from hilltops, and
even on Barra and its neighbouring islands, islet locations are unusual.

The greatest concentration of brochs on South Uist is at the north end
where four of them are situated in two pairs in the Iochdar area. This is interesting because of the likely importance of this area in earlier centuries as the
population centre of the Uists and, to reinforce this picture, there is a similar
concentration of brochs just across the water along Benbecula's south coast.
Whether all were in use together or in paired sequences is unknown but the
brochs either side of the strait form the densest concentration in the Uists.

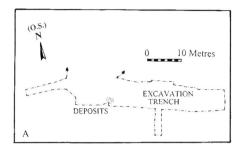

The LBA/EIA occupation (stippled) prior to the construction of the broch (phase 0) *c.* 700–400 BC.

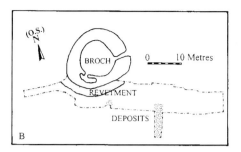

The construction of the broch and associated features and deposits (phase 1a) *c.* 150–0 BC.

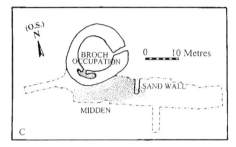

Occupation of the broch and deposition in the midden and wall chamber (phases 1b-2) *c.* 0 BC–AD 200.

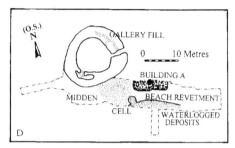

The construction and use of Building A, the beach revetment wall and final depositions on the midden and within the chamber, filling of the gallery and the waterlogged deposits (phases 3-4) *c.* AD 200–400.

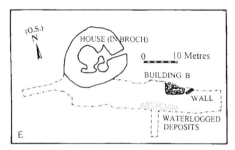

Use of Building B and the house within the broch (phase 5) *c.* AD 400–600.

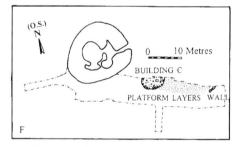

Deposition of layers on top of the platform, use of Building C and the late wall to the east (phases 5-6) *c.* AD 500–800.

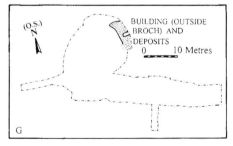

The building to the northeast of the broch and associated deposits (phase 7) *c.* AD 1300–1600.

50 The main phases of occupation at Dun Vulan

Further south, there is another pair of brochs south of Geirinis – Dun Mhor to the east and the broch still visible under Cille Bhannain church to the west. There are two possible brochs at Staidhlaidhgearraidh and the suspicion of a broch underneath the medieval walls of Caisteal Bheagram in Dreumasadal but otherwise, moving southwards, the next broch is Dun Altabrug in Ormacleit. It is supposed to be close to the site of another, Dun Gallan, in Stoneybridge but no trace of that survives. South of Dun Vulan and Upper Loch Bornish is another on Eilean an Staoir at Milton, and two possible sites in lochs at Aesgernis and Gearraidhsheile. At the south end of the island there is one at Smercleit and a possible broch at Dun Duichal in Cille Pheadair.

DUN VULAN

Our excavations at Dun Vulan were aimed at tackling some of the questions, listed at the beginning of this chapter, that were being asked about brochs in the 1980s and early 1990s. Dun Vulan is unusual for the Western Isles in that it had an ancillary settlement on its east side *(48; 50)*. This and the broch itself were being eroded by the sea, which had shifted the formerly protective shingle bank onto the broch and its outbuildings. A strip excavated along the beach revealed the extent of these exterior buildings and allowed an examination of the chamber and intramural staircase within the broch's south wall.

The broch was constructed on an islet of machair sand by laying down a raft of pitched rubble onto the sand and then building the 4m-thick walls on top *(51)*. It was a huge structure, much larger than the largest Cladh Hallan roundhouse, with an internal diameter of 11 metres. From its doorway on the east side, the visitor entered through a 4m-long passage roofed with large, flat stones into a large circular room. By moving to the south they came to a doorway in the wall which led into a boot-shaped chamber from which a stone staircase curled sunwise upwards within the wall *(52)*.

This staircase inside the broch wall probably led to an entry at first-floor level into the main room of the building. Only the bottom six stones of the stairway have survived but part of the scarcement – the protruding stones on which the edges of a wooden first floor once rested – still survives as evidence for this upper floor. Well-preserved examples in the Northern Isles indicate that this was the floor on which people lived and worked whilst the ground floor was used for storage and perhaps sheltering a few sheep or cattle.

Around this upper floor there was a passageway within the wall (which only survived to this height on its north side), entered through a door on the north side. The broch was reoccupied in the Pictish period (see chapter 7) and our excavations have left intact the interior layout of this later period *(53)* so that future archaeologists will be able to explore the ground level of the broch and the foundation offerings beneath it. In the meantime, the modern visitor can

51 The broch wall of Dun Vulan

52 The wall chamber and staircase of Dun Vulan

see the outlines of those later rooms and can also walk on top of the slabs that form the roof of the ground-floor passageway into the broch.

The one part of the broch's original internal structure that has been excavated is the boot-shaped chamber within the south wall. This provided a sequence of layers dating to between about 50 BC and AD 400. Pieces of a human skull from the lower layers of the chamber probably derive from a foundation offering, placed below the floor surface which was probably a raised floor constructed out of timber planks. The builders should have known not to build their foundations on sand because, soon after the broch was built, its southern wall subsided and the carefully laid steps of the staircase were snapped and pulled out of position. The outer wall was propped up by the construction of a buttress wall but the staircase was never repaired and presumably the inhabitants lived with this defect.

Like the roundhouse walls at Cladh Hallan, there was domestic rubbish incorporated into Dun Vulan's stone walls, including a very large and fine but broken quern-stone. These were probably deliberate deposits, incorporating material from earlier buildings elsewhere into the new.

Outside the broch, the occupants created a huge midden of rubbish on the south side, just in front of the doorway. This turned out to be an archaeological

goldmine because it has preserved a large part of the history of the inhabitants' lives within. Starting in the first century BC, the midden provides a remarkable sequence showing how people lived here continuously over about 300 years as a permanent household.

The small size of the sherds and bones in these layers is the result of their having been trampled to pieces within the floors of the broch. Those midden layers which are full of sherds and carbonized barley seeds probably came from rubbish swept out of the first-floor living area, whilst those full of bone fragments probably resulted from butchery and bone breakage on the ground floor or outside. Offcuts and trimmings of antler give us an indication of the tool-making that went on inside the broch but, like their predecessors at Cladh Hallan, the inhabitants were not interested in making much in the way of ornaments. A small carved bone plaque from the chamber, perhaps once a pendant, is one of the few examples of personal decoration.

The most important finds from the midden were the pieces of animal bone and the carbonized plant remains. The bones showed similarities with Cladh Hallan – lots of young calves and lambs – but there were also some interesting differences. Despite the presence of antlers, deer bones were virtually absent. There was a much higher proportion of pig bones than we found at Cladh Hallan and there were greater quantities of fish, particularly larger specimens such as cod. There were also bones of exotic species such as hare, badger and roe deer which must have been imported to the islands. The inhabitants were eating not only lots more pork than their predecessors at Cladh Hallan but also more than their neighbours in the surrounding wheelhouses. In addition, for the pigs there are a larger number of bones from front legs than from back legs which makes it likely that front-leg joints of pork were being brought to the broch. Later on, the inhabitants were also importing domestic cats and chickens.

The carbonized cereal remains were, as at Cladh Hallan, dominated by barley, but new crops such as oats and spelt were now being grown in the surrounding fields. The weed seeds collected with the cereals indicated the same extensive cultivation system as before, planting on the peatlands as well as the machair.

Around the second to fourth centuries AD, two rectangular outbuildings were constructed on the south side of the settlement *(48; 50)*. The first was next to the midden and the second was built a little further out to the east. On Skye there is a peculiar rectangular house at Tungadale on Skye dated to the third century BC, but the Dun Vulan outbuildings are otherwise the earliest rectangular buildings in the Western Isles, a new form of architecture within the curvilinear 'roundhouse' world.

The outbuildings were set on an east–west axis and their floors were paved – a very unusual treatment, since most prehistoric floor surfaces in the Western Isles were made from a soft, peaty matrix. Each had an east-facing entrance

53 Later buildings
inside the broch of
Dun Vulan

aligned over a stone-covered 'drain' or cist, very like the cist beneath the
doorway and wall of the middle roundhouse at Cladh Hallan, except that these
were aligned east–west. Similar Iron Age 'drains' from Orkney and northern
Scotland have been found to contain human bones and these curious stone
structures probably had a significance and purpose greater than merely
removing water and damp.

The striking feature of the foundation 'drain' in the first building was that
one of its covering slabs was made not of stone but of part of the cheek bone
of a blue whale: we found an identical use of whale bone in the slabs covering
the Cladh Hallan 'drain', which had been constructed more than a thousand

54 The 'drain' with its human jaw fragment

years earlier. The foundation 'drain' of the later outbuilding had no such features but contained a fragment of a human jaw which dated to the period of the foundation of the broch, many centuries before the drain was constructed *(54)*.

Dun Vulan's outbuildings might have been successive storehouses – their paved floors and 'drains' would have provided some protection against the pervasive damp. When the buildings went out of use, in around AD 300 and AD 500 respectively, pieces of human skulls were laid as closing deposits on the abandoned floors of each of them. Again, these human remains were already ancient when they were placed here: they date to the second or first centuries BC, the date of the broch's foundation.

The two outbuildings were constructed against the side of a long wall that formed the southern edge of the settlement in front of the broch. A small sub-circular room built into this long wall, with access to the water, might have provided a storage space for boat equipment. The area outside the long wall which the circular room opened onto has remained waterlogged for 2,000 years. In its wet mud we found pieces of wood, decayed vegetation, pollen grains and beetles. By analyzing these different threads of evidence, we were able to work out that there had been a second midden here, formed not of household waste like the other, but of seaweed and herbivore dung.

3 The Polochar standing stone

Previous page
1 The machair plain at Bornais

2 The landscape setting of Reineval tomb

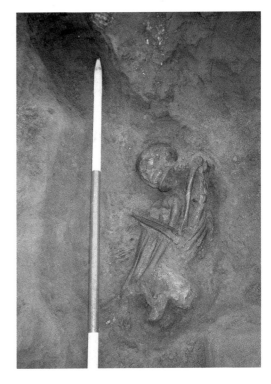

4 The large stone circle of Callanish, Lewis

5 *Left* The cremation burials at Cladh Hallan

6 *Below* The composite skeleton of a man, formerly mummified, buried at Cladh Hallan

7 *Above left* The three roundhouses at the north end of the terraced row at Cladh Hallan

8 *Above right* The double roundhouse north of the track, Cladh Hallan

9 *Left* The cist or 'drain' and broken quern beneath the doorway and wall of the middle roundhouse, Cladh Hallan

Opposite page
10 The monument to Flora Macdonald within one of the blackhouse ruins at Airigh Mhuillin (Milton)

11 The wheelhouse T17, Alt Chrisal, Barra

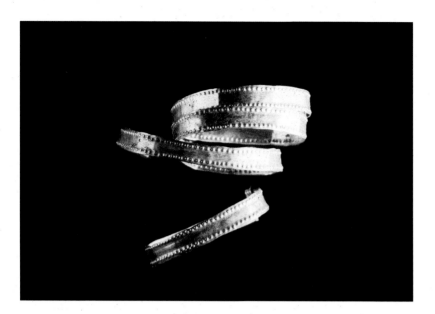

12 A gold strip, twisted into a spiral, from Cille Pheadair

13 A copper alloy spiral fitting from Cille Pheadair

14 Combs from Cille Pheadair

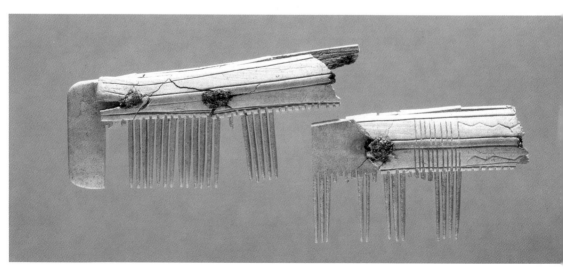

15 The house on Mound 3 at Bornais

16 Excavations on the Hill of the Son of Angus

Following page
17 The ruins of Cille Donnain church on its peninsula in Loch Cill Donnain

18 A blackhouse (House E) under excavation at Airigh Mhuillin (Milton) in 1996

It must have been very smelly and would have been a useful source of fertil-izer for manuring the machair fields. Curiously, there was no evidence that it had been dug into for such a purpose and it seems to have been left to fester.

The pieces of wood from this manure heap turned out to be some of the most important discoveries of the excavation. Some pieces were the broken handles of tools (*55*) and other pieces were trimmings or unworked lumps. The wooden finds divided into two groups. One group, which included the tool handles as well as sticks and branches, came from very slow-grown ash and willow. These had come from local trees, probably from some of the very few remaining in the valleys on South Uist's east coast. By now, these patches of woodland, too small to show up in the pollen cores from that side of the island, were probably the last vestiges of a carefully managed resource.

More interesting was the other group of wood remains, which consisted of tamarack larch. This species of tree is not native to Britain, being found on the other side of the Atlantic, in Canada. The holes in these pieces of wood made by the 'shipworm' (actually a boring mollusc *Teredo navalis*) are testament to the long time that this driftwood spent in the sea, on its journey from the coasts of Labrador, carried by the Labrador current to the Sargasso Sea and thence to South Uist by the Gulf Stream.

The presence of this driftwood is instructive. It may not be the best building timber but it can be trimmed to shape and lashed together to form the long spars that are required to build a roundhouse roof. In the case of a broch, it is not just huge quantities of stone that were needed to raise a tower 6 or even 12m high, but enough timber to provide for a roof and for flooring of the top storey and any wall chambers. Canadian logs still arrive at a regular rate on South Uist beaches and are gleefully burnt in all-night summer beach parties. Back in prehistory the trees would have washed up, roots and all, to be claimed, shaped and probably carefully stored away for future building programmes. If the evidence from Dun Vulan shows us that driftwood was available if not plentiful, we are still left with the mystery of the wheelhouses' stone piers. Were these really necessary if there was adequate driftwood? Or were they needed because the rights to driftwood salvage were claimed by the broch households?

55 A wooden artefact from Dun Vulan

Amongst the pieces of wood from Dun Vulan there was a small branch of purging buckthorn. Today this tree's most northerly range is Morecambe Bay in Lancashire and it is unlikely to have been growing any further north in the Iron Age, or to have been brought on ocean currents. It is most probably an imported piece, valued for its medicinal and possibly magical properties.

At that time, Morecambe was firmly within the Roman Empire so, if there was trade with the Western Isles, why did the local inhabitants want medicines rather than all the trappings of Roman culture – the pottery, the glass, the coins, the dress items – that were there for the asking? Very few Roman items appear to have ever reached South Uist: a Roman brooch was left within Kissling and Lethbridge's abandoned wheelhouse at Cille Pheadair and our project found another within a wheelhouse at Cill Donnain. No other artefacts from Roman Britain have ever been found. It seems that the people of the Western Isles, secure in their own traditions and identity, were not lured by the trappings of the Roman world.

WHEELHOUSES AND SOUTERRAINS

There are almost as many wheelhouses excavated on South Uist as there are known brochs *(56)*. Kissling and Lethbridge's site on Cille Pheadair machair was not the one that they had initially chosen but they had beginners' luck. Within the *bruthach sitheanach* – the brae of the fairy hill – they found a complete wheelhouse missing only its roof. No other stone building on the machair has ever survived intact to this degree since abandoned houses were normally 'robbed' for their stones to build the next house. Why had this particular house been spared the usual treatment? Lethbridge noticed that the floor and hearth had been carefully swept before the whole edifice filled with windblown sand at some time around AD 200. The remains of the wheelhouse can be seen today; its walls still stand to almost their original height but its piers have fallen down.

Two of the mounds excavated in the rocket range project on Drimore machair, A'Cheardach Mhor and A'Cheardach Bheag (translated as the big and little smithies), proved to be wheelhouses. In 1984 another two wheelhouses were partly excavated at Hornish Point, eroding onto the beach out of a large settlement mound where prehistoric remains can still be seen in the sand cliff.

Our own SEARCH project also included the excavation of a small wheelhouse on Cill Donnain machair and a badly damaged example at Bornais. The former is located on the northwest edge of a large settlement mound, and is a tiny house with an interior only 5m across *(57)*. Its internal features included a hearth and a long stone-lined trough. It was built around AD 200 and was used for two or more centuries. When excavated, it had already sadly been robbed of many of its stones, but those that remained have now been re-erected in the grounds of Kildonan Museum.

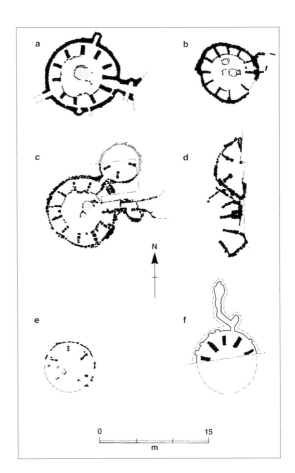

56 Plans of the wheelhouses of South Uist
a) Cille Pheadair; b) A'Cheardach Bheag; c) A'Cheardach Mhor;
d) Hornish Point; e) Cill Donnain;
f) Glen Usinis

57 The Cill Donnain wheelhouse

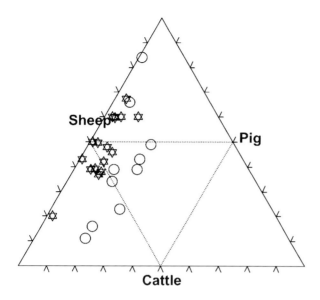

58 Graph of animal species percentages from brochs (circles) and wheelhouses (stars)

The midden layers deposited within and on top of this wheelhouse have provided a very useful index of the economy of the Cill Donnain settlement, which can be compared with Dun Vulan. The wheelhouse had no foundation deposits, which is unusual given that such votive offerings of animals and pots are known from wheelhouses at Sollas on North Uist and Cnip on Lewis. Unlike Dun Vulan there were no human remains associated with either the founding or the closing of this house.

The animal bones in the midden layers are very similar in species and proportions to those from Hornish Point and from other wheelhouses excavated to modern standards. Sheep predominate, followed by cattle, with a very small percentage of pigs. As mentioned before, Dun Vulan had a much higher percentage of pig bones and this is a feature of most broch assemblages which distinguishes them from wheelhouses *(58)*. Also, unlike Dun Vulan, Cill Donnain produced little fish and no exotic species. Otherwise the tools, ornaments and other artefacts were much the same, except for the Roman brooch.

The Bornais wheelhouse was badly damaged by later activity but enough of it survived to give evidence of its layout. It was unusual in having its door on the west side but the living area seems to have been on the south side as in east-facing roundhouses. At some point in the fourth or fifth century AD it burned down, leaving burnt roof timbers in a lattice formation on the ground. Amongst the artefacts left inside were heaps of hammer stones, parts of a large pot, animal bones, parts of a small crucible, and various items that had been kept in the roof such as a beautiful whale bone axe-head, scorched in the blaze. A group of coprolites (preserved faeces) in the centre of the east wall may show where dogs had been tethered.

One of the interesting aspects of house construction in the Iron Age is the continued significance of the sunwise ordering of domestic space that was initiated in the Late Bronze Age. Most Iron Age houses have doorways to the southeast or east, but a significant proportion of brochs and wheelhouses have west-facing entrances (and one or two to north and south) *(49; 56)*. In fact, for brochs throughout Scotland, half of them have west-facing entrances. The reasons for this reversal of the standard orientation are probably many and complex. Early historical texts from Ireland indicate that the king sat in the east so that the doorway to his house must have faced west. The arrangement of space within west-facing roundhouses is sometimes rotated around 180°, like the wheelhouses of Tigh Talamhanta on Barra and Clettraval on North Uist. Alternatively their interior space might be arranged as a mirror image, as seen in the Bornais wheelhouse.

Putting one's doorway on the west side of the house is not a good idea in the Western Isles. The full lunacy of such a building decision can best be appreciated by standing in the doorway of the Clettraval wheelhouse, positioned near the summit of a small mountain on North Uist, and looking directly into the teeth of the westerly winds. Curiously, the majority of these peatland wheelhouses have west-facing doorways, whereas the only west-facing houses found on the machair so far are Bornais, and Cnip on Lewis.

There are some clues as to why these 'oppositional' contrary arrangements were chosen. Cnip has produced a unique artefact, part of a musical instrument, and we may wonder whether certain houses were specially designated for night-time revelry. Clettraval itself is located in a special place, built into the back of a Neolithic long cairn, and perhaps such a place was inhabited by religious specialists whose job it was to monitor the nightly movements of the heavens. Classical writings on Druids mention that they worked at night and slept in the day. Another possibility is that many of the remote peatland wheelhouses, such as the fine example in Glen Usinis, might have been inhabited intermittently at special times of the year such as when the animals were taken to the hill pastures.

As Clettraval and numerous other examples make clear, west-facing doorways must have been chosen for some very strong reasons that outranked the practicalities of comfort. This development of an architecture of opposition and difference did not undermine the principles of sunwise order but elaborated on them. It might have gone hand in hand with greater specialization of activities and roles.

The remote wheelhouse in Glen Usinis on the island's east coast can only be visited on foot and is far enough to recommend an overnight camp. The determined walker is rewarded, however, by a fine building and two souterrains, one in close proximity to the house itself. These underground tunnels are known from different parts of Britain – in Cornwall they are called fogous – and occur as far afield as Denmark. Even in cases where new and untouched examples are unearthed, their long stone-built chambers invariably contain no finds that may shed light on their former purpose. Theories abound as to their role as hiding places, religious shrines or storage spaces. There are five recorded for South Uist. Martin Martin describes one, since destroyed, at Ludag at the south end. Besides Glen Usinis, the surviving examples are one east of Hornish Point (not accessible), another east of Loch Stulaval and one near Loch Skiport. Their distribution appears to be entirely coastal – but they are not found on the west coast – and we are inclined to think that they were something more than underground storage rooms.

THE NEW LAND APPORTIONMENT

The numbers of known wheelhouses on South Uist are just the tip of an iceberg. We probably have a reasonably accurate record of those in the peatlands because their massive forms are easily visible even after substantial robbing. But it is those on the machair that mostly remain hidden in the 25 or so settlement mounds dating to the Middle Iron Age and which are spaced at regular intervals of about a kilometre to a mile along South Uist's west coast.

Within some of these, such as those excavated on the rocket range, there might only have been a single dwelling, but in others there were more. From Lethbridge's records and our own geophysical survey of the 'fairy mound' in which the Cille Pheadair wheelhouse lies, it is likely that another two complete wheelhouses remain to be unearthed one day. The settlement mound at the Udal on North Uist similarly contains three. Even though many settlement mounds have been quarried away, particularly in the Cladh Hallan area, it is likely that 50 or more wheelhouses survive untouched on South Uist alone. This large number of households within 25 settlement mounds represents a huge growth in population in comparison to Late Bronze Age and Early Iron Age populations.

To some degree, the visibility of these Middle Iron Age settlements is due to the ease with which their decorated pottery can be recognized. Nonetheless, their distribution along the entire length of the island represents a marked change in land apportionment. At some point around 200 BC, the entire social landscape started to be transformed. Rather than being concentrated in certain parts of the machair, as is the case for the Bronze Age and Early Iron Age, settlements were established at regular intervals along its length.

Before 200 BC each settlement area was as much as 10km away from another but in the two or three centuries after 200 BC the hitherto empty spaces along the machair were settled with houses every kilometre or so. This filling-up of the machair with settlements must have forced each community to extend their cultivation and grazing lands eastwards onto the peaty soils of the blacklands. Instead of primarily exploiting strips north-south along the machair, Iron Age people now farmed east–west strips across the island. It is likely that the shieling system of summer grazing camps came into being at this time.

The shift to a new settlement layout suggests some kind of ordered division of land. What is most interesting is that the placing of Iron Age settlements conforms to the positions of many of the townships that survived until the Clearances in the nineteenth century. These were mostly organized so as to ensure that each township had access to a longitudinal strip of machair, peatland and mountain as well as to sections of east and west coast. The basis of South Uist's townships could be over 2,000 years old.

How did the brochs fit into this new land deal? Most are some distance from the more fertile soils and, apart from Dun Vulan, are not particularly close to the wheelhouse settlements. Instead, they sit in peatland and moorland areas that would have been summer grazing grounds. Most intriguingly, they lie on or very close to township boundaries. The huge scale of the materials required in their construction means that many more people were involved in building a broch than could live in it. They might well have been community enterprises to establish and protect claims to certain grazing areas, initiatives of prehistoric versions of today's grazing committees. Alternatively, they were inhabited by lineages that could call on corvée labour or other such obligatory services from the remainder of the population, not so much chiefs or lords as leading families. The evidence from Dun Vulan hints at dietary and economic differences as well as ceremonial distinctions such as the keeping of human skulls.

CHAPTER 7

BETWEEN
THREE KINGDOMS
The Pictish Period, c. AD 400-900

The Pictish period is the first era in Scottish history for which we have depic-
tions of people, evidence of writing and knowledge of people's personal
names. The only lifelike art from the Western Isles before this period is a
drawing of a deer on one of the sherds from the Cille Pheadair wheelhouse.
Contrary to early modern period representations of the Picts, they were not a
tribe of painted, hairy Mel Gibson-lookalikes but were rather elegant and well-
groomed people, fond of their mirrors and combs, or at least that is how they
depicted themselves.

For the first time, we have some inkling of the political powers in the land
and their geographical extents. The Picts were not a single ethnic group but a
political confederation of many groups forming a kingdom in eastern Scotland.
This was divided into two, with a southern part around Tayside and Fife and
a northern part on Orkney and Shetland and the northern mainland. Current
ideas about why the Picts came together at this time revolve around the
political and territorial pressure exerted first by the Romans and then by the
Scots or Scoti, who established a kingdom, based in Argyll, known as Dalriada.
It is generally thought that these Scoti were Irish incomers, but not all experts
agree on this. To the south of the Forth were the Britons in the western
lowlands of Galloway, Ayrshire and Clydesdale and the Angles to the east and
in Dumfriesshire.

A third political grouping whose existence influenced life in the Western
Isles were the Irish, divided into kingdoms, some of which were just a few
days' sail from the islands. The political groupings of the communities on the
northwest coast of the Scottish mainland, Skye and the Inner Hebrides are
not well understood. The reach of the kingdom of Dalriada might have
extended as far north as Coll and Tiree, whilst the number of Pictish symbol
stones on Skye hints at some degree of affiliation with the kingdom of the
Picts.

As boat technology improved in the post-Roman world of the North Sea
and the north Atlantic, so places that were formerly distant became easier to

reach. Long-distance contacts had been part of Hebridean life since the Neolithic and now their world was becoming even larger. Trade goods and artefact styles indicate connections in this period with the Anglian kingdom of Northumbria, the Irish kingdoms and the northern part of the kingdom of the Picts. Intriguingly, one of the reactions to these expanded horizons was for the people of the Western Isles to retreat into the security of their own past, using their heritage as a source of political comfort when facing the uncertainties of the world around them.

Once it became clear to scholars that the changes in material culture – architecture, pottery, dress items and other portable artefacts – associated with this period were not due to boatloads of Picts arriving in the Western Isles and imposing their culture on the locals, archaeologists began to realize that Hebridean society changed more subtly after AD 400 than a full-on migration would have entailed. Many of the old brochs and wheelhouses continued to be inhabited, but only after substantial remodelling and with new arrangements of internal space. Pottery became plainer and returned to styles similar to those in use over 500 years earlier. Personal appearance started to matter more than the appearance of one's home.

Gradually the entire character of Hebridean society changed, as it shifted location from the edge of empire to a new position between three kingdoms. Technically the Pictish period did not begin in the Western Isles until the seventh century AD since there is no indication of Pictish influence in the islands before this date. The preceding centuries (fifth–sixth centuries AD) are known as Late Iron Age period I, in contrast to the Pictish period (Late Iron Age period II) of the seventh–eighth centuries. Of course, the Pictish period in northern and eastern Scotland began in the Late Iron Age period I and, for convenience, we use the term 'Pictish' here also to describe houses and settlements from the fifth and sixth centuries AD in the Western Isles.

SETTLEMENTS

The sequence of occupation revealed by our excavations at Dun Vulan shows the seamless transition from the Middle Iron Age into the Pictish period, the first half of the Late Iron Age (the second half of the Late Iron Age being the Norse period). The broch continued to be inhabited and there was also a dwelling outside its walls, built on top of the earlier of the rectangular outbuildings. Unfortunately this house outside the broch had been badly damaged by the sea before the excavations began and its plan could not be recovered in full.

It consisted of at least one room, with walls either curved or round, containing a rectangular hearth. The laid, soft floor had been covered with a thin spread of quartz sand, just as blackhouse floors were treated a century or so ago.

The hearth was a formal affair of baked clay surrounded by a rectangular arrangement of upright stone slabs. The clay had been laid when wet and a rectangular lattice of finger channels had been drawn across its surface. This concern for the solidity of the hearth – a rectangular form within a curvilinear house – seems to have been an important feature of domestic life in the islands in this period. Certain of the old ways at Dun Vulan continued. When this house was abandoned in around AD 600, human bones about 400 years old were laid on the floor and left there to be covered by debris (or they had perhaps been stashed in the roof, being deposited on the floor when the roof collapsed).

The floors and hearth of the Pictish period house constructed inside the broch walls remain to be excavated but its plan is clearly visible. Pottery from construction layers within its walls shows that it was built after AD 400. The builders reused the east entrance into the broch and employed a new configuration of rooms, fitting them into the existing circular space of the ground floor's interior rather like a contortionist squeezing into a trunk *(53; 59)*. Just past the entrance there is a small circular 'guard cell' on the south or left-hand

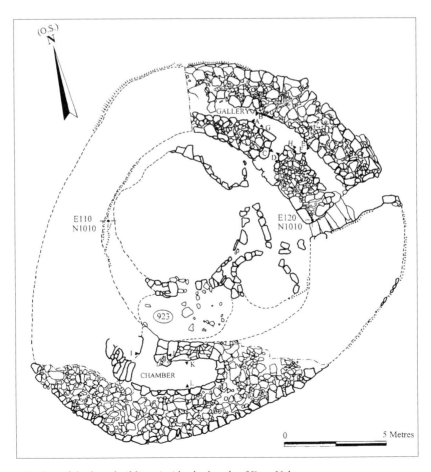

59 Plan of the later buildings inside the broch of Dun Vulan

60 The hearth at Bornais with its surrounding metapodials

side. Moving round slightly to the right one enters the main room, a large circular space about 6m across. From our knowledge of other, excavated examples of houses of this period, there is likely to be a hearth at its centre.

Moving across the large circular room to its southwest side, the visitor goes through another doorway into a back room of curved walls, squashed against the broch's inner wall face. At the rear of this back room is the partly filled-in doorway that leads to the abandoned chamber and broken stairs inside the broch's original wall. The chamber and stairs could still have given access, albeit tricky, to the ruined wall top of the old broch.

The broch had been repaired at some time between AD 200 and AD 400 by bringing soil from another settlement at least a mile away to the east (we know this because of the pollen surviving in that soil). This had been packed into the intramural gallery on the north side to give the building greater solidity. Why the packing material could not have been obtained from the broch's immediate vicinity begs some questions. It is a simple mixture of rubble and soil mixed with peat, which could have been obtained from the adjacent Ardvule loch itself. Today we may think of something like a cheaper builder from further away putting in a tender to undercut the local firm. Back then, it might have been more a matter of staking a claim to the broch by incorporating some of one's ancestral home into the walls of the new property. Earlier cases of incorporating old 'rubbish' into the walls of houses occurred when building Dun Vulan (see chapter 6) and over a thousand years earlier at Cladh Hallan (see chapter 5). This was almost certainly a symbolic act as much as a practical measure, designed to establish continuity between the old and the new.

The use of stonework within the new build is also interesting. Like other examples at Loch na Berie, Cnip on Lewis and Dun Cuier on Barra, the Dun Vulan house was built in such a way that there was a new line of walling insulating its interior space – once it was built, the inhabitants of the new house never came into contact with the broch wall face. This addition of new lining walls might simply have ensured that there were no weak bonds in the stonework, or prevented water seeping down the old walls of the broch into the new house, but it serves to emphasize the extent to which the new building took over and occupied the ruins of the old.

In comparison to the Middle Iron Age settlement mounds, brochs and wheelhouses, there are certainly fewer settlements of this Late Iron Age period in South Uist. Eight settlement sites have been found on the machair and excavations have demonstrated that the wheelhouses of A'Cheardach Mhor and A'Cheardach Bheag were reused in this period, as were two other wheelhouses on Bornais and Cill Donnain machair. The small number of Pictish period settlements found on Barra and its surrounding islands has been interpreted as the result of depopulation.

Yet the evidence is problematic for two reasons. Firstly, the Plain Style pottery is, by its very nature, difficult to identify, especially when just a few sherds are found during the surface survey of an ancient settlement. Secondly, if a large number of Middle Iron Age buildings continued to be occupied in this period, the only way of identifying that later occupation is through excavation – and the vast majority of such sites remain unexcavated. We can extrapolate from the proportion of sites known to have been reused in the Pictish period: since so many excavated Middle Iron Age sites *were* reused, it suggests that, for the unexcavated sites too, we can expect that most of them were also inhabited during the Pictish period. Additionally, many of the small duns and crannogs on islands in lochs remain unexplored and some at least may date to this period.

Our view is that South Uist's machair was as densely populated as before. The inhabitants did not disappear; rather, they reused the villages and houses of their predecessors, and are therefore difficult for us to identify. In the eight cases where new settlements sprung up, all but one are directly adjacent to

Middle Iron Age settlement mounds. This exception is a small mound, probably the remains of a single house, between the Ormacleit and Bornais settlements.

Whether the Iochdar area lost its pre-eminence in this period is difficult to say but by one of the Pictish period mounds there was the site of a metal-working workshop. It has not been excavated but another, at Eilean Olabhat on North Uist, gives some idea of the likely items produced – fine silver and bronze jewellery in the form of pins and brooches that were probably made for the wealthier members of society. By an unusual quirk of fate, the Iochdar site is not that far from today's 'Hebridean Jewellery' workshop in Carnan! The presence of metalworking at Iochdar almost certainly served a rather different purpose than today's jewellers. These items were not made for sale, as they are today, but as gifts for the elite to exchange with one other in forming alliances and to present to loyal retinue as a reward for their services. We get an idea of this giving of gifts by the rich and powerful in this period from Beowulf's description as the 'giver of rings'.

The largest Pictish period settlement is on Frobost machair. It is much bigger than its Middle Iron Age predecessor a couple of hundred metres to the south, and it contains a deep sequence of layers, some of which have been exposed by recent quarrying. Whether this was the developing, new centre of the island is difficult to say but we have not yet identified such a large settlement in the Iochdar area. If the island's centre of political or economic power had indeed shifted to Frobost, near its geographical centre, this need not indicate devolution of all political power away from a Uist-wide centre of control focused on Iochdar, at the north end of South Uist and south side of Benbecula. The establishment of large settlements within each of the islands could indicate the imposition of a second tier of authority to which the inhabitants owed a more local allegiance. Alternatively, political authority might have been more closely associated with individuals rather than specific places, and larger settlements need not equate to greater political power.

BOSTADH AND BORNAIS

One of the most interesting discoveries on Lewis in recent years has been a Pictish period settlement, eroding out of the machair at Bostadh beach *(61)*. Tim Neighbour's team from Edinburgh excavated a series of dwellings that appear at first sight to be a jumbled mass of curving walls, niches, small rooms and passages. On closer inspection, the pattern of 'guard cell', central room and back room – noted in compressed form at Dun Vulan and other reused sites – can be unravelled from the plan.

This arrangement of interior space is also found in the Pictish 'jelly baby'-shaped houses at the Udal and at Eilean Olabhat on North Uist. Comparable

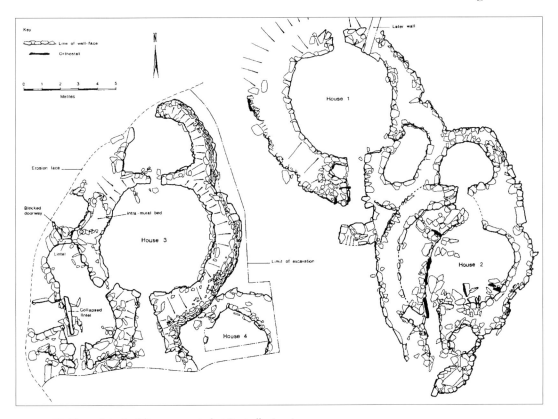

61 Plan of the buildings excavated at Bostadh, Lewis

houses of this period have been found in Orkney, at the site of Buckquoy, and in Antrim, where the site of Deer Park Farms has the remarkably preserved remains of a wooden-walled double roundhouse. After the Bostadh excavations were completed, Jim Crawford was able to build a reconstruction of one of the houses at a nearby location and it is a definite 'must' for the visitor.

The architecture of this period thus demonstrates some links with the Northern Isles but also its connections to a wider and looser network ranging across western Scotland and Northern Ireland. Just inland from Dun Vulan, on Bornais machair, there is a group of three settlement mounds *(62)*. All were used in the Norse period but each had different histories prior to that. The southernmost (Mound 1) was in use during the Middle Iron Age and Late Iron Age period I, ending in the fourth and fifth centuries. The middle mound (Mound 2) developed in the later Pictish period (seventh to eighth centuries), whilst the northern mound (Mound 3) accumulated only in the Norse period (see chapter 8).

Within Mound 1, a Middle Iron Age wheelhouse was converted into a new dwelling in the fourth or fifth century AD. Some of the piers were retained but large sections of walling were rebuilt to form a curious partially rounded,

62 Plan of the three settlement mounds at Bornais

partially rectangular house. Thanks to later stone robbing and modern-day rabbit burrowing, the full details of the architecture are not clear but the doorway seems to have been initially to the west and later repositioned to the south.

The original wheelhouse had suffered a catastrophic fire in which the roof caught light and collapsed onto the floor *(63)*. This was probably not a deliberate act to mark the abandonment of the house, say, on someone's death, since

63 The burnt-down roof timbers at Bornais

64 The die placed in the ashes of the roof at Bornais

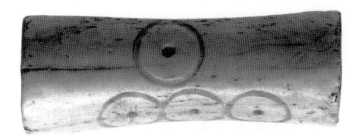

the roof would have been a valuable source of reusable timbers and carbon-enriched turf for fertilizer. Why the collapsed roof was left as a charred mass of timbers lying on the floor is unclear.

Two items that were found unburnt among the charred timbers were a bone gaming die (dice is actually the plural) and a cow's astragalus (heel-bone) which was finely decorated with an incised pattern on one surface. The six-sided die *(64)* is not the same shape as modern dice (in which all the sides are square) but is a parallelepiped form with four long rectangular sides and two smaller square ends. Because of their shape, these dice do not tend to land on one of their ends but this one had! It was sticking up out of the ashes and, together with the astragalus, had clearly been placed there once the embers had cooled.

We associate dice with games and gambling but in more ancient times these dice, together with astragali, might have formed a diviner's kit. Perhaps this die had been cast and a verdict given to continue living in the house, because someone constructed a new hearth directly upon the burnt roof timbers. This solid hearth had around it a rectangular arrangement of stone slabs and one of its ends was marked by an elaborate hemispherical setting of cattle anklebones (metapodials), which extended along the long sides of the hearth *(60)*.

This arc of metapodials at the end of the hearth was constructed from a carefully ordered sequence of 14 bones. The array is divided into metacarpals (forelimb) to the north and metatarsals (hind limb) to the south, with this strict pattern being interrupted by the placing of a single bone of the opposite type towards each end of the arc. Another 14 bones were arranged along the two long sides. The metapodials along the sides are all proximal (the 'tops' of the bones, from the end which belongs nearer to the torso), and the edging also includes a few fragments of scapula and a single sheep tibia. There is only one matching pair of metapodials along one side, and these were placed next to each other. Most of the metapodials in the arc at the end of the hearth were distal halves ('bottoms' of the bones). Although metapodial bones can be easily identified from their proximal ends as forelimb or hind limb, this is harder to do with the distal ends. With their tops broken off, constructing this elaborate pattern would have taken some considerable thought. Within the A'Cheardach Bheag wheelhouse, the U-shaped hearth had been edged with 17 deer jawbones in the Middle Iron Age.

The Bornais hearth bones must have come from a good number of adult cattle – between 7 and 12 animals – whose meat-yield would have been more than 1,500kg. Were these bones the by-products of a single huge feast or were they collected bit by bit from a series of smaller feasts? The bones may have been used to display the feasting tally of the house's occupants, or perhaps they were magical talismans protecting the hearth, the very core of the home. Whatever their purpose, they are indicative of a greater change in the use of animal carcasses inside dwellings. A number of Middle Iron Age wheelhouses and brochs contain the complete, partial or disarticulated skeletons of animals buried under the floor, behind the walls or in other spots. That practice was replaced by a growing interest in collecting sets of single bones. At the end of the occupation of the settlement outside the broch in the seventh or eighth century at Dun Vulan, for example, someone dumped a large collection of cattle astragali and toe bones.

ARCHITECTURE AND ARTEFACTS

Despite the adoption of a new multi-cellular architecture, the style can hardly be considered as a thrusting new development in comparison to what had gone before. The bold and sophisticated engineering involved in broch-building and the construction of wheelhouse piers was a thing of the past. Houses were generally smaller and not as imposing, suggesting that it was less and less important to live in the kind of place where large-scale entertaining could be laid on to impress visitors and retinues.

How people presented themselves to others was much more focused on personal appearance. The earlier generations of the Middle Iron Age certainly made pretty, decorated pottery but their dress ornaments were simple and few. Their descendants were far more preoccupied with looks. Antler combs for coiffuring their long hair (and removing head lice) and a dazzling variety of pins for adorning clothing and hair are the standard finds from settlements of this period. Many have been found at Bostadh and there is a Pictish-style comb and pin from Mound 2 at Bornais *(65)*.

It may seem that with houses so diminished in terms of their power as entertainment venues, the people of the Pictish period were all dressed up with nowhere to go. Yet they lived at the hub of a network of sea roads that could take them south to Ireland, southeast to Dalriada, east to Skye and north to Orkney and Shetland. The bones of deep-sea fish found in the Pictish period levels at Dun Vulan, matched by similar finds in the Northern Isles, indicate that boats were making long-distance voyages far from land on a fairly regular basis. A Scandinavian ornament of this period (known as the Vendel period in Scandinavia), found recently at Ath Linne in Harris, also hints at even longer sea voyages, although it could have been brought to the islands centuries later as an antique heirloom.

No remains of boats from this period have been found in the region but evidence from Scandinavia and England shows a growing mastery of seafaring at this time, with larger vessels more suited to ocean voyages. There is every reason to expect that similar developments were underway in this part of the world, perhaps already utilizing the timber from the Scottish mainland's forested coastline since so little woodland now survived on the Uists.

The attractive pots of the preceding period, the Middle Iron Age, were decorated with incised lines and zigzags, curved channels, ring-headed pin impressions, dots and stabs. These adorned the upper half of the pot, below its rim. Beneath these motifs, around the belly of the pot, there was usually an applied cordon, a band of clay attached to the body of a pot which had been repeatedly pinched between thumb and finger to produce a chain of S-shaped prominences. By about AD 400 this use of a decorated cordon was the only decoration that had survived (except for occasional applied arches) and is sometimes also present around the neck as well as the belly of the pot *(66)*. After about AD 600 the cordon was gone and decoration on pots was limited to occasional finger-impressing of rim tops and lines of tiny dots impressed along the rims.

For the archaeologist this is hugely annoying: not only is most of the pottery plain and therefore difficult to identify to this period, but also these

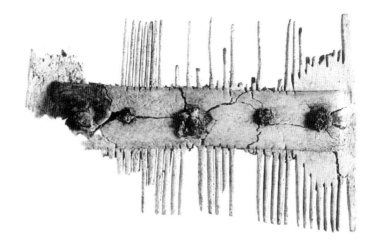

65 The Pictish
comb from
Bornais

66 Late Iron Age
or 'Pictish' pottery

Pictish period pots look very like much earlier vessels of the Late Bronze Age and Early Iron Age. Their shapes are also similar, with the Middle Iron Age globular pots being replaced by wide-mouthed jars. The clay fabric of the Pictish period pottery is slightly better fired than the Late Bronze Age–Early Iron Age ceramics, but otherwise the two types are almost indistinguishable.

The fact that the finger-impressed and dotted rims are common to both periods, separated by a thousand years, may just be due to chance. Alternatively, this is no coincidence and the potters were returning to ancient roots, adopting and recycling styles they would have seen on pots found in old middens dating from an era which they may have perceived as ancestral and traditional. The penchant for living in the ruins of earlier buildings also fits well with this sense of retro-chic. The buildings reused in the Pictish period were sometimes many centuries old, as at Eilean Olabhat on North Uist where a house was built in the ruins of an Early Iron Age building. We may like to think that it is only our own civilization which has played around with neo-Classical, Gothic, Celtic and many other reinvented ancient styles, but invariably it has been done before!

CILLE PHEADAIR KATE AND DISPOSAL OF THE DEAD

Inhumation burial and cremation were both practised during the Middle Iron Age but for the Late Iron Age we only have evidence for inhumation. At the Udal the Pictish period settlement was built on top of a whole field of Middle Iron Age cremation pyres of the first few centuries AD. Most other graves from the Middle Iron Age are long cists, stone-slab arrangements around an extended or near-extended skeleton (lying flat, with the legs straight), and these are often grouped in small cemeteries.

There is a good example of one of these cemeteries at Galson on Lewis, which contained 14 skeletons of men, women and children all dating to between the first and sixth centuries AD. At An Corran on the small island of Boreray, three burials of the Middle Iron Age included one in a long cist and one in a short cist. On South Uist there are a few such finds of long and short cists that could date to this period but most were reported a long time ago and are not well recorded. The largest cemetery found so far is a group of long cist burials which were exposed almost a century ago on the beach east of Tipperton House in Smercleit township, at the south end of the island. Today there is no trace of them.

In 1998 Mark Brennand, one of our archaeological team, was walking along the beach at Cille Pheadair. England had lost a crucial football match that afternoon so, rather downcast, Mark had decided to take the long route home from the pub. But even on a day off, an archaeologist can't help looking for new sites. Mark noticed a line of three upright stones within a mass of beach shingle. The next morning we cleared the loose shingle to reveal a small square cairn, only 2.5m across *(67)*.

This Pictish burial monument had been constructed by setting lines of stones on edge, with each corner marked by a tall, upright stone. However, only one of these four corner-posts remained. Inside the kerb of upright stones, a floor of stone slabs had been laid over the top of the body within the grave beneath. These slabs in turn had been covered by small beach pebbles. The grave pit underneath the cairn had been covered with another row of stone slabs and lined with upright stones *(68)*. Within this stone-lined grave we found the extended skeleton of a woman aged about 40, lying with her

67 Cille Pheadair Kate's cairn before excavation

head to the southeast and looking towards the west *(69)*. The cairn itself was on a different alignment – on the cardinal points – so the body lay at a diagonal angle beneath the cairn.

Cille Pheadair Kate, as she came to be known across the island, became an instant celebrity. As word spread, people flocked to the beach to see the excavation and, a few weeks later, many turned out to fill the church hall to capacity to hear the presentation of our season's results. Kate had several surprises for us. She died around AD 700 and was buried simply within this cist with no grave goods other than a beach pebble which had been placed in the area of her groin. There was no evident cause of death but her life had been a hard one, resulting in arthritis in her back, her jaw and the thumb of her right hand. She had lost four of her teeth whilst alive and two of these, the lower frontal incisors, had been removed many years before her death. Such a practice of deliberate tooth removal is known as tooth evulsion and it has been performed in many parts of the world as a form of beautification or as a rite of passage marking one's entry into adult life.

We do not yet know whether this woman was a resident of South Uist or came from far away but strontium, sulphur and oxygen isotope levels in her teeth will one day reveal this. The question is not unimportant because the style of her cairn is not only Pictish, of a sort found generally across eastern Scotland and the Northern Isles, but is most closely matched by two burials at Sandwick in Shetland. Whether she came from these distant islands or not, her cairn displays knowledge of burial traditions that were more common in these far-away places.

The burial was not a straightforward or quick procedure as such matters are today. Kate's body showed some strange arrangements of her bones. Her arms were by her sides and her fingers were where they should be at the end of her arms. Yet her chest cavity contained the bones of her right hand. How had her arm and finger bones ended up by her waist when the bones in between were somewhere else? Her sternum (breastbone) was missing. The corpse had also been twisted onto its left side at some point and an extra stone upright had been jammed against her spine to keep her in this new position.

When we sieved through the contents of the grave fill, we found the tiny bones of mice. They displayed signs of chemical etching that result from ingestion by an owl. Owls vomit up the bones of their prey in owl pellets. We could deduce that the grave had been left open for some time after burial, perhaps with a loose arrangement of slabs on top, so that an owl had been able to use it as a roost and deposit a pellet into the open grave. During this period, someone came and moved the body, turning it on its side and moving her rotted right arm from its position across her chest. As they did so, the hand must have fallen off and the detached finger bones were hastily placed at the end of the arm. Presumably the sternum was taken away as a memento, a talisman or as something to be disposed of elsewhere.

We do not know whether this interference with the corpse was clandestine or sanctioned, or whether it was done for reasons of robbing the grave or

68 The burial of Cille Pheadair Kate, after the stone covering slabs had been removed

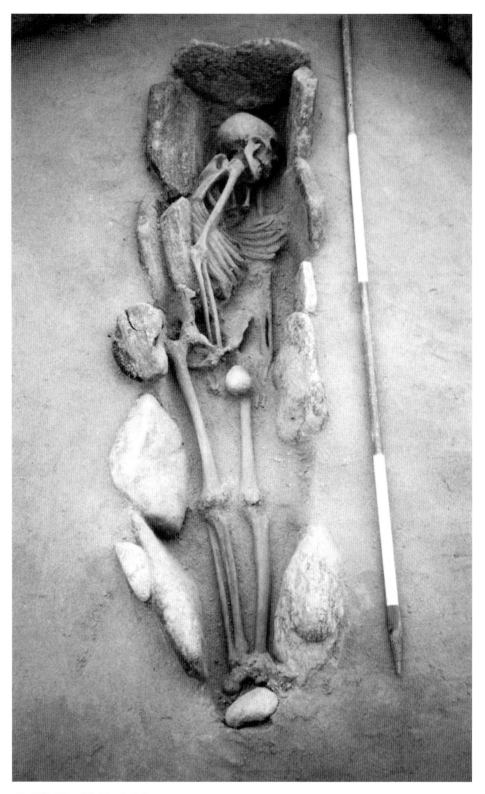

69 Cille Pheadair Kate's skeleton

quieting a troubled spirit. Perhaps, like removing a heart for burial elsewhere, the modifications happened whilst the sternum was being taken.

DIET AND LIFESTYLE

Although greater quantities of fish were being caught in this period, Cille Pheadair Kate was not one for eating much seafood. Carbon isotope levels in bones indicate the source of protein in the diet and Kate's carbon isotope level is among the lowest of any of the 30 individuals analysed from South Uist. This indicates that marine protein only formed a very small percentage of her diet. She was not alone in this: the only other human bone from this period is a skull fragment of a man from a likely burial just north of the Cill Donnain wheelhouse, dating to about AD 600. He displays a similarly low intake of marine food. Isotope studies from other coastal populations in the Western and Northern Isles, together with larger quantities of fish bones in settlements of this period, indicate that some people were now eating a lot of fish. This suggests a growing polarization in diets among the population and could indicate some developing class differences prior to the Viking period.

THE PICTISH STATE AND THE CHRISTIAN CHURCH

There are three other square cairns now known in the Uists and southern isles. One was found at Aird Ma-Ruibne in North Uist during the construction of the Berneray causeway. Another two have been found on the small island of Sandray and a third lies next to the large, possibly Neolithic cairn at Tobhta Mhor na Leaccaich on the south coast of South Uist. All are fairly rough and ready structures in comparison to the Cille Pheadair cairn but they hint at connections with the world of the Pictish kingdom to the north and east.

The long-vanished Picts have left us a record of their civilization in the form of carved stones, engraved with images of mirrors and compasses, animals, people and geometric shapes. These symbol stones have been found mostly in eastern Scotland and the Northern Isles but occur in many other parts of Scotland. There are two Pictish symbol stones from the Western Isles, one from a burial mound on Pabbay off Barra. Another symbol stone is known from Benbecula. A further five stones from Skye make this a notable concentration outside the heartland of the Pictish kingdom, and the new finds of square cairns help to support the idea that Skye and the Western Isles enjoyed some form of political alliance with the power to the east.

As well as carving images on stones, the Picts also used a form of writing, a 20-character alphabet known as *ogham* or *ogam*. It is found mostly on carved stones, as a series of notches cut along the straight edge of a long corner. Very

70 The *ogham* inscription on the Bornais bone

occasionally it is carved onto small portable artefacts such as spindle whorls (spinning-weights) and carved bones. Many years ago, Erskine Beveridge found an animal bone engraved with *ogham* script in a reused wheelhouse at Bhac mhic Connain on North Uist. It reads as MAQUNM?DENCOT and may relate to a person's name.

In 1996 Jerry Bond, another of our field team, spotted an *ogham* inscription on a bone which he picked up from the surface of the excavations on the Pictish house at Bornish. Unfortunately it had broken in half long ago and, try as we might, we could not find that missing half. The *ogham* signs can be translated as EIHNE— (or —EQBIE if turned round) and, once again, are relatively garbled and meaningless *(70)*.

Cille Pheadair Kate was not buried in a Christian fashion and this suggests that the fruits of St Columba's mission, spreading out from Iona where St Columba had established his monastic community in AD 563, had not reached everyone (if indeed anyone) in South Uist by AD 700. At this time Christianity in the Scottish islands might well have been characterized more by communities of hermit monks living in remote locations rather than by proselytizing priests going out to convert the populace. Religious communities from this period are known on the very inaccessible island of North Rona and possibly on the Shiant Isles, recently excavated by a SEARCH project member, Patrick Foster.

There has been much written and hypothesized about the place name 'Pabbay' since it may indicate the location of early monastic sites. A Norse-derived word meaning 'isle of the papar (priests)', it has been suggested that it was used by the Viking invaders to identify places inhabited by these remote religious communities. Apart from the isle of Pabbay at the south end of the Western Isles, there are a handful of 'papar' names in the Western Isles. One of these is the islet of Pabbay within Lochboisdale on South Uist. This is a small rocky island whose traces of human presence include a group of curvilinear earthworks near its highest point. These could well be traces of an early monastic establishment but only future excavation will tell. Another monastery is likely to lie underneath the medieval churches at Howmore, where a Christian gravestone of the seventh–ninth centuries lies amongst the ruins. There is another early Christian cross slab in the Cladh Hallan cemetery.

CHAPTER 8

VIKINGS

The Viking and Late Norse Period

795-1266

On a bitterly cold and wet February day in 1994 two of us (MPP and JS) were walking up and down the two settlement mounds next to the Iron Age and Pictish site on Bornais machair. No one else was foolish enough to be out and about that morning. We were doing it because we had identified these low hillocks as settlements from the shells and bones we had picked up in rabbit burrows the previous summer but, so far, we had not found any pottery at all. We were hoping that this could just be our first discovery of a settlement of Vikings because we knew that they used very few pots. The only excavation of a Viking settlement on South Uist, at Drimore on the rocket range back in 1957, had produced just five fragments of pottery.

The wind was blowing in from the sea so strongly that it was almost impossible to look at the ploughed ground without being blown over. We could only stay on our feet when facing into the wind. We must have looked deranged as we slowly made our way across the mounds, leaning into the gale at 45° and then staggering back, bustled by the wind, to begin the next segment of the survey next to the line that we had just walked. It was slow work but by lunchtime we had half-filled two small plastic bags with sherds of pottery. Retiring to the public bar of the Borrodale Hotel, we ordered Guinness and waited for our fingers to unfreeze.

The sherds were covered in mud but with a bit of rudimentary cleaning we were able to inspect our treasure. Nearly all of them were plain and featureless but three tiny sherds turned out to be just what we were looking for. Completely flat, they had impressions of blades of grass embedded into the clay on one side only. These were tiny fragments of grass-marked Platter Ware, flat circular plates very similar in size and shape to a thin-crust pizza base *(71)*. Made only during the Viking period, these clay plates were prepared for firing on a mat or surface of grass, so their undersides have these characteristic impressions. The surface of the plates was then stabbed and pierced to provide holes for the heat to rise. On these griddles, nestled in the ashes of the fire, the Vikings baked their barley and oat cakes. Today, you can still buy such

71 Platter Ware, the distinctive Norse style of baking tray

cakes at the bakery in Stornoway, but the tradition of making them has lapsed in South Uist.

Platter Ware is exclusive to the Inner and Outer Hebrides. It was first recognized as a regional Viking type by Alan Lane, who was studying the pottery of this period from the Udal excavations. In the Northern Isles, these baking plates were made not of pottery but of an easy-to-carve soapstone known as steatite. For us, Platter Ware was the key to unlocking the mystery of South Uist's Viking settlements. Bornais is a Norse place name, literally the 'borg' or broch on the 'ness' or promontory, named after Dun Vulan (the site described in chapters 6 and 7). We had actually matched an archaeological site with its original Norse name.

There were many other Norse place names to be found along the machair which could be matched with archaeological sites. The place name Frobost contains the 'bolstadr' component meaning 'settlement', whilst Dreumasadal is a composite of 'dal' for dale and the Gaelic word for a ridge. Dalabrog, the dale of the cairn, has already been mentioned (in chapter 3) and there are in all 12 township place names which have Norse or part-Norse derivations. Even the townships with Gaelic names (such as Drimore and all the Cille or 'church' names) have Norse period settlement mounds on their machair. The small islands around South Uist – Orosay (a common name for small coastal islets) and Eriskay for example – all have the Norse '–ay' element, meaning island. The name of Uist itself is almost certainly not Norse but much older. The sea and the settlements appear to have been renamed by the Vikings but many of the names of the inland streams, hills and mountains have Celtic or Gaelic origins, perhaps reflecting those aspects of the islands in which the Norse were least interested.

Since Gaelic names probably post-date the Norse names, it is interesting that so many Norse names have survived. The high proportion of Norse-derived place names on Lewis and Harris has been taken to indicate that Norse influence was greater here than in the Uists but it actually merely reflects what happened to names *after* the Norse period. Just why so many of South Uist's Norse township names have survived requires explanation, even though their survival has not been as commonplace as on the islands further north. This difference may relate to a greater degree of settlement disruption in the Uists in the fourteenth and fifteenth centuries.

One of the Norse-derived place names on South Uist is Peighinn nan Aoireann (Peninerine). It is a small township to the south of Howbeg and north of Stoneybridge but does not have any machair or any trace of Norse or earlier settlement. Its name derives from 'pennyland'. The Norse assessed the productivity of land against a standard weight of silver. Twenty penny lands made an ounce land. Peninerine was the pennyland where mass was said, and this land, presumably provided a levy to support the Church. Christianity brought tributary obligations, rendered to the parish priests at Howmore and Cille Pheadair and to the Bishopric on the Isle of Man.

The people we refer to generally as the Vikings originated in Scandinavia. In eastern Scotland and England the Viking impact came largely from Denmark, although the Danes were also active in the western seaways and seized Dublin in AD 851. The Danes fought the Norwegians in Ireland and were defeated by them in 853. It was the Norwegian invaders who settled in the Western Isles, where they made a profound impact on language, population and culture. Despite having a Gaelic language and culture today, people from Uist are essentially the direct descendants of Vikings. Julian Richards' *Blood of the Vikings* television series reported on a large-scale DNA sampling programme and demonstrated that many of today's Hebrideans share a particular gene with contemporary Norwegians.

In 795 the Vikings attacked the monastery founded by St Columba on Iona. Three years later they plundered throughout the Hebrides and continued to attack Iona in the early ninth century. This moment is considered by historians and archaeologists as the beginning of the Norse period, of which the first half is the Viking Age (AD 795-1000) and the second is the Late Norse period (1000-1266). The date of 1266 is chosen to mark the end of the Norse period because in that year the Western Isles were transferred from Norwegian rule to the Scottish Crown. The Scots had defeated the Norwegians at the battle of Largs in 1263 and, in the subsequent treaty signed at Perth, the Hebrides were handed over to King Alexander of Scotland.

The beginning of the Viking Age is the first time in South Uist's ancient past when we can be sure that there was a large influx of incomers, the first since that initial Mesolithic/Neolithic settlement of the islands. The genetic and linguistic evidence is incontrovertible. Yet the issue of whether the arrival of the Vikings was a full-scale, bloody invasion or a more gentle long-term migration is not at all straightforward, and archaeologists still argue about exactly what happened.

From his excavation results at the Udal on North Uist, Iain Crawford argues that the Viking invaders took over root and branch, killing the local men and enslaving the women and children. Crawford interpreted a timber structure excavated at the Udal as a small Viking fort and also reckoned that the stone-walled Pictish period houses were razed and levelled for the invaders' turf-walled longhouses to be built directly on top. Barbara Crawford (no relation) has worked with the documentary sources and considers that there was a much greater degree of assimilation and integration of locals and incomers, certainly on the Uists.

The early Viking raids seem to have been conducted by pirates – Vikings or 'emporia people' (the word 'viks' or 'wicks/wichs' refers to the trading emporia or ports of Scandinavia and Britain) were essentially outcasts, the fugitives and rebels of the Scandinavian world. One of these early pirates was Onund Wooden-leg who plundered in the Hebrides in 869 and fought a sea battle off Barra. He used Barra as his winter base from which he waged war and extortion in the summers. Another fugitive from Norway who arrived in the Western Isles via Orkney was Ketil Flatnose; he set himself up as Lord of the Hebrides before moving on to Iceland.

By the late ninth century there was an intensification of Viking activity, together with state intervention aiming to stamp Norwegian royal authority across the islands. King Harald Thickhair of Norway mounted an expedition to the Hebrides and slew many Vikings – he had sworn not to cut his hair until he had cleared them out and thereafter became known as Harald Finehair! One of his many sons was the well-known Eric Bloodaxe who plundered the Hebrides before setting himself up in York. Later Eric recruited the Vikings of the Western Isles and Orkney to plunder the Inner Hebrides and lands further south. In the late tenth century King Olaf Tryggvason also fought in the Hebrides. His conversion to Christianity earned him sainthood and could well have had a profound effect in changing the attitude of his subjects on South Uist and elsewhere in the Western Isles towards the still new Christian religion.

After the battle of Clontarf in 1014, the Norwegians and the Danes were driven out of Dublin. Despite the development of a self-determining, emergent kingdom of Man and the Isles which included the Western Isles, the Earls of Orkney (who were Norwegian) continued to claim overlordship of the Western Isles. With the death of Thorfinn, Earl of Orkney, in or before 1064, the kingdom of Man and the Isles gained its independence. Later, however, the island kingdom was reappropriated by King Magnus of Norway who appointed his own governors on Man and on Lewis. His nickname of 'Bareleg' apparently derives from his adoption of a Western Isles style of dress, going bare-legged with a short tunic and over-cloak. In 1098 Magnus led an expedition to put down revolt throughout the region and, among other targets, probably attacked South Uist, since it is recorded that he 'ravaged Uist with fire'. From then on until 1266 the kings of Man and the Isles remained tributary to Norway, although in the period between Magnus' death in 1103 and 1156, ties to England seem to have been more significant.

South Uist had to provide warriors and ships to fight in battles and expeditions over several of the bloodiest centuries of recorded history in Ireland and the north. Many men of the Western Isles served in the Norwegian army and must have fought in Ireland, the Hebrides and England. In 1066 South Uist was on the side of the invaders, not the defenders. Uistmen and other Hebrideans joined the Norwegian and Orcadian warriors in the fleet assembled by Harald Hardrada, king of Norway, which sailed on northeast England. The plan was to defeat Harold Godwinson's army and take the English throne, restoring Harold's traitorous brother Tostig as Earl of Northumbria.

At the battle of Stamford Bridge, outside York, most of the Hebrideans died along with Tostig and his scheme. Harold Godwinson's victorious but exhausted army marched south immediately – within twenty days, near Hastings, they had fought again, and lost. The Norman invaders seized power in England and from that year on, the power of the Scandinavian north was on the wane. Even in South Uist, economic and social relationships began to divert towards Ireland and England as these countries themselves looked more towards France and the Continent.

One of the key problems with the Norse period in Scotland is that the earliest archaeological evidence of Viking settlement, apart from a few sites such as Drimore, is hard to date any earlier than around AD 950. This is a century and a half after the early raids on the Western Isles. It is likely that the lack of Viking settlements in those 150 years is due not to some problem with finding them but to the fact that such settlements didn't exist. The Vikings were certainly present in the area during the ninth century but it seems they chose not to live there at that time. Most of the Viking colonization did not occur until the second half of the tenth century and after. Our excavations of Norse period sites at Bornais and Cille Pheadair fit well with this later date of settling down and, therefore, most Pictish period settlements presumably remained in use, still occupied by local people, after 800. The radiocarbon dates from the Pictish village on Bostadh beach show that it was abandoned around 900 to 950.

The Norse period raises some knotty issues about archaeology, history, language, genetics and ethnicity. The simplistic equation of material culture (architecture, dress, cuisine and lifestyle) with ethnic identity (roots, 'race, creed or colour', nation, tribe, etc.) cannot be sustained – bungalows originated in India, for example, but people who live in bungalows in Britain do not necessarily come from India themselves. In the same way, wielding a Viking sword did not necessarily mean that the sword's owner was of Scandinavian descent though it might have let them think of themselves as Vikings. Ethnicity is not some sort of biological constant: it can be manipulated to suit the occasion, so that particular strands are sometimes emphasized over others. It too is an artefact with which people choose to play up their historical and genetic roots (or, rather, selected aspects of those diverse roots) or to play them down, or even invent new ones!

The Norse period in the Western Isles is essentially a prehistoric period – the few documentary sources that we have are not only very limited but are also written from the outside – and we are thus largely reliant on the evidence of material culture as recovered through archaeology. Given the difficulties of reading that material record in terms of Norse and Hebridean ethnic identities, what clues do we have about the nature of the Viking impact?

NORSE PERIOD SETTLEMENTS AND CERAMICS

At the beginning of the SEARCH project there were few clues as to where Viking settlements could be located. Some thought the east coast was a likely area since the deep-sea lochs on that side look not unlike fjords and might have served as a home from home for Norwegian settlers. But the Viking period house on Drimore machair, together with the machair location of the Udal on North Uist, pointed to the west coast as the more likely settlement zone. We have found 23 Norse period settlement mounds on South Uist, making it one of the most densely identified Viking landscapes with associated place names anywhere in Europe.

The relationship of these Norse period villages to previous settlements of the Pictish period and Middle Iron Age is a close one, since Norse period mounds are mostly immediately adjacent to these earlier sites, if not on top of them as is the case for one of the mounds at Bornais. One or two, such as Cille Pheadair, are different in that they do not seem to have been located near any earlier settlements.

The general pattern of South Uist's Norse period settlements does indicate a strong degree of continuity from the Pictish period. Yet there was at least one Norse village which was strikingly different from any settlement dating to preceding periods of the island's history. The three mounds at Bornais form the centre of a group of eight Norse period settlements within Bornais machair. This is the densest distribution of machair settlement for any period and suggests that this township might have been the largest community and centre of power on South Uist at that time. As far as we can tell, there were no longhouse communities living in the peatlands, but some of the shieling sites up in the hills probably date to this period. A couple have been found on Barra, one within the ruins of a wheelhouse at Alt Chrisal and the other at Ben Gunnary.

Clay pots were not a favourite form of container anywhere in the Viking world. More robust materials such as metal, wood and soapstone were preferred for the cauldrons, buckets, bowls, platters and other containers used in everyday life. Despite its scarcity *vis-à-vis* earlier periods in the Western Isles, pottery was actually relatively widely used in this part of the world when compared to other areas settled by the Vikings. Between them, the sites of Cille Pheadair and Bornais have yielded about 20,000 sherds of Viking pottery.

The fact that potting continued here as a valued activity providing a useful product does suggest a degree of continuity with older traditions, a continuity not found in the other Viking domains such as Orkney. The grass-marked platters, small bowls and round-based cooking pots of the Norse period are certainly very different in style from the flaring and open-mouthed jars of the Pictish period, but a small number of these Pictish jar styles continued to be made in the Norse period and were used alongside the Norse styles. The Pictish and Norse potting technologies were also similar in that they both involved building the pot by fitting slabs together but the slabs of Pictish pots were joined together by tongue and groove whilst the slabs of the Viking pots were fitted as overlaps.

Drimore

When the Viking house at Drimore was excavated in 1957, it turned out to be a very odd shape *(72)*. It should have been a rectangular house – Vikings lived in longhouses – but its two long walls were built in different styles and the west end had a curiously irregular curved shape. There were also several adjoining walls which seemed not to be part of the main structure. One of the interesting aspects of some of the later walls of the Drimore house is that they are free-standing, not revetted into the sand. Only the lower courses of these walls survived. The long-gone upper courses could have been made of turf, a building style typical of Viking longhouses, but the surviving stone-built lower courses were very unusual. Such stonework is definitely not a typical feature of the timber and turf longhouses known from other parts of the Viking world. Inside the longhouse, a very long hearth ran half the length of the interior, along its centre.

The excavations were carried out in difficult circumstances with little time and a high water table. This was also the first time that standard archaeological techniques were employed in the tricky machair sand, which has unusual properties which challenge the excavator and take some getting used to. Just a few years earlier, Kissling and Lethbridge had conducted their archaeological

N

d

c

a

socket

b

e

metres | 1 | 2 | 3 | 4 | 5 | 6 | 7 | 8 | 9 | 10
feet | 5 | 10 | 15 | 20 | 25 | 30

72 Plan of the Drimore longhouse

'excavations' on the Cille Pheadair wheelhouse by watching gangs of workmen simply shovelling out sand, as fast as they could be persuaded to work.

Some interesting artefacts were found at Drimore. Combs made of deer antler come in distinct styles, very specific to time and place, and a complete antler comb dates the Drimore house to sometime between 800 and 1000. The other finds include a silver plaque (possibly for adorning a Pictish comb), 16 steatite bowl fragments, seven steatite spindle whorls, 11 pins and a collection of knives and other tools, all made of bone. The site of the house was never a high mound and it seems to have had a relatively short-lived period of occupation, probably earlier than the Bornais and Cille Pheadair houses.

Bornais

The Bornais mounds have revealed a very different picture. The Norse settlement developed on top of a Pictish settlement (Mound 2), which is dated to the seventh and eighth centuries by a very distinctive antler comb and a bone pin. This Norse settlement was located about 100m north of the settlement (Mound 1) discussed in the last chapter, which dates to the fourth or fifth centuries AD. As time passed, the settlement expanded, new buildings were established to the north and east (Mound 3 and Mounds 2A and 2B), and the earlier settlement to the south (Mound 1) was reoccupied *(62)*.

Geophysical survey by project member Mike Hamilton has given us some idea of the number and density of buildings at Bornais. A resistivity survey, which measures the degree of soil conductivity, has identified numerous areas of high resistance: these are areas of the dry windblown sand that fills up abandoned houses. Magnetometer survey, measuring magnetic variation, picks out the rubble of abandoned houses because gneiss, the local stone, is very slightly magnetic. When compared to each other, the two types of geophysical survey reveal five groups of farmsteads containing as many as 23 buildings in total *(73)*.

The earliest structure so far discovered is a longhouse-like building with postholes where wooden posts once stood. Post-built houses had last been constructed on South Uist in the Bronze Age, so this was a somewhat unusual find within a Viking settlement. However, this alien style of building is strongly suggestive of the adoption or importation of a lifestyle with its roots in Scandinavia. We cannot, of course, be certain whether it indicates incomers fresh off the boat, or Hebrideans adopting a new way of life.

The next construction on this spot was a very large stone-walled building *(74; 75)*. It was about 20m long (east to west) and over 5.5m wide inside and seems to have been built as a free-standing structure. Its long walls are slightly curved, to form the classic bowed shape known so well in the Scandinavian world during the Viking Age. It was built just after AD 1000 and was probably an important person's farmstead which could also have doubled as a communal hall. Placed within the biggest mound within the large Bornais community,

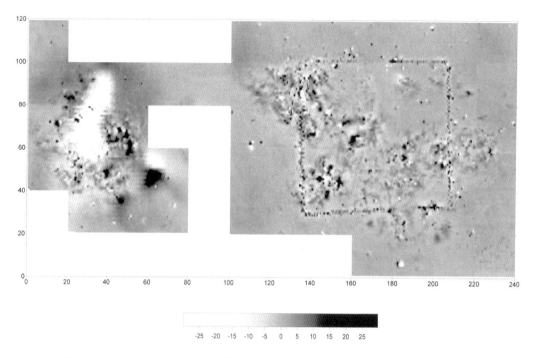

73 The magnetometry survey plot for Bornais

this might well have been the meeting place and feasting house for everyone on the island, as well as supporting a household of between 20 and 30 people.

When this great longhouse was abandoned in the twelfth century, all kinds of artefacts were left inside: two iron cauldron handles, a whale bone plaque, an antler comb, a carved antler tip and a bone collar from the neck of a leather flask. This collar is engraved with a marvellous depiction of a lion-like creature, in a Scandinavian style known as Ringerike *(76)*. Other carvings of this type of animal are known from Scandinavia and this item most likely came from Norway.

Over a period of about a century the longhouse was heavily modified with smaller, poorly constructed (and badly robbed-out) walls being constructed at its east end. Eventually these walls were cleared away altogether and another large house, 13m long and 6m wide, was built here, probably in the late twelfth or early thirteenth century *(74; 77)*. This time the house was oriented north–south. It was quite different to the previous two houses built on Mound 2 because it had straight sides with corners at right angles. The entrance to the house was located at the north end of the east side and was a passage over 2m long. Inside there was no long central hearth, as in the earlier houses, but a series of discrete circular ash heaps. This sequence within Mound 2 indicates that these buildings were clearly the centre of the settlement, but excavations on the other two mounds demonstrate a long period of activity from the tenth

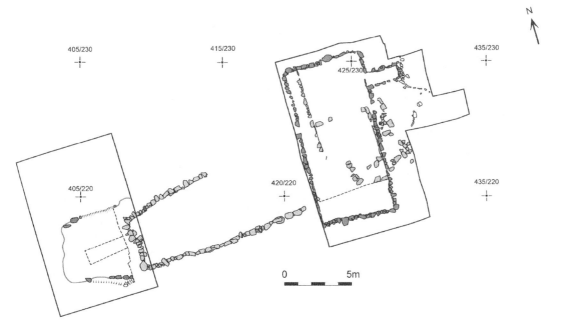

405/230

415/230

425/230

435/230

405/220

420/220

435/220

0   5m

N

74 The large longhouse with bowed walls (House 2) and the later house (House 3) at Bornais

75 House 2 on Mound 2 at Bornais

76 The carved animal
in Ringerike style
from Bornais

77 House 3 on
Mound 2 at Bornais

to the fourteenth or fifteenth centuries with crafts which included comb-making and corn-drying (see chapter 9).

The village at Bornais appears to have started in the tenth century with the take-over of a native (Pictish) farm by an incoming Norwegian family. Initially it was probably a single farm, belonging to an important Viking leader but, as time progressed, it grew into one of the largest settlements along the western seaboard of Scotland. It seems to have retained its status well into the period of Scottish rule, after 1266, only to be abandoned in the early fifteenth century.

Cille Pheadair

In the early 1990s fierce winter storms on South Uist coincided with high tides and washed away huge sections of the sand cliffs on the west coast at Cille Pheadair. This particular stretch of coastline has been eroding for some time. Historical records indicate that the church of Cille Pheadair was washed away by the sea in the nineteenth century and, in recent years, the land is being eroded at a rate of about 20m every quarter of a century. In 1977 an archaeologist, Elizabeth Eames, was on holiday here and noticed a settlement eroding out of the cliff. The iron nails amongst the finds indicate that it was from the Viking period or later but we shall never know its precise date because it was entirely washed away without further investigation.

The storms in the winter of 1993-1994 revealed the edge of a second settlement – from the Norse period – which had been completely and deeply buried beneath the coastal dunes. It was found by Callum and James MacDonald over that winter and we realized that we did not have long to wait until the sea also swept this site away forever. In 1996 we began the first of three seasons' work excavating this small settlement mound to recover the entire history of what had once been a small, single farmstead.

The Cille Pheadair wheelhouse lies about half a mile to the north, together with an assortment of Middle Iron Age settlements and sites of other periods, some distance from this Norse period farmstead. The area in which it stands was originally the end of a long peninsula or promontory of machair, which would have been similar to the promontory that can be seen today at Bailesear on North Uist. At the end of that promontory, Pictish Kate had been buried about 300 years earlier. During the Bronze Age and Iron Age the area to the east of this peninsula had been a tidal cockle strand open to the sea but by the Norse period it had become a freshwater or brackish inland loch.

This sandy coastal ridge was being ploughed shortly before the Norse period farmstead was established. The first building on this field was a rectangular wooden structure. Just how big it was will never be known because part of it had already been washed away by the sea by the time our excavations began. It might well have been a small longhouse, built north–south, perhaps with two interior lines of posts supporting the roof. Its doorway was on the south end of the east wall, facing inland, and the two holes for the door posts contained specially placed deposits of a comb, a bone pin and a pair of vertebral discs from a whale.

The wooden house might well have been a short-lived temporary dwelling, because it was replaced by a completely different arrangement. The builders removed the old house's floor and all but the bottoms of the postholes. They dug out a large, rectangular, house-sized trench, also arranged north–south, and piled up the sand around it to form a bank which was revetted with a low stone wall on both faces *(78)*. There was an entrance to this sunken enclosure on the south end of its east side. Probably as part of the founding of the farmstead, two lines of large pits were dug inside the enclosure. Many were filled back in empty, some had household rubbish in them and one contained some special finds that included iron fittings from a wooden chest, a dress pin and a comb.

A stone-walled longhouse was then built inside the enclosure, somewhat shorter than the length of the original house trench *(79)*. This farmhouse was the first of four longhouses built on the site. It had a long central hearth and its upper walls would have been made of turf. Its occupants were very tidy: most household rubbish was regularly swept out of the door but a small number of bones and sherds accumulated in the dark southeast corner of the house. Fortunately for the archaeologists, the house had earth floors so enough tiny debris remained were it fell on the soft surface to provide a good idea of how the dark interior was organized.

The cooking was done at the north end of the hearth, the spot furthest from the door and the best place to sit and survey what everyone else was up to. We can be confident that cooking was women's work in the Norse period and this dominating location gives some idea of the power and status of the mistress of the house, perhaps greater than women had enjoyed in earlier periods. To her right, someone – presumably her husband – sat and worked at whittling, grinding and polishing activities. The beds were most likely arranged along the long west and east sides of the house. The area at the south end was used as a store. There was a cat in the house at some point – it left some faeces in a dark corner – but it seems not to have caught the mice whose two tiny skeletons were found against the walls.

Around 1100 the house was replaced by another on a much larger scale *(80; 81)*. It was 14m long inside and now consisted of two rooms – the main room and a small square annexe or back room to its north. The entrance passage was also longer and had a wide forecourt at its outer end. To our good luck, the people who lived in this house were much more untidy than their predecessors. The cooking area was in the same place, covered in tiny sherds of broken cooking pots and pieces of slates used as lids. The platter baking was done slightly further into the hearth, where the fire was hotter.

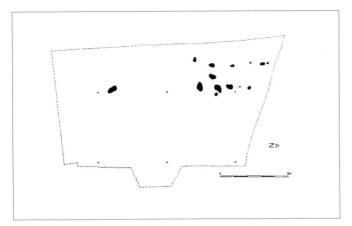

78 *Left and below* Plan of the sandwall enclosure and earlier postholes at Cille Pheadair

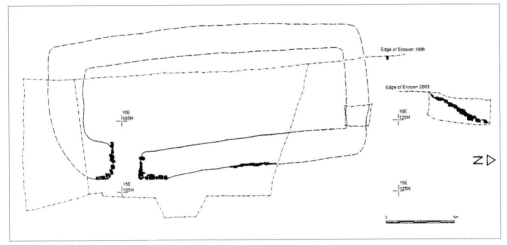

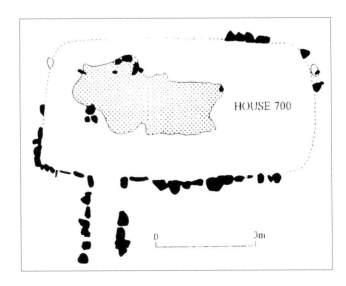

79 Plan of the first stone-walled house at Cille Pheadair

80 The second stone-walled house at Cille Pheadair

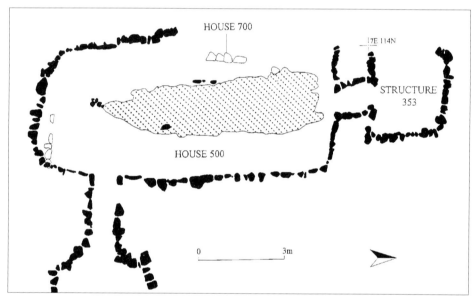

81 Plan of the second stone-walled house at Cille Pheadair

On the cook's right-hand side, again, lay a knife, pounding stones and debris from sharpening tools on whetstones and whittling antler. The husband – if this is who sat here – was also in charge of lighting the fire because tiny chips of flint from his strike-a-light lay here. The children probably sat along the long east side of the hearth. The family's beds were visible as a row of sleeping hollows along the west side of the house. On the east side just inside the door, a wooden chest or dresser had once sat. All that remained of its presence was its outline where a new floor layer had been laid around it. The

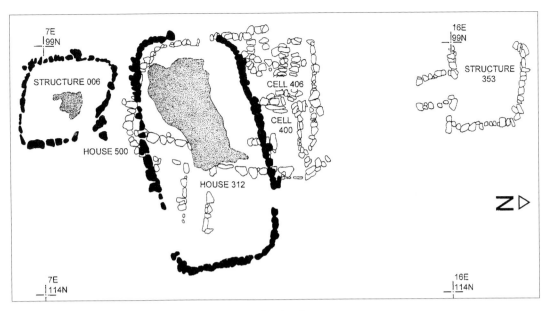

82 Plan of the third stone-walled house at Cille Pheadair

south end of the house contained dung which suggests that a couple of sheep or cows were kept here. What is interesting about this indoor byre is that it is just like the use of space in blackhouses inhabited in recent centuries and recorded by Werner Kissling, in which a cow and a couple of calves were often over-wintered in the house.

The back room was for storage. Potting clay was kept on its west side and tiny shells of *Spirorbis* indicate that dried seaweed and possibly dry driftwood were kept here for feeding the fire. Dogs were allowed in the house and they left their calling cards in various places, especially at the south end near the door. When the house went out of use, 'closing deposits' of a comb and a bone pin was left in the woman's place – closing deposits identical to those we had found left in the first longhouse when its inhabitants abandoned it. This time, another offering were left in the space between her and her husband. It was a tiny bone cross, planted into the edge of the hearth after the fire had gone cold for the last time *(83)*.

The longhouse was modified around 1200: the main room was turned into a much smaller dwelling and the back room became an outhouse, reached by a pathway from a new doorway at the north end of the east wall. The longhouse soon went into decay and abandonment; the main residents now were owls which deposited their pellets into the ruins. After the ruin was levelled and covered over by sand, someone built a pair of sheds on the site. The large, thick-walled storage pots found in this phase give us an idea of what these small buildings were used for. Presumably the owners of the sheds lived some distance away and visited only occasionally.

83 The two bone crosses from Cille
Pheadair

After using the site just for storage, people came back to live here again.
The next longhouse was built east–west, with its doorway at the east end of
the north side *(82)*. The arrangements for living and working around the long
fireplace were the same as in the first two houses except there was an extra
space on the left-hand side of the cooking area where sharpening, grinding and
whittling were also going on. Presumably this was the place of an older child
learning the ways of adulthood. Spinning was also being carried out by those
sitting on the long side of the fire – presumably the children. Other activities
included pottery-making and flax-beating. A new square outhouse was positioned against the south side of the longhouse and it was used as a storage room
and bakehouse for making platter cakes.

This longhouse had two rooms. The eastern third of the interior was
divided from the rest of the house by a wall or barrier of wood. This had not
survived but we can deduce where it once stood from the patterning of sherds,
bones and hearth ash which had built up against it. This end room was not a
byre, of the sort identified in the earlier longhouse, and could have been a
storage area. At the end of the house's use, the presence of human faeces and
high phosphate values in the earth show that it was used as an impromptu
lavatory. This east–west longhouse, and the final house built on top of it, did
not contain any foundation or 'closing' offerings as the earlier ones had. This
change in customs marks the moment when the old pagan beliefs had finally
waned in the face of Christianity.

The last house was built across this one on a north–south axis *(84;86)*.
Towards the north end it had two opposing entrances, one to the west and one
to the east. The west door led towards the rebuilt outhouse and the east door
led out to the fields. The floor was well swept and kept extremely clean but
the few surviving scraps of micro-debris indicate a pattern of use similar to the
earlier houses. A penny of King John of England (1199-1216), cut in half, was
dropped in the ruins, probably long after its issue, towards the end of the thirteenth century.

84 The fourth stone-walled house at Cille Pheadair

AGRICULTURE, ECONOMY AND VOYAGING

The long-term mainstay of dairying, which had been in place for 2,000 years, came to an end with the Viking period. With the exception of the Udal, the Uist settlements show a shift to a beef-rearing economy in which cattle were now slaughtered at around two years old. The other major change was the advent of fishing as a major part of daily life. Even the dogs and cats were eating fish (along with mice). More particularly South Uist was specializing in herring fishing. This type of activity required co-ordination of boats and organization for long voyages, and the thickness of the shanks of the many iron boat rivets from Cille Pheadair and Bornais indicate that most of the boats were between 6 and 12m long, with a few larger vessels of up to 18m. Another change was the new emphasis on the cultivation and processing of flax to make linen.

In the meantime, the Norse inhabitants of the Northern Isles were pursuing a different course, intensifying their dairying and concentrating their fishing on cod, saithe and ling. The change in the Uist economy might well have been deliberate, enabling these islanders to diversify into new products which could more easily find a market in the globalizing world of Norse trade, stretching from southern England to Norway.

The products coming in to South Uist from the north were soapstone – made into bowls, spindle whorls and line sinkers – and whetstones from Norway, and ivory from Greenland. After a while, around 1100, these were no longer in use at Cille Pheadair and its imports now included pottery from Wiltshire, procured most probably in Bristol or Dublin. Pins of bone, copper alloy and iron in Irish styles also hint at other connections with Ireland. Gold and silver were also being obtained from afar and it is curious that the small Cille Pheadair farmstead is far wealthier in precious metals and fancy metalwork than the great village at Bornais *(colour plates 12 and 13)*. Its range of combs *(colour plate 14)* is also very different from those at Bornais even though they are of the same period. This may well suggest that identities were very localized within South Uist – perhaps even then there was a difference between the south end and the rest of the island. The people of Bornais retained contacts with Scandinavia into the thirteenth and fourteenth centuries, using imported ivory and some fine combs that were almost certainly made in Norway.

Burnt plant remains from Bornais indicate that the new crops of flax and rye were cultivated on a large scale. This might have required agricultural expansion in the Norse period onto soils previously underused, probably on the machair as well as on the fertile strip between machair and blackland. We discovered ploughmarks under Mound 2A at Bornais as well as under the Cille Pheadair settlement, providing evidence of this greater use of the machair for cultivation.

One of the artefacts missing from the Uist settlements is querns. Grinding stones are essential for processing cereal crops so querns are naturally common in previous periods and their absence from the Norse sites is striking. The answer is most probably that the milling of barley and oats was being carried out in specialized watermills. Several are known on Lewis and there should be similar undershot watermills up in the hills of South Uist along the stream courses. None have yet been found, not for want of looking.

The long-distance connections implied by many of the artefacts can be compared with the various references in Icelandic sagas and other texts to voyages made by Hebrideans around the north Atlantic. Unfortunately these rarely specify where in the islands these individuals were from, except in cases such as Alfdis the Barra-woman.

CHAPTER 9

MEDIEVAL CHIEFDOMS
The Medieval and Early Modern Period
1266-1700

In 1995 a great discovery was made. It wasn't dug up. It wasn't even found on South Uist. It was a large carved stone and it turned up in a dead man's London flat. His family took the stone to the British Museum who got in touch with the National Museum of Scotland. Immediately one of the curators, David Caldwell, recognized it as the lost armorial stone of Clan Ranald *(85)*. It had been stolen by the young man and an accomplice in 1990 from a chapel at Howmore, on South Uist, and had finally resurfaced. It was carefully restored and then brought back to the island in 1997 to be reinstated, this time in the safety of the Kildonan Museum. To the accompaniment of pipes and under the watchful eye of Historic Scotland's inspector of monuments, the stone was ceremoniously carried into the museum.

The Clan Ranald are a particular branch of Clan Donald, whose descendants are found not just in South Uist and western Scotland but throughout the world. Their ancient ancestor is Somerled, Thane of Argyll, who lived in the mid-twelfth century in the southwest part of Scotland. There is much discussion as to whether he was a true-born Gael — a noble successor to the kingship of the vanished kingdom of Dalriada — or of mixed Norse blood, though the general consensus is that all the leading families of the region were at least part-Norse by this period. Somerled is reckoned to have laid the political and military basis for the Lordship of the Isles in a series of military campaigns and naval engagements, from his base on the island of Islay. By 1158 he had taken all the Hebridean islands from the King of Man.

The Clan Ranald crest of arms is composed of what looks like a bird on a stick, a large horse-like animal, a hand holding a Celtic cross, a castle, and a ship. The bird is actually a sea eagle standing on a thistle, and the other animal is in fact a lion. The cross-bearing hand signifies the blessings of the Church whilst the castle may represent one or more of the Clan Ranald strongholds. The carving of the ship is a representation of a Hebridean galley. Its symbolism was so important that it was often used on its own to represent the Lord of the Isles. Unlike the Viking longships, this new style of warship possessed a rudder,

85 The Clan Ranald stone

to give it greater manoeuvrability compared to the old-style steering oar, and a raised fighting platform on the mast from which archers could pour their fire on the unprotected decks of enemy ships. These ships, known as *nyvaigs* or *birlinns*, were not particularly large but they were very successful. By the time of his death in 1164, Somerled could launch a fleet of 160 of them.

Somerled was succeeded by three sons, Dugall, Reginald and Angus. We know that they ventured as far south as Bristol, a route which was already being used earlier in the twelfth century when someone brought a Wiltshire tripod pitcher to the farmstead at Cille Pheadair. After Somerled's death the King of Man recovered much of his territory but whether this included Uist is uncertain. Somerled's rule had passed to Reginald and thence to his son Donald who died in the mid-thirteenth century.

In 1266, the Treaty of Perth forfeited the kingdom of Man's lands to the Scottish Crown and granted an amnesty for all the Norse chieftains of the Isles, appointees of King Hakon IV of Norway. They could either leave for Norway or remain under Scottish rule. Donald had had a younger brother, Ruairi (who was probably long dead by 1266) and it was his descendants, the Clan Ruairi or MacRuairis, who were in control of the Uists by 1300. Ruairi's son Dugald was already known as 'King of Innesgall and Argyll' before 1266 and fought in Hakon's army before eventually settling in Norway. Dugald's brother Alan inherited the MacRuairis' estates and the title of King of the Hebrides - 'Rex Hebudum'. A charter of 1343 indicates that the Uists, Barra and the Small Isles were united into a single lordship within the MacRuairi territories which included the area between Ardnamurchan and Glenelg on the mainland, known as Garmoran, as well as the southern half of the Outer Hebrides.

The MacRuairis were a force to be reckoned with in the thirteenth and fourteenth centuries, committing acts of piracy and raiding Skye and Lewis. In 1308 Lochlan MacRuairi was captured by the Earl of Ross, who wrote to Edward II of England: 'Lochlan is such a high and mighty lord, he'll not answer to anyone except under great force or through fear of you.' Earlier, in the early thirteenth century, the Clan Ruairi made alliances in Ireland with the Kings of Connacht and others, later providing 'galloglass' mercenaries there.* In 1318 a MacRuairi 'King of Innse Gall' was killed at the battle of Dundalk.

The succession from Somerled passed from Donald to Angus Mor to Angus Og and thence to John of Islay, the first Lord of the Isles, who lived in the mid-fourteenth century. Through a well-chosen marriage to Amie MacRuairi, the heiress to the Clan Ruairi lands, he managed to take over not just Uist and Barra but Eigg and Rhum in the Inner Hebrides and even more of the western mainland. His three sons by this marriage were John, who died young, Ranald who was to become founding ancestor of Clan Ranald in the 1370s, and the youngest son Godfrey.

John's lust for power was greater than his love for his wife and around 1358 he divorced her in order to secure a better political alliance. He married Margaret, daughter of Robert the Steward (who as Robert II would become King of Scotland in 1371). People in the islands were not best pleased because Amie was well liked. Her sons Ranald and Godfrey were now disinherited; Ranald was bought off by being promised his mother's lands as well as Benbecula and various parts of the Scottish mainland.

Godfrey was not so easily mollified and left for Uist. Ranald later attempted to evict his brother's people, the Siol Gorrie, from South Uist. He died in 1386, before Godrey; the influence of the Siol Gorrie eventually waned and Ranald's line became the dominant power in the islands. Amie spent the rest of her life in various building projects on Benbecula – Caisteal Borve (Borve castle) and Teampull Collumcille (St Columba's church) – as well as a chapel on Grimsay and, further afield, the castle on Island Tioram at Moidart that would become the main stronghold of the Clan Ranald.

In the meantime, John's succession passed in 1380 to Donald, his eldest son by his second wife, Margaret. During the fifteenth century, South Uist continued to be part of the Lordship of the Isles under, successively, Alexander and John. John was the fourth and last Lord. He died in lodgings in Dundee,

---

* 'Galloglass' is an anglicization of the Irish Gaelic term *galloglaigh* or 'foreign warrior', first mentioned in 1290.

deeply in debt, in 1503 having forfeited the Lordship to the Scottish Crown in 1493. He had given the old MacRuairi lands (which included South Uist) to his brother Hugh of Sleat, with Boisdale (the southern third of South Uist) being granted to MacNeill of Barra. Yet Clan Ranald were not prepared to give up their lands and were eventually granted heritable possession. In 1505 Hugh of Sleat's son John signed his lands over to Ranald 'Bain'. Despite attempts by Angus Og and Donald Dubh to revive the Lordship, all pretence was finally over by Donald's death in 1545.

Over four centuries, ownership of South Uist passed from the kings of Norway to the kings of Man, the Clan Ruairi, the Lord of the Isles and finally to the Clan Ranald. Of course, political history is often about people who may never have set foot on South Uist, let alone spent much time there, and about events far away that affected the island's destiny. Archaeology offers another dimension; the study of the lives of the ordinary people whose voice is rarely heard in the documents and charters of the time. They may be entirely anonymous but the records of their lives still remain to be found within the ground.

The medieval and Early Modern period, between 1300 and 1700, is only now beginning to yield up archaeological evidence. Yet we have more evidence from the periods before and after: as archaeologists, we still know more about prehistoric life on Uist than we do about medieval houses and villages, a situation that can only begin to be rectified by large-scale excavation of a medieval settlement. Until then, we must continue to rely on the documents written by and for the elite which give no voice to the common people.

THE END OF CILLE PHEADAIR AND BORNAIS NORSE SETTLEMENTS

For archaeologists, 1266 is an arbitrary date that does not make much sense in terms of our excavated settlement sequences, although the transfer of the islands' ownership from Norway to Scotland might well have had a profound effect on island life thereafter. People certainly continued living in the Cille Pheadair farmstead after this point as well as in the much bigger settlement on Bornais machair.

Cille Pheadair
At Cille Pheadair the last longhouse was probably inhabited at this time (see chapter 8). Its sunken floor, low internal stone wall and upper turf wall were all features found in earlier buildings but its pair of opposed doorways, stone hearth surround, and eavesdrip gully were new features *(84; 86)*. Viking pottery styles were still in use and Platter Ware sherds now formed almost half of all the pottery, having been around 5 per cent of the assemblage two

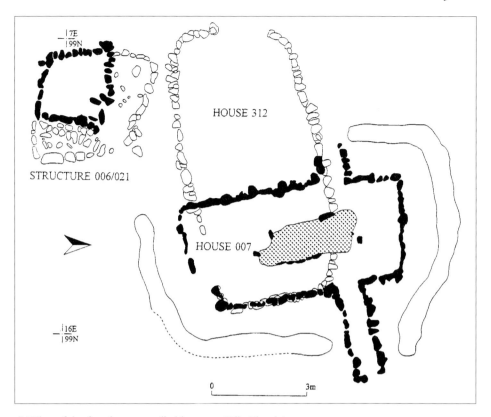

86 Plan of the fourth stone-walled house at Cille Pheadair

centuries earlier at the start of the farmstead's life in the early eleventh century. In the final phase of occupation, however, the use of Platter Ware declined dramatically and shapes of pots changed; they were now made with footed bases (in which the base protrudes slightly).

By this time, the last longhouse had become a ruin and was sub-divided into two small shacks, one at either end, which were temporary shelters rather than dwellings, judging by the lack of domestic rubbish that was being produced from them. Their small, rectangular shapes recall the field bothies and shelters of much more recent times and perhaps they were used by whoever now had the rights over this abandoned farm and its fields, treating the old farmhouse as a temporary base when coming across from their own farm.

Bornais

At Bornais, the occupation on the three large mounds ended with houses on each of the mounds in the fourteenth century. One of these was a small longhouse built on Mound 3 *(89; colour plate 15)*. Unlike the last Cille Pheadair longhouse, it was not sunk below the ground surface but sat on top of it. Its

87 Opposite above The grain-processing barn and kiln at Bornais

88 Opposite below The hearth of the house at Bornais under excavation

89 Above Reconstruction drawing of the house on Mound 3 at Bornais

lower courses were, however, built of stone and presumably these formed a stubby base on which the interior wall timbers rested. Like the last Cille Pheadair longhouse it was oriented north–south but had only a single doorway, towards its north end on the east side. The hearth was not only enclosed by a setting of stones, it was almost square rather than long *(88)*.

Careful recording and analysis of the floor deposits of this house have given us a remarkable picture of how it was inhabited. Cooking was organized not at the north side of the hearth as it had been in the Cille Pheadair longhouse, but at the hearthside nearest the doorway. There was no space for overwintering of animals and the south end of the house was probably the sleeping quarters, with beds arranged around the walls. Food remains were concentrated at the north end.

Just to the east of Mound 2 (on Mound 2A) excavations have revealed an area rich in the debris of craft activities. Several small furnaces were surrounded by ash dumps containing large quantities of slag or clinker. Just what was being processed here is uncertain because this is not metalworking slag, despite the large quantities of recycled nails found in this excavation trench.

In the final phases of the house in this part of the settlement, during the fourteenth century, people were producing antler combs. These were made from red deer antler and large quantities of waste from this activity were left on the floors of the building and also in the middens of rubbish dumped on the east side of the settlement mound. The waste consists of the unusable parts

90 Comb-making debris from Bornais

of the antler (tines and crown) as well as rough-cuts that broke during the various phases of manufacture *(90)*. The composite combs being made here had several basic components, with each component made as an individual piece: small, rectangular pieces of antler were needed for the teeth plates and long, thin pieces were made into the comb's side plates.

The side plates were then riveted together, with between three and six teeth plates held securely between them. The teeth plates were not cut into shape until *after* the comb was fully assembled: a mistake at this point rendered the comb useless. So any slip by the maker and the whole exercise was wasted – a new comb would have to be started from scratch. Comb-making evidence like this is common in Viking towns such as York and Trondheim but it has never before been found in a rural setting, suggesting that Bornais was an important community within South Uist with connections possibly further afield.

On the northern edge of the settlement there was no such evidence for craft specialization. Excavations here revealed a small rectangular building 8m by 4m, associated with an outhouse. This outhouse was used in the fourteenth century for processing crops: the grain was winnowed (or cleaned) in the draught created by opposing doors, and there was a kiln on the south side of the building for drying the grain *(87)*. Many grains of barley, oats and rye had been charred by the kiln and these littered the floor of this outhouse in large quantities.

This grain drier had an important role in the settlement's agricultural practices and many of its products were probably consumed in the adjacent building and other longhouses. The floor of this adjacent house was covered in dense concentrations of fish bones, mostly of herring but including cod heads. Fish, as well as cereals, were an important contribution to the diet in the fourteenth century and before.

HOUSES AND ORIENTATION

Visitors to South Uist today are sometimes puzzled by a figure of speech about the island's geography: if one goes to the south end of the island, one goes up and conversely to go north is to go down the island. This classification of space is not influenced by the topography – the north end of South Uist has the higher mountains, not the lowest land – but rather is an example of how all societies make symbolic and metaphorical maps of space. English readers may remember, for example, that one always used to go *up* to London, no matter where the journey started in physical terms.

In the days of the blackhouses, similar terminology was used to describe movement within the house itself: one went up towards the hearth, or down from the hearth to the doorway. The interesting thing about the last longhouse at Cille Pheadair is that the hearth is placed to the south of the doorway and thus fits in well with this more recent verbal classification of space.

One further possibility is that these post-Norse longhouses were also organized so as to embody the shape and geography of the island itself, so that the identity of the islanders was given physical form through the house itself, which was treated as a microcosm or map of the island, best approached from the east. Whatever the symbolism and metaphorical meanings of the house in this period, the disappearance of the long hearth may indicate the end of traditions of larger-scale hospitality. Small hearths were to become the standard, surviving as interior features of the Early Modern and later houses.

One of the curious aspects of Norse and later architecture is the switching of orientations between the cardinal points. Longhouses were built on either an east–west alignment, or a north–south alignment. John Hunter, an archaeologist working in Orkney, noticed on one site there that the earlier houses were east–west and the later ones were north–south. He devised an elaborate argument proposing that this was due to a shift in the wind patterns. Perhaps longhouses were best constructed with one of the two shorter walls facing into the prevailing wind, and so he surmised that the westerlies had been replaced by southerlies at some time around 1000.

Our own evidence from South Uist makes any attempt to explain house orientation according to prevailing winds far from convincing. Cille Pheadair shows a shift from north–south to east–west, and then to north–south again. At Bornais, the earliest houses were both east–west and were then replaced by a north–south house. To make matters more confusing, the east–west long hall at Bornais is the same date as the north–south longhouses at Cille Pheadair, and some of the north–south houses at Bornais are the same date as the east–west house at Cille Pheadair. Just five miles apart and with similarly exposed locations, these Norse period settlements cannot have been subject to completely different wind systems. So what could possibly account for this switching between cardinal points?

There are no known Viking Age graveyards on South Uist but a group of burials from Cnip on Lewis reveals that this same arrangement of orientations, either east–west or north–south, is found within graves. It is also found in longhouses throughout the Viking world, from Sweden to Greenland to Dublin, regardless of terrain and wind conditions. Anthropologist Dennis Doxtater has suggested that these consistent orientations derive from the symbolic significance of the four cardinal directions, recoverable from the sagas. North is the direction of the spirits (the gods and ancestors) whilst south is the domain of the living and the mortal. He also interprets the east–west axis as the path of life, from birth in the east to death in the west, and a gender axis of female in the east and male in the west. Working on medieval Norwegian cases, he argues that the farmhouse (*stue* or *salr*) should be aligned east–west whilst the *hov*, a loft and/or meeting place, should be orientated north–south.

Yet this does not fit the South Uist evidence. Our own view is that, whilst environmental factors such as wind are not satisfactory explanations, the symbolic argument as it stands is not entirely persuasive although it points us in the right direction. Medieval and later houses on South Uist, including many blackhouses, share this orientational predilection for the cardinal points but no one has yet worked out why.

In Britain today the only buildings which still maintain a respect for the cardinal points are churches which, as we know, are aligned east–west with the chancel at the east end. And then we find another anomaly – echoing the Hebridean Norse tradition of switching between north–south and east–west, South Uist's Catholic churches at Dalabrog and Bornais are both oriented north–south. Neither is older than a couple of centuries but no one knows why their orientations are as they are.

THE CHURCH IN SOUTH UIST

With no certain evidence of Christianity in South Uist before the poignant placing of the carved bone cross into a longhouse hearth at Cille Pheadair around 1100, it is possible that the population did not convert until the Norse period. There is a second, broken cross from the middens at Cille Pheadair *(83)* but no similar finds from Bornais.

The term 'cille' is often taken to mean a monastic cell or chapel rather than a parish church but the distribution of Uist place names beginning with 'cille' or 'cill' is most definitely matched by the recorded parish churches and chapels. Beginning at the south end of the island is Cille Bhrighde (or Kilbride), the chapel of St Brigit. Its remains now lie underneath the caravan site at West Kilbride and a skeleton in the former graveyard was once found when posts for a washing line were being put up.

91 The remains on Dun na Cille include a long east–west building and two smaller ruins

Further north is Cille Pheadair (Kilpheder or the parish church of St Peter). This is first mentioned by Dean Munroe in 1549 as one of the five parish churches of Uist. As noted in chapter 8, it was washed away by the sea in the nineteenth century. A second church site, whose remains consist of a long east–west building and a couple of outbuildings, sits upon a crannog known as Dun na Cille in the loch east of modern-day Cille Pheadair *(91)*.

Somewhere in the Frobost area Timothy Pont, the first mapmaker of South Uist, recorded a 'cille' (he actually wrote 'Gill') in the 1590s but there is no other record or material indication of such a place. Slightly further north, he and others knew of Cille Donnain (Kildonan or the chapel of St Donnan). This is an interesting dedication because St Donnain was an early Celtic saint but, of course, many centuries had passed between his life and the church's foundation.

Moving north, Aird Mhicheal at Stoneybridge (Staoinebrig) can be equated with Munroe's mention of 'St Michael's'. He is a reliable source on these matters because he was 'High Dean of the Isles' and would have known and probably even visited these places. There is no sign of the chapel but its remains are probably buried within the modern graveyard – the walls of a large east–west building are visible but these may be from a later blackhouse.

92 The chapels at Howmore

The ecclesiastical centre of the island was Howmore (Tobhta Mor), named as Howf by Munroe *(92; 93)*. In the fourteenth and fifteenth centuries it was a place of learning with an international reputation and is recorded as a parsonage dependent on the Abbey of Iona in the sixteenth century. The Howmore mound, perhaps built on more ancient remains, supports not one church but five different chapels: Teampull Mor (St Mary's); Caibeal Dubhghaill (Dugall's Chapel or the Chapel of the Kindred of the Son of Dugall); Caibeal Dhiarmaid (St Dermot's Chapel); Caibeal na Sagairt (Priest's Enclosure, demolished in the nineteenth century); and Caibeal Chlann'ic Ailein (Clan Ranald's Chapel).

St Dermot's was also known to the traveller Martin Martin in 1695 as St Columba's whilst St Mary's was the parish church. These are the only fully standing medieval ecclesiastical buildings on the island and their forms are inspired by Hiberno-Romanesque designs, with steep gables and inward sloping doorways.

Howmore is first mentioned in the fourteenth century but some of its remains are much older. St Mary's was built in the thirteenth century and Clan Ranald's Chapel is thought to have been built after 1574. Around that date, Eoin Muideartach (John Moidartach), chief of Clan Ranald, left funds to erect

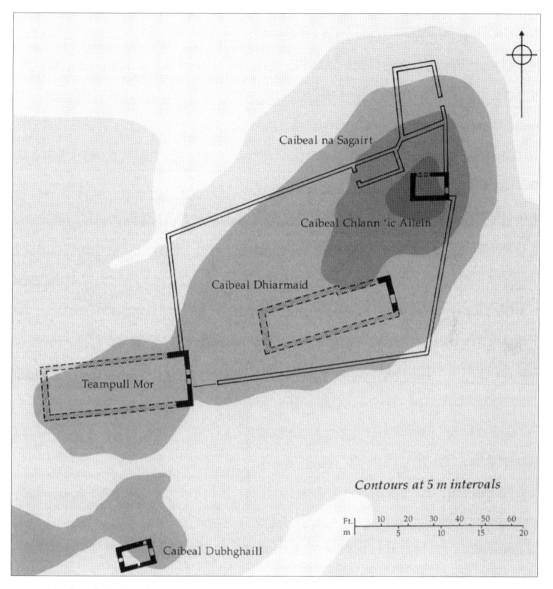

Caibeal na Sagairt

Caibeal Chlann 'ic Ailein

Caibeal Dhiarmaid

Teampull Mor

Contours at 5 m intervals

Caibeal Dubhghaill

93 Plan of the chapels at Howmore

a chapel at Howmore in Uist, where his body lies buried. The armorial stone which was removed in 1990 from inside the Clan Ranald Chapel had probably sat previously above the doorway of this or another chapel.

A recent architectural survey by Andrew Reynolds of the University of London has identified two earlier phases of the Clan Ranald chapel, the earliest predating the thirteenth century and contemporary with the construction of Caibeal Dhiarmaid and Caibeal Dubhghaill. The mound on which some of the chapels sit is artificial and may contain a sequence of earlier monastic buildings, presumably associated with Howmore's early Christian grave slab which dates to centuries before any of the existing chapel ruins, somewhere in the seventh-ninth centuries (see chapter 7). Eoin Muideartach was, as far as we know, the first of many clan chiefs to be buried in what was probably already an ancient graveyard. According to oral traditions, a Viking princess also lies buried at Howmore.

Further north from Howmore is Cille Bhannain (Kilvannen or the church of St Bannan) whose ruins lie on top of a broch. Near the north end of the island is Cille Amhleidh (Kilauley or the chapel of St Olaf) but there is no sign of its remains, which are probably buried beneath the modern houses at Kilauley.

The chronology, history and archaeology of South Uist's churches are sorely in need of further research. How many of them have origins in the Columban and Norse periods? Why and when did Howmore become an important centre? When Munroe was writing in 1549 he declares that the only parish churches were St Peter's (Cille Pheadair) and the Howmore churches. In 1695 Martin Martin records St Peter's, St Donnan's (a variant English spelling of Donnain), St Michael's, the Howmore chapels (St Mary's and St Columba's), St Bannan's and St Jeremy's. This last name may be a reference to St Olaf's but it is more likely to be St Diarmaid's.

Martin also alludes in passing to some interesting customs that show how understandings of the prehistoric tombs and standing stones were incorporated within Christianity. He says that 'near a mile south of Columba's church' there was a stone 8ft high and 2ft wide, known as the Bowing Stone, supposedly put up 'when the inhabitants had the first sight of the church… and there bowed and said the Lord's Prayer'. This might well have been a much earlier stone, possibly even moved and set in this place. More definite is his reference to the Neolithic chambered cairns: 'There are several big cairns on the east side of this island, and the vulgar retain the ancient custom of making a religious tour round them on Sundays and holidays'.

The clerics whose writings recorded these ancient churches are our best historical sources for this period of South Uist's history. Munroe travelled in the islands a few years before the Scottish Reformation in 1560. Timothy Pont, also a cleric, was here after the rise of Protestantism. During the 1600s Roman Catholic missionaries came from Ireland to South Uist – Catholicism was banned so priests maintained an underground movement until the more tolerant times of the Restoration. In 1650 Father Dermot Dugan came to work in the Uists and Barra. He was warmly received by Clan Ranald and received help from two assistants but, having spent many years in Paris, he was not impressed by the food or the accommodation:

> The meat which the islanders do sometimes eat makes one disgusted, for they are content to half cook it on the embers, and then they throw it on the ground on straw which with them serves for a table, table-

cloth, and plate so that we scarcely ever eat it. In the summer it is necessary to sleep on the ground exposed to the weather, against which we protect ourselves as best we can with our cloaks... but even when we reach some cottage we often do not find any straw to lie on.

He died in 1657 at a shieling in Cill Donnain, still known today as Aird Dhughain. Standing on a promontory into the loch south of the Kildonan Museum, the shieling consists of a small group of ruined buildings. It is as a result of the work of Father Dugan and the other Lazarist and Franciscan missionaries of the seventeenth century that Catholicism is the main religion of South Uist and the Southern Isles today.

As well as Howmore, early burial grounds are known at Cille Donnain and Cladh Pheadair. Cille Donnain was still remembered as a place of burial in 1881 when the first Ordnance Survey map recorded it as such. Cladh Pheadair (St Peter's graveyard) lies on the boundary between Cille Pheadair and Dalabrog, and is now within the modern graveyard of Cladh Hallan. Cladh Pheadair is just east of a large machair dune and has produced skeletons over the years. On the land now covered by the dune there was a settlement in the sixteenth to seventeenth centuries and, nearby, an inn which is remembered in oral traditions and recorded on William Bald's map of 1805.

Inside the graveyard walls of Cladh Hallan, two large mounds – one at the top of the hill close to the trig point and the other north of it at the bottom of the hill – mark ancient burial places similar to the mound with the symbol stone on Pabbay off Barra. One of these ancient burial grounds at Cladh Hallan has a gravestone which probably predates the Norse period.

Our archaeological research into the early Church has concentrated on the church of Cille Donnain. On a promontory on the south side of Cille Donnain loch lie the ruins of a long rectangular east–west building with a small square chancel at the east end *(94; colour plate 17)*. It is identical in size and plan – but not in orientation – to the largest longhouse within the Cille Pheadair farmstead. However, it has a door midway along its west wall which is definitely not a characteristic of a Norse or medieval dwelling in this region as far as we can tell. Its plan can be matched closely with those of Late Norse chapels in the Northern Isles and it was probably built around 1100-1300.

The church does not sit in isolation but is surrounded on its northwest side by a row of four small, conjoined cellular buildings. Out on the adjacent island, known as Eilean Mor, is another small complex of buildings. This arrangement is reminiscent of the larger political and religious centre at Finlaggan on Islay, centre of the Lordship of the Isles, but Cille Donnain's significance was religious rather than political. Our limited excavations were designed to find out whether the site was founded on a broch, as happened at Finlaggan, and whether the row of cells was an early religious building contemporary with the church's construction. As it turned out, there was no broch and the cells were

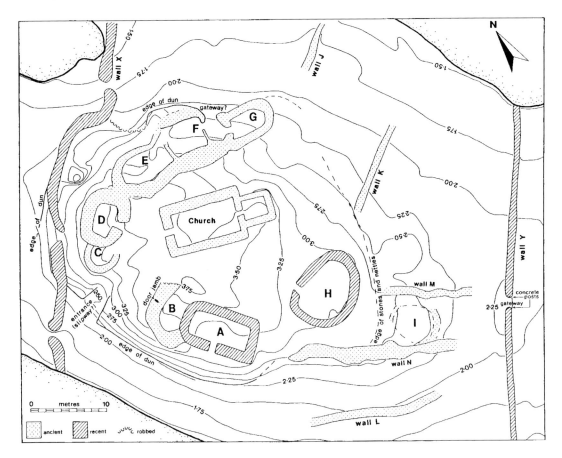

94 Plan of Cille Donnain church

built after 1500, when a large quantity of settlement midden was heaped up around the church to enlarge the promontory and deepen the graveyard.

Pottery

We do not know where the settlement was that produced this rubbish but, together with the finds from the final years of the Bornais and Cille Pheadair settlements, it provides us with an idea of the pottery used during the period 1300-1500. The pots were hand-made – the potter's wheel never reached the islands – and is characterized by everted (splaying outwards) rims. It is very similar in form and decoration to pottery of this period in Ireland known, not surprisingly, as Everted Rim Ware. In the fourteenth century it was entirely plain but some pots in the fifteenth and sixteenth centuries were decorated with incised, cordoned and dotted motifs that recall the styles of the Middle Iron Age.

We also found one or two sherds of wheel-made green-glazed pots, made either in southern Scotland, Ireland or England during the thirteenth or fourteenth century. Handmade pottery continued to be produced in South Uist until the seventeenth century, possibly until the early 1700s, but pottery-making was certainly finished by 1790. Elsewhere in the Western Isles, in Lewis and Harris, the tradition continued into the nineteenth century; the coarse pots made during this late period are known as Craggan Ware.

The sixteenth- and seventeenth-century pottery was decorated, mostly with fine pinpricks and impressions below the high-collared rim or along the top of the rim. It is again very similar to the Irish ceramics of the period, known as Crannog Ware. Two decorated pots of the sixteenth or seventeenth century were found smashed in the ruined entranceway of the Dun Vulan broch and seem to have been part of a not-very-Christian offering that included a horse's leg and a cat. Attitudes to cats might have been a little odd at this time: Martin Martin records that people of the islands consulted oracles in three ways, of which the third was to put a live cat on a spit and roast it until 'a very big cat comes… and answers the question.'

TOWNSHIPS: FROM MACHAIR TO PEATLANDS

The Norse period was the last time that the complete string of township settlements hugged the machair. Thereafter there was a gradual process of with-drawal from this zone onto the peatland edge. As the Bornais settlement was abandoned, so another village sprang up about 600m away to the east, sitting on a low grassy knoll between the current sites of Bornais church and Bornais House.

In the townships of Aesgernis, Machair Mheadhanach, Baghasdal, Smercleit and Stoneybridge, the Norse settlement was succeeded by medieval occupa-tion on the machair, either on top of the Norse period village or immediately nearby. Cille Pheadair, Dalabrog, Frobost, Cill Donnain, Ormacleit, Howmore, Dreumasadal and Drimore all seem to have moved off the machair at this time. The map drawn by Pont in the 1590s and a later map by Joannis Blaeu of 1654, schematic though they are, show that all these township settle-ments were located east of the machair zone.

Today the only settlements on South Uist's machair are a few farms and houses at the northernmost end of the island. Otherwise this strip of sand is abandoned, used for agriculture but not for houses. The last townships to move were Machair Mheadhanach (Iochdar) after 1600 and Baghasdal after 1800. We know that Baghasdal was abandoned because of the 'fever', but there are no accounts as to why the others were left.

There are several sources of evidence to pursue in order to reveal the reasons for the abandonment of all the machair settlements. It is possible that cultiva-tion of the machair largely ceased in the medieval period, replaced by a pref-erence for the peatlands, but there is not yet any definitive evidence. There is documentary evidence of terrible sand blows in the late seventeenth century onwards but most machair sites had already been given up by this point. The water table on the machair might also have risen, making conditions too wet in many areas.

Did the island suffer from similar conditions around the thirteenth and fourteenth centuries, when the first of the machair villages were abandoned? Yet the Bornais and Cille Pheadair settlements show no such traces of incursions of windblown sand at that time. Was a worsening climatic situation – a long period of storminess from 1400 – to blame? On North Uist, Ian Armit thinks that the opposite happened – here, many settlements moved *onto* the machair at this time. So what was going on?

One possibility is that this was an economic change to do with the transition to beef farming that began during the Norse period. It was perhaps sensible to relocate villages to the junction of the machair and peatlands, in order to make better use of the grazing land on the peat and in the hills. Whether the Treaty of Perth in 1266 had anything to do with this settlement shift is unknown, but what is striking is that the successor settlements on the peatlands seem to have been smaller than their predecessors. It appears that there was a major depopulation of the island after the Norse period and this might just have been caused by one of the conditions in the Treaty. Ordinary people, as well as the Norwegian chiefs, were free to leave their farms and move from the islands. Perhaps people emigrated to take up farming in other parts of Scotland, but there might have been other causes of population decline.

One of the major themes of studies of early Scottish history in recent years concerns the formation of the townships. Robert Dodgshon has carefully researched the historical sources for the islands and the western highlands and considers that the township as a working community, resource base and tax-paying entity did not exist much before 1500. His approach is directly counter to previous notions which viewed the township as a sort of 'primitive communism' of closely knit kin groups formed in the mists of prehistory which was only upset by the introduction of modern capitalist farming in the eighteenth century and after.

Unfortunately the problem of the origin of townships has not been tackled by either side from an archaeological perspective and any generalizations are not going to speak for all cases. South Uist – and the Uists in general – may well be different from much of the rest of the region on account of its large areas of fertile land, but our own evidence shows that townships had their origins as settlement nuclei at the end of the Early Iron Age, more than 1,500 years before Dodgshon's estimate. Now, in certain aspects Dodgshon is most probably correct; if the township is to be defined in terms of its tenurial tax payment to the lord, then such a feudal arrangement might well not have come into existence until South Uist passed into the rule of the Lordship and eventually the Scottish Crown.

The idea that a dispersed system of settlement was reorganized by rounding-up communities into *bailtean* may work for other islands but it certainly does not characterize the settlement process in South Uist. Not only is there just one *baile* place name (Bailedubh in Gearraidhnamonie) but there was never really a period of nucleation. The shift to the spatial structure of the township system had occurred on the machair during the last centuries BC and, because of these specific conditions, the settlements were already divided on the machair into clusters. The territories of these early settlement clusters remained largely constant except for a degree of fissioning that occurred after the Norse period.

The spatial patterning of townships did not, however, remain static between the Middle Iron Age and the Early Modern period. There were relatively few changes until the Norse period (other than the shift in central places from Iochdar in the north to Bornais near the centre of the island) but thereafter a whole series of transformations took place. Bornais was no longer the principal settlement on the island: this appears to have shifted to Howmore and its adjacent neighbours, Caisteal Bheagram in Dreumasadal and the small castle on Loch Druidibeg known as Dun Raouill.

Caisteal Bheagram is first mentioned in 1505 in the title of Ranald 'Bain' – 'Ranaldo Alansoun de Ylandbigrim' (Ranald Allanson of Island Bheagram). It is a square blockhouse, not much bigger than a broch, sitting on a small island in the loch north of Howmore *(95)*. A causeway once linked it to the loch shore.

The new arrangement of townships was created by the splitting of existing ones either into two halves or by creating an adjacent *gearraidh* township. *Gearraidh* ('garry' or 'garth') is a post-Norse name (*gart* becoming garth) given variously in the Uists to home pasture, or the strip between the arable and the hill pasture, or the pasture between the arable and the grazing. All the *Gearraidh* townships on South Uist – Gearraidhnamonie, Gearraidhsheile, Gearraidh Bhailteas (Milton) and Gearraidhfleuve – are without machair and have no settlements within them that predate the medieval period. In the case of Gearraidh Bhailteas, we know from oral tradition that it split from Frobost and documentary records show that it was already in existence by 1493. Upper and Lower Bornais are a split township but this split had already occurred in the Middle Iron Age.

At the time that Timothy Pont drew his map of South Uist on the sixteenth-century equivalent of the back of an envelope – it is a barely legible draft and part of it has been written over with no reference to the drawing – none of the *gearraidh* townships were named except Gearraidh Bhailteas. The same is the case for Blaeu's 1654 map but this was probably based more or less directly on Pont's lost final version. The full set of names appears on the map drawn by William Bald in 1805, shortly before the Clearances.

One of the interesting features of the Pont and Blaeu maps is the marking of an inland waterway joining up the freshwater lochs to provide access by

95 Caisteal Bheagram at Dreumasadal

water to most of the length of South Uist. It is said that the chief of Clan Ranald could sail on this inland waterway from Howmore to Benbecula. The machair was certainly the main routeway by foot, until the modern road was built, and perhaps the machair track and the waterway were used in tandem until the waterway became blocked in the late sixteenth or seventeenth centuries.

Bornais – Bhac na Mhic Aongheis (Hill of the Son of Angus)
We have been able to investigate the settlement process from the Norse period until the Clearances in one township, Bornais, by excavating the post-Norse successor settlement on that grassy knoll known as Bhac na Mhic Aongheis *(colour plate 16)*. This is remembered as the site of the nineteenth-century tacksman's house (tacksmen formed a middle management of leading farmers and bailiffs) and, from the mid-1600s at least, was the farm of the hereditary factors (land agents) of the clan.

The pottery from this site shows that it was settled from the fifteenth-sixteenth centuries onwards until the late 1800s. We excavated traces of longhouses very similar to the last house on the Bornais machair settlement, built with a single stone course on which turf walls had been piled. One of the longhouses ran east–west with a doorway towards the west end of its north side, thereby providing a parallel house plan, rotated anti-sunwise at 90°, to those found in the last phases at Bornais and Cille Pheadair. The full dimensions of a second longhouse could not be ascertained but it contained a circular hearth. Such buildings, once the turf has decayed or been carted off, leave no signs above ground, and so the identification of these medieval and Early Modern township settlements off the machair requires considerable detective work.

Gearraidh Bhailteas – a new foundation

The documentary record of Gearraidh Bhailteas (also called Milton today), in existence by 1493, conforms well to the pottery that was found during excavations here. Unlike the Hill of the Son of Angus, the houses here were built with walls that contained substantial quantities of stones and they survive today as outlines of impressive longhouses organized on east–west and north–south orientations. The houses are arranged in close proximity to each other on a small knoll which is surrounded by acidic and boggy land. We have no certain idea of how long the settlement was occupied but a medieval copper alloy dress pin and pieces of factory-made ceramics, from opposite ends of the chronological spectrum, indicate activity in the fourteenth-sixteenth centuries and again in the 1800s.

CHIEFDOMS AND SURPLUS EXTRACTION

The medieval settlements have yielded very little evidence of what people wore. This is partly because those excavated have been on peatlands and thus any bone pins and the like have not survived in the acid soils. Martin Martin tells us that by 1695 people in the islands were wearing woollen plaid of different colours and stripes so that 'every isle differs from each other'. Bone or wooden pins were used to fix the plaid at the breast and a leather belt went around the midriff. The traditional dress of women, still worn 'by some of the vulgar' was a white plaid called *arisad* covering the body from neck to heels and pinned at the breast by a silver or copper-alloy brooch. Leather shoes were worn but he describes ancient footwear as a strip of leather attached by thongs from toe to ankle. Martin Martin also refers to an archaic dress style worn over a hundred years earlier by persons of distinction; this was the *leni-croich*, a yellow tunic that reached to below the knees and was tied with a belt around the waist.

The ancient 'persons of distinction' included the chieftains and Martin Martin talks about these in the past tense in his chapter on 'Ancient and Modern Customs'. In return for the allegiance of clan members, the chief had to provide land and military protection for his kin. The kinship group was held together by two principles: the inalienable right of the lower orders to have access to ancestral arable lands (known as *duthchas*), and the deference and loyalty owed to the clan chief who held lands in trust for the clan.

The clan was divided into 'septs' (*sliochdan*) that were themselves sub-divided into smaller groupings (*cloinne*). These inhabited the individual townships (*bailtean*) and each *cloinne* in its *baile* was headed by a close relative of the chief. This was the tacksman: he was granted a tack (a lease) of land on a hereditary basis in return for rent and military service. Most of the population were either tenants of the tacksman or were cottars, who occupied small patches of land as sub-tenants or as squatters.

The chieftain had a retinue of young men whom he would lead on cattle raids against neighbours with whom they were feuding. Feuds could be endless, since each raid encouraged a counter-raid, although Martin says that he had not heard of this practice 'for these sixty years past'. From the later sixteenth century well into the seventeenth century there was a long-running feud with the MacLeods. In 1593 the eighth chieftain of Clan Ranald, Iain Mor Moidartach, died and whilst his grandsons were jostling for the succession, a warband of 120 MacLeods landed on the east coast of South Uist at Acairseid Falaich and marched on Howmore to avenge an insult.

One of the grandsons, Angus, led a victorious Clan Ranald counterattack at the Abhainn Roag, southeast of Howmore, and was killed, so his brother Donald, who had avoided the fighting, became the ninth chief. On a trip to Ireland in 1595 he was captured on Mull by the MacLeans but released after payment of a ransom. In another feud against the MacNeills of Barra, Donald successfully drove them out of the southern, Boisdale end of South Uist in 1610.

The chief's retinue included not only young warriors but also quartermasters, look-outs, armour-bearers, smiths, physicians, orators, poets, bards and musicians. When cattle were slaughtered, the carcass was even divided into allotted portions: the hide for the quartermaster, the head for the smith and the feet and entrails for the workers in the 'cultural industry' – poets, bards, orators, musicians and physicians. Often these positions were hereditary. The MacMhuirichs of Howmore served the Clan Ranald as bards for many generations.

All of these people took some feeding, especially at feasts which were held to consolidate alliances and also during periods of feuding. To provide this, clan chiefs had to extract supplies from their kinsmen who tilled and farmed the land on which this extended kinship group, the clan, lived. Such supplies were obtained from the farmers in the form of food rents which would feed the retinue as it travelled around the islands, provide a store to be doled out in times of crisis, as well as cater for feasts and feuds.

In the period 1577-1595, about the time that Timothy Pont was compiling his map of South Uist, a written report describes something called *cuid-oidhche*. This was a render of hospitality for the chief and his retinue. It was already of some antiquity at that date and was paid irregularly, since it was due only when chief and retinue turned up. In the 1577-1595 report, each island was expected to provide a set amount of meal (oats), bere (barley), cattle, chickens, malt, butter and cheese. The Uists supplied 2,800 stones of oatmeal per annum.

Martin Martin refers to something he calls *calpich*, a duty paid by all tenants to the chief, and to *eachfuin horizeilda*, the right of the chief to choose a horse from a deceased clan-member's estate. There were also exports from South Uist during the seventeenth century and one account records the movement of 20 barrels of salted salmon and 200 otter pelts.

Although cash rents were coming into being from the sixteenth century onwards, the traditional system remained in place throughout the Early Modern period in South Uist, and Clan Ranald was one of the last in western Scotland to introduce regular rents. By the early 1700s it was still cattle and not cash that was the island's currency, and cows were paid as rent. The chiefly retinue system also continued. A document of 1718 records such positions on South Uist although many might have been honorific: falconers, fowlers, foresters, pipers and genealogists. Clan Ranald also had a boatwright and a mason at this date.

The extraction of surplus from kin groups working the land and the receiving of tribute from feuding, alliances and warfare are classic aspects of chiefdom societies around the world from many different periods of history. In return, the chiefly elite redistributes wealth to retinues and followers through gifts in the form of feasting and small valuables. During the 1400s Angus Mor, chief of Clan Ranald, was known for dispensing silver rings to his followers. Such a system of redistribution almost certainly goes back to the Pictish period a thousand years before (see chapter 7), for which we have evidence both of feasting and of making high-status silver jewellery in the power centres of the islands. The high numbers of pig bones, especially from front leg joints, at the Iron Age broch of Dun Vulan (see chapter 6) also raises the likelihood that food rents had an even greater antiquity, albeit extracted at a much smaller geographical and political scale.

If the chiefdom system was actually of some antiquity, going back at least a thousand years before the sixteenth century, it was also in the process of change as chieftains became landlords. This gradual undermining of the chiefly economy by the pressures and demands of an encroaching market economy is excellently documented by Robert Dodgshon in his book *From Chiefs to Landlords* and he demonstrates that the process was effectively complete before the Clearances and the subsequent shift to commercial sheep farming which occurred in the 1800s.

One of the main catalysts of this change was the passing of the Statutes of Iona in 1609, followed by the Acts of 1616. The 'statutes of blackness', as they have been called, undermined the political independence from the Crown of the clan chiefs and ushered in the collecting of rents. They could be described as introducing the Scottish chiefdoms to feudalism. Chiefs' offspring were to be educated in English, away from the islands, clansmen without title to land or unable to gain income through trade were outlawed, and retinues were banned. Even bards were prohibited. There followed the 'years of woe' in which chiefs raised rents on all their lands except for the home farm – for South Uist this became Howbeg – on which they were themselves required to live.

CHAPTER 10

'THE AGE OF IMPROVEMENT'

The Early Modern Period 1700-1900

During the 1930s a group of archaeologists came to the Western Isles to see with their own eyes if the daily life of Hebrideans could provide a glimpse into the lives of Ancient Britons 2,000 years ago. One of the archaeologists, Cecil Curwen, was so taken with the simple lifestyle and rustic charm that he wrote an article entitled *The Outer Hebrides: a cultural backwater* in which he set down a series of points as to how the way of life of these, in his eyes, historical leftovers may help archaeologists reconstruct the more ancient past.

We can laugh now at the cultural arrogance of a more innocent age when the islanders were seen by outsiders as a modern 'primitive people', stranded in the past by poor communications and an inherent conservatism, whose mid-nineteenth-century culture 'was more like that of the pre-Roman Iron Age in southern England than any succeeding phase'. Those archaeologists would have been surprised to discover that, 70 years on, the period of the blackhouses would itself be a subject of archaeological research in its own right and no longer just a modern parallel used to illuminate someone else's past.

In any case, Curwen and his colleagues were hopelessly wrong about the link with Ancient Britons for two reasons. Firstly, as this book has demonstrated, there has been an awful lot of cultural 'water under the bridge' over the last 2,000 years since the age of those Ancient Britons. Secondly, by the 1930s the lives of the islands' inhabitants had been remorselessly and irrevocably transformed by the demands and pressures of the industrial age. The perceived 'remoteness' of the Western Isles was a product of modern economic and social changes: the islands had become incorporated into a market economy whose centres were now far away in mainland Scotland and England, and were thus geographically on the fringe.

The conditions of Hebridean life were intermeshed with the workings of profit, markets, industry and capital in a way that was utterly different from the social relationships that pertained in the Iron Age. The simple technologies of spade cultivation (with the *caschrom*), grinding querns, and parching grain directly over the fire (known as 'graddaning') may appear at first sight to be authentic residues of a former, timeless way of life but the archaeologists were forgetting to separate outward appearance of form from the social matrix in which these artefacts and practices were embedded. As Robert Dodgshon has recently argued, these apparently archaic technologies might well have been actually *created* by the rise in labour-intensive strategies that accompanied the transition to a market economy.

Those early archaeologists would probably have wondered what point there was in doing archaeology on the remains of the eighteenth and nineteenth centuries. Do we not have all the information we need, in written form? There is a vast quantity of records for South Uist's recent past, notably the Clan Ranald papers in the National Library of Scotland, so why bother digging up a few old blackhouses to find out what we already know? The reason is, of course, that the voices of the vast majority of the men and women of the modern past are silent from the point of view of the written records.

The material remains of their houses, their belongings and their labour are the only vestige of ordinary people's lives and the only medium through which their stories can be retold in the present. Otherwise, our only record of island life from the point of view of those who lived on the land comes from fairly recent times: a few words spoken by the common people are recorded in the representations to the Napier Commission (the Parliamentary Commission into Crofting) in 1884 and life towards the end of the period is recorded in Angus MacLellan's eloquent stories and in surviving songs and tales.

The history of South Uist over the last two centuries is sufficient to fill a large book and it may be useful here to provide a potted history from the time of Martin Martin's visit. The themes of this period include the completion of the change to a market economy, the transformation of clan chiefs into landlords and their kinsmen into tenant farmers, the population explosion and subsequent Clearance of many of the population to British North America, the adoption of new farming methods and the introduction of the potato whose failure caused famine and crisis, and the rise and fall of the kelp industry.

The intertwining of politics and economics, and the relationship between Scotland and the rest of the British Isles, are evident in the disaster of the Jacobite revolt against George II, followed by the Scots' participation in the British army's wars of empire. In broad economic terms, the islands and highlands became producers of black cattle to meet the Royal Navy's require-ment for salt beef, and then later wool, mutton and kelp, but the region remained underdeveloped, becoming an 'internal colony' of the British state with its produce fuelling the expanding economy of lowland Britain.

One of the most interesting maps of South Uist is that drawn by William Bald in 1805. After the highly schematic attempts of Pont and Blaeu it is the first representation of the island which we can recognize as geographically accurate, or at least reasonably so. It is interesting for two reasons. Firstly, it provides a good impression of the townships, their settlement locations and

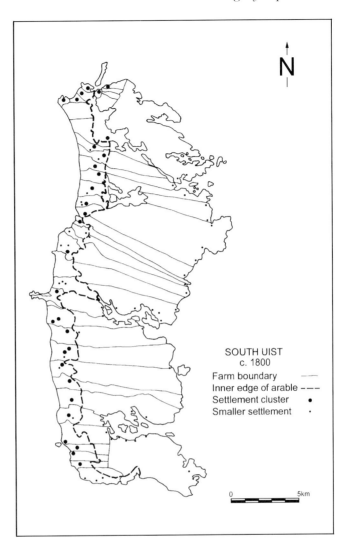

SOUTH UIST
c. 1800
Farm boundary ———
Inner edge of arable - - -
Settlement cluster •
Smaller settlement ·

96 A schematic redrawing of William Bald's map showing townships and township boundaries in 1805

their boundaries, particularly in the Iochdar region, before they were reorganized later that century after the Clearances *(96)*. Even so, our own excavations in Bornais have shown that Bald's marking of settlements is not always in the right place nor is it necessarily precise in terms of size and density.

The second aspect of interest is the reason why Bald was asked to compile the map in the first place. It may at first glance be simply a map but it was also a first step towards agricultural assessment, a weapon in the armoury of the improvers who were advising their landlord clients on how best to extract more profit. Ever since the Statutes of Iona in 1609, chiefs' sons had been required to be sent away to school on the Scottish mainland. The result of this practice was the creation of an aristocracy with lessening ties and interests in the islands and growing tastes for expensive, urban living which left them little in common with their island kin.

Extravagant lifestyles cost money and rents needed to be paid to support such requirements. The problem with places like South Uist was that, in terms of the cash economy, they were now a long way from anywhere. Until the steamships arrived, there was no quick way of getting agricultural produce to markets to sell at competitive rates. Equally the quality of produce was not necessarily as good as that grown in the lowlands within easier reach of the cities.

Food tribute needed to be converted into cash rents by getting produce to markets and Dodgshon suggests that the state's interference in Hebridean society – preventing feuding, curtailing feasting and reducing retinue sizes – might well have contributed to the chiefs' need to raise more and regular rents. He sees the decline of the chiefdom system as causing a divergence in interests: the once unified clans were split into two social groups, landlords and tenants. The tenants needed to maintain their self-sufficiency, especially in crop production, to ensure their own long- and short-term survival, whilst the chiefs needed produce which could be sold for cash, particularly the black cattle and latterly sheep.

Dodgshon shows how tension developed, as tenants increased their acreages of cultivation whilst landowners attempted to raise more stock on the same lands. By Bald's day the result of these conflicting aims was that even South Uist, a fertile island compared to many, with larger townships than most, was seriously over-cultivated.

The clash of interests limited the amount of over-wintering fodder available to the tenants; those who raised a few animals were often hard put to feed them through the winter. There are harrowing stories of crofters having to carry their starved and enfeebled cattle in their arms to move them out of the byre and into the fields in spring because the beasts were too weak to walk. Such accounts led a few archaeologists to presume that this situation was caused by environmental, rather than economic, pressures and therefore some writers have attempted to deduce erroneously that dairying would not have been possible in earlier times if fodder were so limited.

At the same time as the landlords were attempting to maximize profits, so their occasional insolvency was causing them to mortgage off blocks of farmland to intermediate tenants, the tacksmen, who could then collect the rents on that land for themselves. The system known as 'wadset' is the granting of land in return for a lump sum and a small annual 'feu' payment. By the 1600s Clan Ranald was busy wadsetting land to retainers in exchange for loans, leasing farms as tacks to the highest bidder or using land as collateral.

In 1672 Clan Ranald granted Upper Bornais in feu charter to Ranald MacDonald, whose father was the clan's factor or land agent, a position that became hereditary. The charter required annual payment to Clan Ranald of twelve bolls of meal, ten stones of butter and five stones of cheese. Upper Bornais was a valuable farm not only because of its extensive cultivable areas on its west side but also because it included land on both sides of Loch Ainort on the east. Loch Ainort was South Uist's principal harbour in the seventeenth century and had a tax-collecting house at its head and an inn on the north side near Bagh Lathach. It had access to South Uist's inland waterway and was also lined with slipways and fish traps. Its tidal zones might even have been used to make salt for preserving fish and beef.

In the mid-1500s, when Donald Munroe wrote about the Uists, the townships of South Uist were overshadowed economically by North Uist. Yet from the beginning of the eighteenth century to the early nineteenth century, the townships of South Uist were among the largest and most productive in western Scotland. During this period the population expanded considerably, rising from just over 2,000 people in 1750 to over 7,000 by 1851.

Ways of coping with this nightmarish and inexorable hurtle towards the island's natural population limit (what archaeologists call 'carrying capacity') included the use of spade cultivation of runrig – lazy beds or strips of soil piled into a corrugation of ridges and furrows – on the thin acidic soils of the black-lands which had hitherto been avoided, the increased use of seaweed on machair soils and manure on peatland fields, diversification into kelp produc-tion, and the introduction of the potato. Women in particular bore the brunt of the increasing workload. In addition to raising children, looking after the animals and tending the hearth, their daily round included the carrying and stacking of peat, loading carts, pushing barrows, and carrying seaweed fertil-izer onto the fields. Many suffered ill health as the result of being worked like draught animals.

Environmental circumstances were not always conducive to high agricul-tural yields. In 1697 a massive sand blow caused devastation in the Uists, covering fields in deep sand and causing the abandonment of the settlement at the Udal. In the early years of the nineteenth century, inhabited parts of South Uist were again engulfed in sand. Clan Ranald had to import grain from the mainland in 1812 and 1815 to prevent starvation. In 1816 the crops failed completely while in 1817 many cattle and horses starved or were slaughtered because of a lack of fodder. In 1822 a violent storm caused the sea to break through the coastal dunes and flood the fields around Aesgernis and Gearraidh Bhailteas. The prehistoric landscape at Cladh Hallan was also buried below deep sand dunes in this century.

One of the ways out of the looming population-subsistence crisis was the kelp industry. Today we use the word 'kelp' to describe a type of seaweed but the word also refers to an extract of seaweed, an alkaline powder used for making soap and glass. It was discovered that this could be obtained from the seaweed that grows on South Uist's west coast. The Napoleonic wars between 1790 and 1815 were, in one sense, good for the island: Spain was the main source of barilla (sodium carbonate produced by burning seaside plants), which had the same uses as kelp, and the war's economic blockades meant that supplies from Spain no longer reached Britain.

Clan Ranald exploited this gap in the market and mobilized the island's population to gather seaweed each summer between April and August. Workers were moved like chess pieces from their traditional joint holdings to be resettled on individual land plots or crofts. Between 1816 and 1818 the township of Cill Donnain was divided into 23 to 26 lots for kelping, thereby creating a crofting township by dividing up into crofts the arable land of an existing joint farm and individual holdings. This pattern was repeated throughout the island.

Each croft was tiny and Clan Ranald was charging exorbitant rents; the crofters could not support themselves on their own agricultural produce and had to gain extra income. As kelp-labourers they were no more than wage-slaves. The price of kelp rose from less than £5 per ton in 1794 to over £10 per ton by 1815. But the bottom fell out of the market in the early 1820s, leaving the crofters as poor as ever and Clan Ranald in search of a new source of revenue.

Redundant kelp-labourers were moved off their crofts in the middle part of South Uist and the land turned into sheep farms. They were re-settled on the small island of Eriskay and on the poor-quality lands in the hills and around the sea lochs of the east coast, where they had to find new ways of feeding themselves with sea fishing and potato growing. In this one transformation, communities were wrested away from their townships which had given them access to the produce of an east–west strip from the machair to the mountains for the previous 2,000 years.

In 1846 South Uist was devastated by a catastrophic failure of the potato harvest. The blight that caused this failure affected harvests over the next five years, resulting in famine. The potato had been introduced, reputedly, in 1743 by Macdonald of Clan Ranald in the face of a storm of protest from the islanders. When they brought his harvested crop to his doorstep in Benbecula, they protested that although he may force them to plant potatoes, he could not compel them to eat them.

By 1800, though, potatoes had become the staple of the islanders' diet and, in just 20 years between 1821 and 1841, the population rose by 1,300 people to a total of 7,327, partly thanks to the nutritional value of the humble spud. Potatoes were easy to grow without complex technology and in areas hitherto unfit for cultivation. They were planted by hand and could be grown in the poorest and most acidic of peatland soils, allowing landlords to relocate entire families at will. This over-reliance was to have tragic consequences when the crop failed.

The results of this failure were twofold. In 1851 Gordon of Cluny, who had bought South Uist from Clan Ranald in 1838, decided to export a sizeable percentage of the starving population to eastern Canada. By 1860 about 5,000 people were left on the island, some 2,700 having been cleared off and transported to Canada from his lands on South Uist and Barra. Another temporary solution was to employ workers on the famine dykes, building unnecessary walls so that they could earn just enough to keep body and soul together.

The history of the Clearances has attracted a lot of recent scholarship and accounts vary considerably in attributing blame or explaining the causes of the events. For the writers of 'people's history', the Clearances were the outcome of class struggle in which the beleaguered tenants are the honest and simple heroes of the hour, victims of rapacious landlords who duped them into exile from their ancestral lands. Economic historians, working from the estate accounts and other official records, see the Clearances as an inescapable consequence of wider British economic developments and 'improvement', and have been criticized as 'landlord apologists'. Yet both positions contain a large measure of propaganda and are reliant largely on the written records, rarely integrating them with the evidence of landscape, settlement and artefacts.

The Clearances were a long-term phenomenon which began in the eighteenth century with voluntary emigration and ended with the dispossessed poor being loaded onto boats at Lochboisdale pier whilst those who tried to escape were hunted down and brought by force to the pier side. By 1851 many of the inhabitants of Uist had already emigrated. Not all emigrants had left destitute and desperate, dragged onto ships and clinging to the end to a sense of clan loyalty that their lairds had abandoned years before. The migrations of the mid-nineteenth century were in part conditioned by a long-lived 'culture of mobility' in the highlands and islands.

In 1772 over 100 South Uist Catholics, led by their factor John MacDonald of Glenaladale, left the Clan Ranald estate for Prince Edward Island after persecution by their Protestant laird, Colin MacDonald of Baghasdal. In 1769 he had expelled the Catholic priest from his estate and threatened to evict tenants unless they renounced their Catholicism. Standing outside the Protestant church on Sundays, he forced passers-by inside with a stick, an episode recalled in the folklore as the 'Faith of the Yellow Stick' (*Cneideamh a' Bhata Bhuidhe*). Religious intolerance accounted for a small proportion of the early emigrants but most left for economic reasons. By the 1840s, Bornais township had been cleared and only the tacksman's family now lived here. Most South Uist townships were cleared but not the little island of Eriskay.

Even after the Clearances, conditions were little better. Evidence presented to the Crofting Commission in 1884 found appalling living conditions among crofters and landless cottars in Dalabrog. During the winter months, a little three-roomed house (with just one room set aside for sleeping) could accommodate eight individuals, more often than not a young family with older relatives. Angus MacLellan's writings also provide a heartbreaking insight into the hardships that crofters faced.

97 Ormacleit castle

ARCHAEOLOGICAL INVESTIGATIONS

The material record for this period lies all around South Uist. The hills and inlets of the east coast are littered with the remains of blackhouses, shielings, squatters' houses, lazy beds and field dykes. Even the machair has small and large settlements and kelpers' cottages. At Baghasdal the remains of the last township settlement mound to be inhabited into the nineteenth century can be seen underneath the ruins of the Protestant chapel with its small graveyard.

The most impressive architectural remains dating to the 1700s are to be seen at Ormacleit castle *(97)*. Ormacleit had replaced Howbeg as the chief's South Uist residence by 1654, and in 1700 Allan Clanranald embarked on a project to build a fine castle, finally completed in 1707. For a visitor looking at the ruins today, it is hard to believe that it was designed by a French architect and had cornerstones of French limestone. Its roof was described as covered with 'shimmering marble' – most likely highly polished schist from the east side of the island.

Allan had spent years in France after the Scottish defeat at Killiecrankie and had there married Penelope MacKenzie, the daughter of a Scotsman and his French wife. Penelope was unimpressed with her new husband's attempt at building a French chateau on South Uist, comparing it unfavourably with her father's stables. But the castle did not last for long. Just eight years later, in 1715, the house burned down on the very day that Allan Clanranald's own life was snuffed out at the battle of Sherrifmuir, or so the story goes.

The most famous island figure of these times is Flora Macdonald. She was born in 1722 in Milton, the township south of Cill Donnain, and lived a long and lively life, including a short spell imprisoned in the Tower of London, dying at the good age of 68. Such was her fame that her funeral cortege was more than a mile long and upwards of 300 gallons of 'mountain dew' (whisky) were drunk by the several thousand mourners.

Daughter of the Milton tacksman, the head of the village, Flora spent much of her life off the island. She married Allan of Kingsburgh, a tacksman on Skye. In the 1770s the couple were early emigrants, moving to North Carolina where Flora lost everything by supporting the British troops in the War of Independence. They then moved to Nova Scotia before returning to Allan's home on Skye.

Her fame mainly stems from her association with Bonny Prince Charlie who was on the run after the battle of Culloden in 1745 and fled to South Uist to escape the troops searching for him. As the story goes, Flora dressed him in women's clothing as a disguise and rowed him to safety over the sea to Skye (the Skye boat song was, incidentally, written down in the early 1900s by an Englishman, Sir Harold Boulton, who had heard a Hebridean boatman singing it).

The Clan Donald Society erected a monument within one of the black-house ruins on the site known as Airigh Mhuillin in Milton township to mark the approximate spot where Flora once lived *(colour plate 10)*. Airigh Mhuillin ('the mill by the shielings') is a blackland settlement of 11 or more structures *(98)*. These were farmhouses, some of which had outbuildings. After excavating five of these it is now clear that the settlement was occupied mainly in the period 1790-1820s and not at the time of Flora's birth in 1722! Just where she was actually born remains a mystery. Perhaps her father's house lies under today's Milton farm or is hidden amongst the medieval ruins of Gearraidh Bhailteas.

The Airigh Mhuillin houses are 'blackhouses' – rectangular in plan with rounded corners to deflect the wind, constructed from double-thick drystone walls covered by a thatched roof. Inside, some but not all of the South Uist blackhouses had a cow byre. There was no chimney and no windows although light could be introduced by setting a small pane of glass into the thatch. Blackhouses are mostly orientated north–south and, although their location in the landscape may appear somewhat haphazard, they were positioned to make good use of the underlying terrain. Even with three small streams (now bogs) running through the settlement, drainage was a problem and each house was constructed with its long axis running downslope.

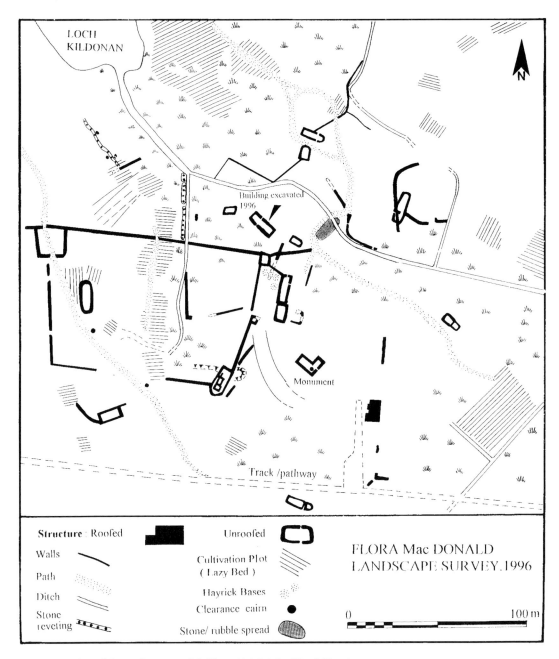

98 Plan of the settlement and fields at Airigh Mhuillin (Milton)

After the best spot was found, the ground was stripped of turf and the house was built with its upper end as the living and sleeping area and its lower third as the animal byre. The house walls are surprisingly massive, constructed of large, coarse blocks and filled in with a tempered earth core *(99; colour plate 18)*. The hearth was in the middle of the house. The fall of slope allowed animal urine to drain along a specially constructed channel and to exit the byre through the end wall or, in some cases, a doorway at that end.

The form of these houses is broadly the same as those from the Norse period onwards but the devotion of a substantial portion of the internal space to use as a byre is new. We may consider that the symbolic understanding of the house was as a metaphorical body, with the upper half the place where people ate, worked and slept and the lower section, the animal half, associated with excrement and urine.

Three of the small square buildings at Airigh Mhuillin contain corn-drying ovens, almost identical to the Norse period example at Bornais, except that the kiln was now inside the barn rather than outside.

The finds from the Airigh Mhuillin houses include wine bottles, bronze implements and factory-made pottery. Bone, of course, has not survived in the acid soils. The handful of tiny scraps of hand-made earthenware are probably manuring rubbish from an earlier time and it is clear that this locally produced pottery was out of use by 1790. One of the houses, House E, was remodelled several times before being used ultimately as a sheep barn *(100)*. It was built on top of a dump of iron slag which filled a depression in the rocks and had been produced nearby in a bloomery for roasting iron ore.

99 A blackhouse under excavation at Airigh Mhuillin (Milton) in 1997

100 Reconstruction of House E at Airigh Mhuillin (Milton)

From this house and others came sherds of factory-made pottery, produced in Edinburgh, Glasgow and Stoke-on-Trent. Along with the rest of Britain in the 1700s, South Uist obtained the new luxuries of tea, tobacco, sugar and molasses, together with the paraphernalia of tea sets and clay pipes. Many of the china plates and bowls had been repaired with lead staples; was this so that they could continue to be used for eating, or were they mainly or even wholly for display?

There were far more round bowls than there were dinner plates or side plates while cutlery was almost wholly absent. There were no teapots, milk jugs or sugar bowls. Perhaps the large bowls and dishes were important for serving potatoes, oats and broth, prepared in an iron cauldron over the fire, and eaten by hand or by drinking from the bowl which was cradled in the lap – there were no chairs and no table and people sat on the floor or on low wooden stools to keep below the level of the peat smoke.

Travelling in the Western Isles between 1782 and 1790, the Reverend Buchanan recorded that:

> The whole family commonly eat out of one dish called the claar. This large dish is between three and four feet in length, and a foot and a half in breadth, made up of deal. They place the straw or grass in the bottom, and pour out the potatoes and fish above that stratum, which they generally collect carefully, with the fragments, for some favourite cow.

The Airigh Mhuillin evidence would indicate that this practice of eating food by hand from a communal long dish was modified to allow it to be eaten from bowls cradled in the lap.

In style, these bowls and dishes are relatively low-status 'industrial' slipwares (i.e. creamware and pearlware crudely 'turned' and painted) and sponge-decorated wares. Even 'seconds' were highly prized. The ceramics were made in the factories of Glasgow and Edinburgh and reached South Uist via the steamships that sailed from the Clyde. Their motifs include colourful flowers and occasional thistles and other Scottish emblems. Before the introduction of the regular steamship passages in the second quarter of the nineteenth century, goods were distributed to the townships as 'job lots' by travelling chapmen and peddlers; the assemblage's striking consistency in the range of forms hints that these ceramic vessels might very well have been purchased in bulk as one such job lot, perhaps bought collectively by the households.

There is no denying that the ceramics indicate circumstances of poverty: people were getting by with the cheapest ceramics and going to some lengths to repair many of those that broke *(101)*. Yet is seems as though the consistency and homogeneity of the ceramics might also have expressed an identity, a closeness of community relations in the face of a lack of fixity and the ever-looming threat of resettlement. In such circumstances, material possessions were more of a hindrance than a comfort. At the same time, the solidity of the houses is surprising given the mobility of residence and perhaps their large sizes and massive walls were designed to provide a sense of permanence in an uncertain world.

The people of Airigh Mhuillin were kelpers. The land was held as a 'tack' and the homes of sub-tenants clustered around the large house of the tacksman to form a township. The tacksman's house was probably the largest, the north–south house which we excavated in 1997. After the inhabitants had attempted to make a living by crofting (though the true crofting system did not start until after the Clearances and farming in this earlier period may best be called proto-crofting) once the kelp industry had collapsed, the land was parcelled up to form a sheep farm in 1827. Only those who worked as farm labourers were allowed to remain on the land.

101 Ceramics repaired with drill holes from Airigh Mhuillin (Milton)

102 Milton House

Long-established patterns of land use and routeways were progressively obliterated and eradicated in the 1800s, especially by the landowner Gordon of Cluny, who might well have been keen not only to open the land up for sheep but to erase the memory of earlier land holdings. New walls appeared, crossing the landscape in straight lines irrespective of topography – the straight lines drawn on maps by improvers. Even where old boundaries were retained, their curving lines were straightened out.

Milton Farm, built in the late nineteenth century, is a very imposing, two-and-a-half-storey building, bringing an alien architectural style to this landscape which it dominates *(102)*. In the 1800s the main land route down the length of South Uist was still the machair track and the house has an elaborate driveway that leads onto it. The farm's high symmetrical façade faces west, towards the track and the sea, reversing the directionality of traditional custom. Since the *sluagh* (the spirits of the dead) pass by night on that side, west-facing windows would provide access for them to attack the living. This house was not only the face of the future but an architectural display designed to intimidate and to flout customary superstition.

In its farmyard the outbuildings included an enormous grain-drying oven. A corn mill was also built further inland to serve Milton Farm. Local sentiments were not best disposed to the new order and many people were reluctant to have to pay for their corn to be dried and milled when they could do this at home for free. Angus MacLellan records in his autobiography how previously when the island's owner had built watermills, many tenants preferred to hand-grind their own grain. The owner then ordered that everyone who possessed a hand quern should permit it to be smashed and officers were sent round to enforce the ruling. The broken quernstones were then thrown into a loch at Ormacleit which thereafter took on the name of the Loch of the Querns.

Given the worsening working and living conditions of the crofters, it is surprising that there was no concerted resistance on South Uist to their exploitation by the landlord. Part of this was a residual loyalty to the clan chief, an institution with deep roots. Also, people found comfort in religion. Between 1820 and 1870 a religious revival swept through the islands and many crofters joined the Free Church to find salvation beyond this earthly vale of tears. After the Parliamentary Commission into Crofting's report in 1883, matters began to improve but it was only in 1917 that most South Uist crofters were granted security of tenure (though to this day most of the land still belongs to the landlord). In that year the sheep farm at Milton was broken up into separate crofts allotted to different crofting families.

Our project has excavated other blackhouses at Frobost and at Kirkidale on the east coast, and some blackhouses at South Glendale were excavated by contract archaeologists in advance of the construction of the Eriskay causeway. We have also investigated the kelp bothy site on the Ardvule promontory, just east of Dun Vulan. Most of those from the period of the Napoleonic wars have been washed away but one site still survives on the eastern edge of Dun Vulan's loch. Further east is a kelp-processing compound of 20 bothies, laid out in a three-sided rectangle *(103)*. These were used in the late nineteenth and early

103 A kelper's house at Ardvule

104 Kelp workers at Ardvule, *c.*1900

twentieth centuries and two excavated hut sites have produced spongeware bowls, bottles, clay pipes, a broken mirror and other assorted items. Letter books in the South Uist Estate Office suggest that in the 1870s the kelp site was occupied all year round and entire families were put to work. A photograph from the early 1900s shows the site in use, with the bothy roofs made of driftwood covered by turf *(104)*.

EMIGRATION: THE NOVA SCOTIA EXPERIENCE

One of the finds from Airigh Mhuillin, left lying outside the doorway of House E, was a bronze military belt plate with the insignia of the Inverness-shire Militia, a regiment established in the Napoleonic period *(105)*. We shall never know the identity of its wearer but it serves to remind us of the importance of military service in highland life and how those soldiers formed the 'shock troops' that carved out the British empire.

Highland regiments played a major part in the wars against the French and Americans and some 23 regiments of the line and 23 of militiamen or fencibles (over 48,300 men) were recruited from the highlands and islands between the outbreak of the Seven Years' War in 1756 and the battle of Waterloo in 1815. If they lived through their military service, soldiers were promised land in the New World when their regiment was disbanded. Land allotment depended on rank: 100 acres for privates and 500 for officers. Cape Breton Island and the

Minas basin of Nova Scotia were the destination of many after the American War of Independence. The Nova Scotia colony had been founded in 1625 by a Scotsman, Sir William Alexander of Stirling, to establish a Scottish version of the English plantations.

Nova Scotia had previously been the French colony of Acadia, whose inhabitants departed to resettle in the southern colonies; their descendants are the 'Cajuns' of New Orleans and Louisiana. By the 1760s the influx of Highland soldiers and planters had changed the colony's character. From the 1770s, Catholic Highlanders, led by their priests and tacksmen, settled in Antigonish and Guysborough counties and the south and west coasts of Cape Breton. Highland Presbyterians began to arrive in 1773, landing at Pictou. The settlements spread westwards into Colchester and Cumberland counties, to the east coast of Cape Breton and to the north and west of the Bras d'Or lake. By 1871 some 50,000 of Cape Breton's 75,000 inhabitants were of Scottish descent and most had arrived between 1800 and 1840, before the famine *(106)*.

Timber and mining were the important industries. The timber trade took off in the 1790s and new shipping routes ferried oak and pine from the eastern Maritimes to Scottish ports, bringing back emigrants on the return trip to boost the assault on the forest. Much of the wealth generated by the timber trade flowed back to Britain to be invested in substantial town and country houses of the rich in England and Scotland.

The first waves of emigrants had the best deals in land allotment, and acquired the larger portions of more fertile 'frontland'. These lots were typically rectangular with a width ratio of 1:5 and fronted onto coastline, lakeside or the fertile strips along river valleys. By the late 1820s the best of this 'frontland' had been settled, mostly by the few relatively prosperous tacksmen who arrived in Cape Breton between 1800 and 1820.

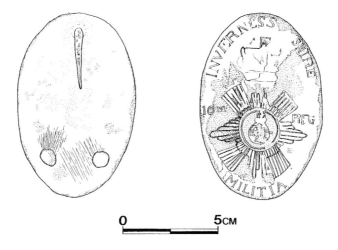

105 A military belt plate excavated from outside a house at Airigh Mhuillin (Milton)

106 Map of Cape Breton, Nova Scotia and Prince Edward Island

The later arrivals had to make do with 'backland', the thin-soiled irregular plots carved out of the rocky uplands. Here they were back in the position from which they had started, once again unable to survive on marginal land. The only difference was that they were at least free of the obligations towards tacksmen and landlords. To make matters worse, however, in 1827 the free land grants were abolished and the land had to be bought. At £200 for a 200-acre plot, most were unable to pay and were forced to squat on land hitherto unallocated. In 1837 almost 20,000 of the 37,000 residents of Cape Breton were squatting illegally on Crown land.

Ways of coping in these dislocating circumstances included the maintaining of the extended kinship networks that had survived from home. In the Margaree district of Cape Breton, 71% of the pioneer population were related to each other before they emigrated. Other communities turned in on themselves and modified their marriage practices to favour close cousin and brother-sister exchange marriages, providing 'no inclination to mix with strangers'.

Gaelic music, language and religious faith were maintained and provided a further sense of identity in difficult times. As a result, Nova Scotia has remained very Scottish, maintaining traditions of wearing kilts, dancing to pipes and fiddles, and distilling whisky. Yet the material elements of traditional lifestyles did not survive. New agricultural methods were needed to clear and farm the densely wooded hill slopes. Furthermore, no one built the stone-walled Hebridean longhouses and, instead, dwellings were modelled on the New England style of wooden-framed houses *(107)*. There was, of course, an abundance of wood, a rare material back on South Uist.

Houses were lighter and brighter than the blackhouses and were not shared with the animals. The hearth was still in the centre of the house but it was enclosed within a stone chimney stack and remained the fulcrum around which daily Gaelic life revolved. Not only was interior space partitioned into several rooms but another major change was the conversion from a horizontal plan to a vertical house form, consisting of a ground floor (with kitchen, utility room and parlour), an upper floor (with bedrooms) and an attic for weaving. The much harsher winters required the building of cellars to store root vegetables and it is these that survive as the remains of those pioneers' homes. One of these surviving cellars is that of the Neil MacPhee house. Born near Ormacleit in 1785, MacPhee and his wife Margaret emigrated to Mabou via Prince Edward Island in the first decade of the nineteenth century.

107 A Cape Breton house of the 1820s

CHAPTER 11

TIME, TRADITION AND CHANGE
A Long-term Perspective

Eight thousand years is a lot of history for a small island. If we estimate 27 years for a generation, a total of some 300 generations have lived on South Uist. Only six generations ago the Clearances were in full swing. The first written records mentioning Uist go back less than 30 generations, in other words less than a tenth of the entire sequence. Archaeology is the only means by which that unwritten history can be told and, even in the historical period, it offers an important material dimension to dispel the historian's reliance on a single type of artefact, the written text.

The archaeological resource, however, is in grave danger. Rabbits are not native to the island but were introduced as recently as the 1780s: within 220 years, they have become a pest of epidemic proportions. Their burrowing on the machair is damaging all but the deepest of archaeological deposits and that rich treasure-house of 4,000 years of unwritten history is gradually being turned into a sand version of Swiss cheese. Our excavations on sites such as Viking Bornais have shown the scale of their destructive abilities, scrambling the evidence of stratigraphic layers and house floors.

The scale of the problem can be appreciated when we realize that rabbit damage has only really become serious since the 1970s, when myxomatosis put people off eating them. From the damage that has been done in just 30 years, we can be sure that the evidence in most of the settlement mounds will be severely compromised within this century. There are small-scale and temporary solutions, such as gassing them in particular areas of the machair, but the rabbits soon come back.

The archaeological quest into South Uist's past, with just 50 years of excavation and modern survey, is only in its infancy. It would be a great shame if rabbits were allowed to destroy within a few centuries an archaeological legacy which has developed over many thousands of years and which we are only just beginning to appreciate. What has been excavated so far is only the tiniest tip of the iceberg in terms of preserved settlement mounds. Future research will hopefully expand on our discoveries and also continue to find ways of better conserving the resource. Our own results can only ever be an interim statement which will change in the light of new discoveries and new excavations. At the same time, archaeology, along with other forms of history, brings present circumstances to bear on writing that past.

What have been the key themes in the island's past? Can any sense be made of the millennia of agricultural struggle, the vain monumental constructions of bygone eras, or the bloodshed of island sons in foreign wars? Or is the only lesson of history that there are no lessons from history?

South Uist's history will always offer, to some extent, the evidence each generation needs to find, to back up whatever lessons and mythologies we may want to impress on others. If we want to emphasize the powerlessness of human communities in battling against the ferocious elements, we can point to the ways in which the climatic and geomorphological changes constrained and affected past livelihoods. We can also tell the opposite story, of human endeavour overcoming these environmental constraints.

There is grist for the mill of Malthusian determinists who can point to the high population growth before the Clearances as an obvious case of population pressure overloading the land's carrying capacity. The same scenario may be recast by a Marxist historian in very different terms, focusing on the enforced bondage of tenants exploited by greedy landlords.

South Uist can be considered today as being on the margins and we may wish to seek out that theme back in the distant past, or to challenge it by drawing attention to periods such as the Viking Age when the island lay on one of the great 'sea roads' of the Scandinavian world. For some historians and archaeologists, the romantic notion of a timeless past of honoured traditions can be celebrated with the evidence that we have gathered; for others it is the changes and transformations that are the real stuff of South Uist's history.

One of the most interesting aspects of the island's past is that relationship between tradition and change. The common perception of Scottish island communities is that they have been drawn into the modern world from a timeless past on the marginal fringe. Our story has shown the inadequacy of such a perspective on the island's history but the power of tradition has certainly been strong in certain periods.

THE INTRUSION OF THE OUTSIDE WORLD

There are four or five moments that we can identify as having brought profound cultural and social change. Some of them, and possibly all of them, were associated with influxes of incomers or at least the influence of outsiders on the existing way of life. The first of these moments is, of course, the point at which South Uist was settled. The evidence is not wholly conclusive but it would seem that people arrived here around 6000 BC and made their living

108 Glac Hurkavat Neolithic chambered cairn

from fishing, gathering and hunting or even managing the red deer that they either brought with them or that had earlier populated these islands by swimming the Minch. These unknown and, to some extent, hypothetical people were the first Hebrideans.

The second moment of great change was the arrival of farming at some point around 4000 BC. The earliest sites of the Neolithic in the islands date to the fourth millennium but not earlier *(108)*. Recent discoveries on the Isle of Man indicate that a Neolithic way of life was already in existence there in the latter half of the fifth millennium BC and we should not be surprised if the same is true for these more northerly isles.

The adoption and spread of domesticated animals and crops seem to have been motivated by more than solely economic concerns, and the speed of their spread across the British Isles appears to have been fast and uniform. Even the Mesolithic communities with plentiful resources of seafood and red deer, such as those of the Inner Hebrides, seem not to have delayed the introduction of the Neolithic way of life, in contrast to the delay which can be seen archaeologically in some areas of Europe, notably in the Netherlands and Denmark.

The arrival of Beakers seems to have been a significant moment for the islanders as well as for the rest of the British Isles. Ideas about a mass migration of Beaker people no longer stand up to close scrutiny and the uses of these new ceramics seem to have fitted into existing social institutions and thereby transformed society from within. Alcohol might have been one of the primary ingredients of a social package that linked people over long distances. The Western Isles appear not to have been slow to catch on to these changes and were as early as anywhere else (i.e. within the first three centuries) in making use of the new styles, as well as proving to be excellent makers of finely decorated Beakers.

The adoption of mainland British roundhouse architecture around 1100 BC is nicely documented at Cladh Hallan where it represents a dramatic change from the boat-shaped and other houses of the preceding millennium. The old ancestor cults were finally done away with as revered and ancient mummies were buried under the floors of the new houses.

This revolution was not simply one of architectural form but of the ideology that animated that form, replacing local ancestral religion with a new set of beliefs founded in universalizing concepts of the movements of the heavens. This was a profound transformation which occurred throughout Britain, in which the domain of the living finally took precedence over the power of the dead. Evidence for copious bronze working and the presence of probably Irish gold at this time indicate long-distance links for this Late Bronze Age community.

It is not until the Viking Age that the outside world was again to intrude into island life. The changes in domestic architecture and other material culture, the change in place names and language, the historical records and the genetic inheritance of today's islanders all serve to highlight the profound impact of the Scandinavian world. Along with the initial Mesolithic settlement, we can be fairly sure that this was a moment when many incomers settled here.

The next period of such change is one that we are still living through. It begins with the arrival of a capitalist market economy in the few centuries prior to the Clearances. Depopulation and repopulation, the gradual collapse of crofting and traditional occupations, the abandonment of traditional domestic architecture and the embracing of the modern world and its material culture are various aspects. It has been a time of considerable displacement, the creation of a Hebridean diaspora, the engaging in military and merchant naval service, and the huge loss of life on the battlefields of empire.

THE POWER OF TRADITION

South Uist and the Western Isles have been caught up in some of the most profound changes that have affected western European society, but it would be ingenuous not to acknowledge that there have been long periods of stasis that may pejoratively be called stagnation or more charitably termed the maintenance of traditional ways.

The main stone circle at Callanish on Lewis was constructed around 3000 BC, earlier than the stone circles of Avebury and Stonehenge, and bears witness to social innovation and mobilization in the Middle Neolithic. During the Later Neolithic the Western Isles seem not to have taken up the material culture of henge monuments and Grooved Ware that developed out of Orkney.

This is particularly surprising when we consider Orkney's relative proximity in terms of sea travel and the influences that Orkney and Shetland had on the islands in earlier times in terms of ceramic forms and tomb styles. It is most unlikely that Neolithic Hebrideans were unaware of these innovatory forms and the new beliefs and practices that they embodied. Passage grave art is another form that characterizes the Irish Sea region and Orkney but simply misses out the Western Isles. Equally, there was anachronistic continuation of the use of the style of pottery called Unstan Ware well into the Late Neolithic, many centuries after it had gone out of fashion in its native Orkney.

The period of the Earlier Bronze Age is, as far as we can judge, one in which there were no such anachronisms. Indeed, the use of mummification at around 1500 BC at Cladh Hallan is a high point of achievement and novelty. However, our evidence is as yet slight for any judgements to be made with confidence. It is rather in the first millennium BC that the iron grip of tradition is gradually tightened. While digging the Early Iron Age layers at Cladh Hallan, we were surprised to find large numbers of deer antlers which had been used as pick-axes and shovels made from cattle scapulae. Elsewhere in the British Isles, these are classically tools of the Neolithic and Early Bronze Age so why were they being used here so much later?

A straightforward answer is that such bone tools as picks, rakes and pokers remained in use simply because they worked well, but elsewhere people were already using agricultural tools made of iron. The question of iron's availability on South Uist in the Early Iron Age is difficult to resolve. Iron artefacts might well not have survived in the machair sand – pieces of iron from Middle Iron Age Dun Vulan were very badly corroded. Yet we found no evidence for iron-working at Cladh Hallan – if it had been taking place, the residues of the process should have survived in the form of slag.

The retention and elaboration of circular architectural forms well into the first millennium AD can be perceived in terms of a cultural resistance to the Roman Empire and its encroachment beyond the frontier. The adoption of broch and wheelhouse architecture from the Northern Isles is undoubtedly innovative yet the continued use of these styles throughout the Roman and post-Roman period also reaffirmed the significance of traditional roundhouse life in the face of the architectural transformations – villas, army camps, amphitheatres, basilicas and other public buildings – that were changing the face of Britain south of the border. This circular architecture was emblematic of a cultural retrenchment that also rejected most of the material trappings of Roman life, preferring instead to import medicinal plants and exotic animals from the south.

In the Pictish period, Ireland and Scotland remained the last bastions of curvilinear architecture. Longhouses and other rectangular house forms were universal domestic living spaces in Scandinavia, England and the Continent. On Uist and the other Hebridean islands, the adoption of a plain ceramic style and the reoccupation of many of the ruins which survived from earlier periods might well have been elements of a deliberately anachronizing strategy, designed to import the past into the present. Rectangular geometry gradually found a place within the architecture of this period but its context was limited to outbuildings, hearths and single elements within otherwise curvilinear houses.

After the Norse period, the longhouse was to remain as the basic form of domestic dwelling until the nineteenth and early twentieth centuries *(109)*. There is no doubt that the 'blackhouses' have their origins in Norse period houses such as those at Bornais and Cille Pheadair. There were certain changes along the way in terms of byre provision, small informal hearths replacing rectangular ones, and variations in stone and turf walling, but essentially the basic architectural form survived with minor modification for a thousand years *(110)*.

The emphasis on cattle rearing for meat and on herring fishing, both of which were important in the Uists and Barra until the nineteenth century, also had their origins in the Norse period. Dodgshon has made an interesting point that the primitive technology of spade cultivation, hand querns and other features of nineteenth-century life might have been products of agricultural crisis rather than traditional methods carried forward through centuries of unbroken tradition. Even if that is the case, the production of hand-made earthenware into the late 1600s or early 1700s and the conservatism of architecture, folk practices and material culture amongst all but the elite were clearly evident to visitors such as Martin Martin and, for the Inner Hebrides, Boswell and Johnson.

Today, we stand on a knife-edge, balancing between innovation and retrenchment. As the folk traditions disappear with each generation and the traditional life is consigned to museums, there are attempts to reclaim the past through the support of Gaelic language education in schools, fostering of Gaelic arts and crafts, and research and education about the past. The way forward is not to pursue one goal at the expense of the other but to grasp both

109 A croft house in South Uist

110 Loch Ainort in 1936, photographed by Kissling

together. Archaeology is one of those primary keys which can unlock stories and secrets long forgotten, and turn them into a resource that will be of value to the local and more global community for the millennia to come.

TRADITIONS AND SOCIAL PRACTICE

If tradition and change have often gone hand in hand and if there were certain moments of profound social transformation, is there anything in South Uist's history that was more long-lasting, enduring over millennia, rather than mere centuries? Is there anything in recent or modern times which actually forms one end of a thread that runs back into the depths of the ancient and prehis-toric past?

Whereas architecture and material culture have changed with the ages along with social institutions and subsistence, one aspect of life that may indicate a long-term continuity is contained in what is inelegantly called 'bodily practices' by anthropologists. We now have some good evidence that the concern with sunwise motions of movement (*deasil*) might have an antiquity of at least three millennia and possibly longer.

The relationship between memory and our bodily movements – ways of sitting and standing, looking and lounging, working and resting, declaiming and recollecting – are sensual actions which fix memories in practice and bodily posture. We don't forget how to ride a bike and we remember implic-itly and sub-consciously the rhythms of work. A good example can be found in nineteenth-century South Uist practices of waulking (fulling) cloth *(111)*.

Along with milking and spinning, the rhythmical activity of waulking was performed by women to the accompaniment of songs and it is thought that as many as 200 waulking songs survived in Barra and South Uist until the 1930s. The process of waulking was described by Margaret Fay Shaw from observa-tions made between 1929 and 1935 (recently republished in 1986):

> The ends of a length of a newly woven cloth are sewn together to make it a circle, and the cloth is then placed on a long trestle table and soaked with hot urine. An even number of women sit at the table, say twelve with six a side, and the cloth is passed around sunwise, to the left, with a kneading motion. They reach to the right and clutch the cloth, draw in, push out, free the hands to grasp again to the right. One, two, three, four, slowly the rhythm emerges.

Margaret Fay Shaw and other folklorists recorded numerous examples of sunwise movement at ritual occasions and in everyday life. After dark on New Year's Eve (Hogmanay or *A'Challuinn*), the young men of the township would walk around the outside of the house sunwise, singing Hogmanay ballads and

111 Wool waulking, *c.*1927-1928 (Keith Henderson)

accompanied by a torch-bearer who passed his brand of smouldering sheepskin three times around the head of the wife of the house.

When fishermen went to sea, they always turned their boats sunwise when setting out. The house and the churchyard were always entered and left in a sunwise direction at weddings and funerals. Before sowing, water was sprinkled over seedcorn in a sunwise direction in order to hasten growth. Harvesting and the grinding of corn in a quern were also practised in a sunwise direction.

Even today the sunwise tradition survives in the stacking of corn stouks at harvest and occurs in activities of recent origin, such as winding wire around a fence post. When we excavated a circular stack-base (a flat stone platform used as a dry base for storing harvested crops) at Airigh Mhuillin, we discovered that its stones had been laid in a sunwise arrangement. Expecting the platform to date to the nineteenth century, we were surprised when a plastic Brylcreem tub, dating to the 1960s, turned up underneath. When the tenant of the croft volunteered that it was he who had built the stack-base, his reply as to why he had laid the stones in that fashion was 'that is how it is always done'. This casual remark reveals the power of such embodied traditions; they are unquestioned and innate ways of doing things that are so naturalized as to require no discursive explanation.

When Martin Martin visited the Isles in 1695 he was fascinated by the sunwise rituals and traditions. Some of them had then already been out of use for as much as 40 years:

> There was an ancient custom in the island of Lewis to make a fiery circle about the houses, corn, cattle, etc., belonging to each particular family: a man carried fire in his right hand, and went round, and it was called *dessil* [*deasil*], from the right hand, which in the ancient language is called *dess* [*deis*]… There is another way of the *dessil*, or carrying fire round about women before they are churched after child-bearing; and it is used likewise about children before they be christened: both which are performed in the morning and at night. This is only practised now by some of the ancient midwives…

Martin Martin describes those sunwise movements still in use at the time of his visit: poorer people circling their benefactor three times, and the rowing of the boat 'sunways' before departing. He was told that the fire rituals preserved woman and child from the power of evil spirits. Martin was a man of the modern world who wanted explanations and also wanted to rid the people of these superstitions. In one case he actually forbade his boatmen to turn sunwise at the start of their journey, in order to impress on them that they would still reach their destination safely.

Moving back further in time, Robert Dodgshon has drawn attention to the Scandinavian concept of sunwise movement, known as solskifte. He shows how it was a principle in the laying-out of medieval townships in northeastern and eastern Scotland and that it played a pivotal role in Norse cosmologies. Rituals focused on the sun as differentiator of light and dark, and celebrated its diurnal and seasonal movements. The rituals of fertility were based upon a recurring movement, starting in the east at dawn and working around sunwise to the west.

Just a decade ago, it might have seemed difficult to find archaeological evidence for a concern with sunwise movement – fire rituals, boat sailings and the like leave no material traces – but our own research (see chapters 5, 6 and 7) has produced some powerful evidence of its importance in domestic life from 1100 BC until the abandonment of curvilinear architecture with the beginning of the Norse period. The sunwise ordering of life within the roundhouse affected daily movement around the house, the diurnal pattern of activities and, most dramatically, the passage of life from birth to death *(112; 113)*.

What was important about this embodiment of the sunwise principle in daily life was that it was part of a broader change from the ancestor-focused rituals performed at public monuments (cairns, standing stones and stone circles) to the incorporation of ritual activities within the house. The very

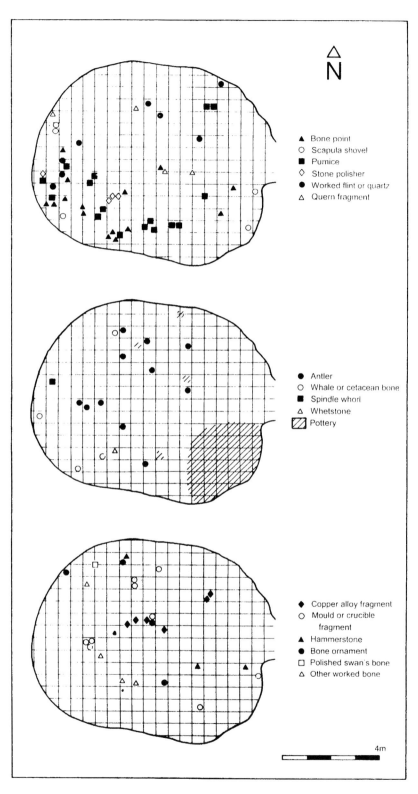

Bone point ▲
Scapula shovel ○
Pumice ■
Stone polisher ◇
Worked flint or quartz ●
Quern fragment △

Antler ●
Whale or cetacean bone ○
Spindle whorl ■
Whetstone △
Pottery ▨

Copper alloy fragment ◆
Mould or crucible fragment ○
Hammerstone ▲
Bone ornament ●
Polished swan's bone □
Other worked bone △

4m

112 Plans of the distribution of artefacts on the earliest floor of the middle roundhouse at Cladh Hallan, showing activity areas

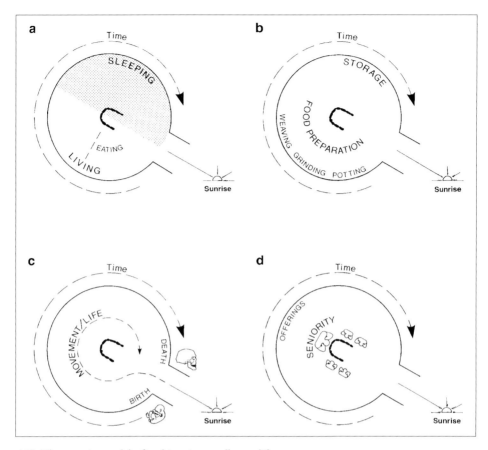

113 The sunwise model of prehistoric roundhouse life

adoption of circular geometry, hitherto reserved for monuments of the ancestral dead, into the domestic setting was part of this transition. It is thus very likely that the significance of circularity and roundness in Early Bronze Age monuments (chapter 4) and even in Neolithic tombs (chapter 3) might well have been linked to sunwise concepts.

There is a significant distinction to be made here between the carrying out of a specific ritual or ritualized act (from a New Year fire ritual to winding wire round a fence post) incorporating the sunwise principle and the existence of the structuring sunwise principle itself. As Martin Martin demonstrated, three centuries ago certain sunwise rituals were already obsolete and we can be sure that others now practised had not yet come into existence. The context of sunwise performance and the degree to which it may be a formal rite or a momentary unacknowledged act are subject to significant change. It is very unlikely that a single sunwise ritual has survived across the hundreds of generations – what has survived is the principle itself which has been incorporated and reincorporated into successive, different ritual and daily practices.

From its association with the monuments and tombs of the ancestors, to the constitution of life within the house in the Late Bronze Age and Iron Age, to the organization of land and fertility in the Norse and medieval periods, to the protective fire rituals and daily activities of individuals in recent centuries, the contexts of sunwise enactment have changed but the principle that motivates them has remained the same.

It is likely that South Uist was one of the few parts of the British Isles where the sunwise order of things continued into or beyond the Roman and medieval periods. Elsewhere it survived only in concepts of clock movement and vague superstitions such as the association of widdershins with witchcraft. In South Uist and the Western Isles too, this adherence to sunwise movement may disappear within the next generation or so.

POWER AND SOCIAL ORGANIZATION

We know a great deal about the political transformation of recent centuries, from chiefdoms into full incorporation of the islands into the economy and politics of the Scottish state, but how much can be said about the prehistory of power? For many years, archaeologists have used anthropological notions of social evolution, postulating a sequence of social organization from bands to tribes to chiefdoms to states.

Bands, in which there is a sexual division of labour but little inequality beyond age differences, are defined as kin-based groupings of normally less than 200 people and are thought to have been the building blocks of hunter-gatherer life in the Mesolithic. Tribes are larger, kin-based groups sub-divided into lineages or clans and deriving from a common ancestor. Hierarchy and inequality are weakly developed whilst labour is sexually divided within a domestic mode of production. The Earlier Neolithic of the British Isles is often characterized as a set of tribal societies.

Chiefdoms are sometimes smaller than tribes. The chief obtains his power by means of his kinship position of seniority in relation to the founding ancestor or deity, and is able to collect tribute from his subordinate kin and defeated enemies, and redistribute largesse as required. Chiefs direct monument building, conduct war and maintain retinues of warriors and other specialists such as craft workers who live off the surplus of others. Chiefdoms are relatively unstable formations since, if one chiefdom prospers, it is invariably at the expense of another. For British prehistory, the chiefdom model with its elites and their specialists has been applied to the period starting in the Late Neolithic and Beaker period until the coming of the Romans. North of the Roman frontier and after the Roman period, it has been considered a feature of the Pictish and early Anglo-Saxon period.

States are the largest social formation, formed of three or four hierarchical levels with the ability to extract tax and tribute to maintain a standing army, a bureaucracy, a judiciary and a religious elite. States differ from chiefdoms in having tightly demarcated territories and boundaries as well as being organized by class rather than by kinship. They emerge in the Viking and Late Saxon periods and become increasingly complex within the Early Modern period.

Critics of this evolutionary scheme have noted that cultural sequences in different parts of the world do not always follow this order of band to tribe to chiefdom to state. Nor do these entities necessarily exist in isolation from each other – states can include chiefdoms within them, as in the case of medieval Scotland. The scheme is also somewhat reductive, taking all the myriad complexities of different societies and trying to cram them into just four categories. For example, some anthropologists talk of transegalitarian societies which are somewhere between tribes and chiefdoms and may oscillate between periods of relative equality and inequality. Nonetheless, the basic scheme is a useful point of departure in looking at South Uist's ancient past.

Of the Mesolithic period we can as yet say nothing but there are a few clues for the Neolithic. Despite extensive monument building, the lack of evidence for craft specialization and the absence of symbols of power – such as gold regalia, special materials reserved for certain people, goods with controlled access for an elite – indicate that people of this period were relatively equal in life. It is the dead who were lauded and for whom surplus was produced rather than any of their successors amongst the living.

It is difficult to know whether the Early Bronze Age followed the same pattern as is seen in, for example, southern Britain, where wealth in individual graves points to major inequalities arising after 2500 BC. Was the stone circle at Callanish the product of a chiefdom society, as Colin Renfrew has argued for Late Neolithic monuments in Orkney? The Callanish region was certainly the religious centre of the islands but there are no conclusive signs of other features that may permit us to talk of Early Bronze Age chiefdoms in the Western Isles.

The Cladh Hallan evidence has produced some rather more concrete indications of a hierarchical society – the differential control of metalworking and the inequalities in wealth between households – but can we yet treat this period as a chiefdom society? The gold penannular ring from Cladh Hallan speaks of differences in the appearance and connections of certain individuals in comparison to others, and the three roundhouses could be interpreted in that 'Celtic' social order of chief, religious specialist and commoner. We are most certainly dealing with the existence of elites in this period and very possibly the Uists were organized into a chiefdom whose centre was at Machair Mheadhanach (Iochdar) at the north end of South Uist.

By the time of the brochs, social inequalities are clear in the architecture and the food debris. Broch-dwellers were 'elevated' both physically and socially above their ground-dwelling peers. They were able to obtain construction labour from others, keep skull trophies and be given food tribute in the form of pigs or portions of pork. During the Iron Age in East Yorkshire, front portions of pigs were given to certain of the dead, who were also provided with the better grave goods. Classical sources record that, in the Celtic world, the champion's portion consisted of the rear end of the pig.

There were many fewer brochs than wheelhouses on South Uist, perhaps a ratio of about 1:4 or more, and this variation in numbers may imply a difference between commoners and a growing chiefly or royal clan, the descendants of the elite which emerged in the Late Bronze Age, whose centre of population straddled the ford between Iochdar and Benbecula.

In the Pictish period, the kingdom in the east of Scotland had many of the features of an emergent state but in the Western Isles there seems to have been little change in power structure from earlier in the Iron Age, other than in the medium of its expression. As social position was bound up less with residence and more with individual appearance, so the significance of dress became more important. At the top of the hierarchy were those who controlled the production of elite metalwork, from which they would have been able to distribute jewellery to reward and encourage their retinues.

The Norse period sees the encroachment of the Norwegian state, first in the 'bow wave' of pirates and fugitives who haunted its expanding margins and preyed off the weak, and secondly in the full imposition of royal rule from Norway and its tributary kingdom of Man. We know something of the ways in which the islands became pawns in the struggle between Norway, Scotland, Man and the Lordship and about the means by which smaller kingdoms or chiefdoms struggled to carve out a power base in the interstices between the larger, more powerful states.

Finally, one of the big surprises of our work has been the early foundation of the land units that were to form townships in the historical period. The townships which once stood on the machair almost all had their origins in clusters of Middle Iron Age and successive settlement mounds. Some of these might have had beginnings in the late Early Iron Age around 200 BC. These proto-townships formed a settlement organization that was only modified substantially in the medieval period when some of them were divided and new ones were created (*gearraidh*) in the peatlands between existing townships.

The evidence outlined above for food tribute associated with the brochs suggests that the Middle Iron Age proto-townships were units of assessment from which a food rent, possibly the origin or precursor of *cuid-oidhche*, was levied at this early date. If townships were much later phenomena (not much before AD 1500) in many or most other parts of western Scotland as Dodgshon has argued, they were of a more respectable antiquity in South Uist and probably throughout the Uists and even much of the Western Isles.

IN THE MAINSTREAM OR ON THE MARGINS?

When the project started, some of our colleagues were very much convinced that South Uist's marginality had had a stultifying effect on the island's subsistence and social organization over the millennia. It was part of a remote island chain a long way from Sheffield (and even from Edinburgh, for that matter!) Its soils were not particularly fertile. The severity of the wind and weather was enough to destroy a harvest at a blow. It seemed to some that the dynamic environmental forces of blanket bog formation after deforestation, and the formation of the machair must have exerted excessive pressures, making it near impossible to make any kind of worthwhile living.

Added to these environmental difficulties, the poverty and hardship of recent centuries could, to the newcomer unaware of tenant exploitation, be misleadingly construed as typical of previous millennia – or even as the zenith of evolutionary progress, an advance over any life lived in the preceding thousands of years. Was prehistoric life on South Uist really so bad? It was presumably always very windy, but the evidence uncovered by our work shows that it was probably not really much different to anywhere else in prehistoric Britain.

Ian Armit's map from *The Archaeology of Skye and the Western Isles* beautifully illustrates the fallacy of the landlubber mainlander's perspective which places the islands on the geographical margins *(114)*. He overturns our preconceptions by putting Shetland at the centre of the map, with north at the bottom. By using such an island-centred geography, Armit shows that the Western Isles are not marginal: they are central to the north Atlantic zone, within 300km of Orkney in one direction and Ireland in the other. Robert Dodgshon has also refuted this concept of marginality, pointing out firmly that it did not exist before the islands became enmeshed in the wider market economy of the nation states of England and Scotland in the last three or so centuries.

Our excavations of Norse period settlements on South Uist have uncovered a wealth of material possessions, gold and silver, and successful subsistence practices which can match almost any other place in the Viking world. Located along the great seaway that formed the western axis of the Norse world, the Western Isles were anything but marginal in that period.

Even in the Late Bronze Age, the many bronze artefacts and the variety of bronzeworking at Cladh Hallan indicate that this island was not poor in metal. Gold-rich Ireland is a few days' sail to the south and could have been the source for copper as well. The Western Isles did not have the gold deposits or fertility of Ireland nor did they produce the monumental and material innovations of Orkney and Shetland – huge chambered tombs, henges, Grooved Ware, brochs, wheelhouses – but the islands were far from marginal in terms of their relationship to these two powerhouses of prehistory.

The other impression we can banish is that those ancient communities lived a hand-to-mouth existence, barely able to produce enough food to make ends

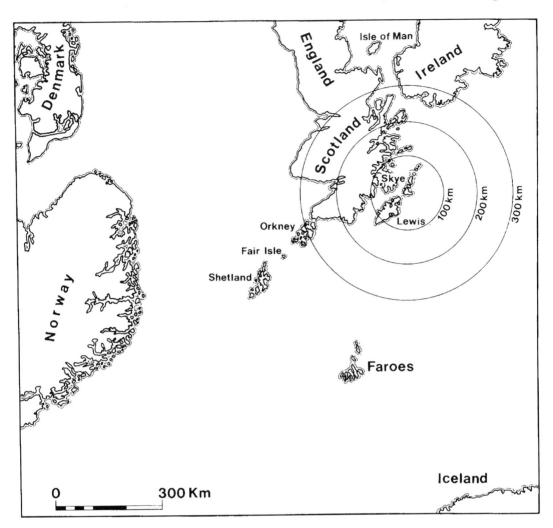

114 Map of the Western Isles with its relationships to Iceland, Scandinavia and the North Atlantic

meet. Our evidence shows that surplus was being appropriated at least as early as the Middle Iron Age and probably earlier in the Late Bronze Age. This was not a subsistence society spending all its energy on survival: even in the Neolithic and Early Bronze Age there was evidently plenty of time available to build monuments for the ancestors and to commemorate the dead.

There has been a tendency to perceive Neolithic people's lives as nasty, brutish and short, yet when one takes into account child mortality (which remained high until the nineteenth century throughout Britain) and the recent reassessment of the ages of the individuals whose skeletons have been found in the Orkney Neolithic tombs, the bulk of the adult population lived into their 40s and beyond. Life was undoubtedly basic and hard but it was not as awful as some writers sometimes like to paint it for shock effect!

This said, there is no denying that the environment of the Western Isles is and has been a difficult one. The catalogue of farming disasters in the 1800s is a reminder of how the wind and weather can take away livelihoods and invite shortage and famine. There is no doubt that living in such places has always required considerable co-operative support, not just from fellow islanders but also from overseas. Alliance building must have been a fundamental political and economic strategy, perhaps more important here than in more fertile and climatically predictable areas of Britain. The flip side of tribute payment was also that communities were insuring themselves against the hard times, economically and politically.

Perhaps the greatest tribute to the past inhabitants of South Uist is that they seemed to live so effortlessly in such difficult conditions, developing excellent ways of adapting to their harsh environment, building extraordinary structures such as the tall brochs, and creating complex social institutions whose existence we are just beginning to discover.

SITES TO VISIT

There are many sites to see but few currently have any formal public access or display boards. In many cases the sites can only be reached by walking across croft land so please be careful to close gates behind you. Take care not to damage any crops, disturb grazing animals, or tread on the chicks of ground-nesting birds. Always take an Ordnance Survey map and compass with you, especially when walking in the hills – broken legs, sprained ankles, hypothermia, heatstroke, and infestations of sheep ticks have all afflicted our archaeological survey teams in the wilder parts of the island.

The best starting place for visitors interested in South Uist's archaeology is the Kildonan (Cill Donnain) Museum where Cille Pheadair Kate's cairn and the wall stones of the Cill Donnain wheelhouse have been re-erected in the grounds.

The Cill Donnain trail

A copy of the leaflet *The Cill Donnain Archaeology and Wildlife Trail* can be obtained at Kildonan Museum. The trail takes you westwards from the war memorial north of the museum, past abandoned nineteenth-century black-houses, out to the broch of Dun Vulan. The Iron Age broch originally had walls 4m wide and stood to a height of 6m or more – today it is filled in to the height of the first floor, so the slabs within the floor of the entrance are actually the lintels over the roof of the passage from the doorway into the ground floor. A Pictish three-roomed house has been squeezed into the broch's circular interior.

You can then walk south to the settlement mounds of Cill Donnain machair and inland to Cille Donnain church, returning to the museum along the road. At Cille Donnain, the church sits on a promontory. Beyond it are small islands in the loch with walls of rectangular buildings that might have been monastic places of retreat.

Machair Mheadhanach, Iochdar

There are 40 archaeological sites on this stretch of machair, ranging in size from surface scatters to enormous settlement mounds up to 80m across and 3m high. The most impressive of these form a long line running southeast from Ardivachar. They date from the Beaker period (Early Bronze Age) to the post-medieval period.

This area lies within the rocket range which has public access except for certain days when red flags indicate that the range is off-limits.

If driving to Ardivachar, park the car by the range entrance and walk from there. The mounds to its southeast are the first of a line that runs in that direction for 2km. They can also be reached by driving from West Gerinish (Geirinis) through the range's southern entrance, past the range headquarters and then taking the second turn to the right (northwards) until the road bends sharply to the left – the mounds are 200m north of this bend.

Cladh Hallan

If coming from the north, take the right fork at the Borrodale Hotel in Dalabrog (Daliburgh), and then immediately turn right again, past the public bar's car park, onto the road that leads westwards towards the sea. Past St Peter's church, turn right again at the T-junction and head for the radio mast. At the radio mast, just before reaching the modern graveyard, turn left along the sandy track and follow it for about 500m. You may find it best to park at the radio mast and walk along this track but it is normally driveable.

As the track swings round to the left you will be able to see the main site on your left (south) and the smaller site a couple of hundred metres further on to your right. Parking is possible on the flat area north of the track but be careful not to get stuck in the soft sand! Alternatively, park on the firmer ground near the beach and walk back to the site.

The main site consists of three Late Bronze Age roundhouses whose walls have been partially reconstructed (these are the northern end of a row of six or seven houses, the remainder remaining buried under the high dune on the south side). The Early Iron Age house on the north side of the track is an unusual double roundhouse with a connecting doorway whose lintels were deliberately lowered when the house was abandoned.

Post-medieval dun in Loch Druim an Iasgair

At the north end of South Uist, take the turn eastwards towards Loch Carnan and the Orasay Inn. Park about 400m west of the junction (south of Cnoc Breac) and walk about 600m southwards to Loch Druim an Iasgair. Within this loch there is an unusual dun (a defended house) of the sixteenth or seventeenth centuries. Its walls rise up from the bottom of the loch about 2m below the surface of the water. This is a very well-preserved site but nothing is known of who built it or why.

Cille Pheadair wheelhouse, Norse settlement and crannogs in Loch Dun na Cille

The Cille Pheadair (Kilpheder) wheelhouse is a perennial attraction but is very difficult to find, especially because it is marked in the wrong place (200m to the north of the correct spot) on the OS map! Drive along the machair track westwards from Cille Pheadair and park at the crossroads where the tarmac ends. Continue on foot straight on (westwards) along the track for 200m until it turns southwards to skirt around the edge of a grass-covered mound. Climb up the mound to find the wheelhouse in its northwest corner. There are another two well-preserved but unexcavated wheelhouses within this mound.

Coming back to the crossroads, take the south track (metalled with chippings and stone) for about 600m to an area where corncrakes live in the summer months. Climb westwards up the coastal dune and look for a grassy hollow on the dune edge. This is the Norse period farmstead excavated in 1996–1998 and remains of a longhouse's stone walls can be seen at the bottom. The sea is eating away at this coastline at a rate of 20m every 25 years and so these remains will soon disappear.

Inland, on Loch Dun na Cille, there are two crannogs. Eilean Chreamh is a small flat platform of stones of unknown date or purpose. It can be approached from a stone causeway on the west bank. Dun na Cille can be reached from the east bank, by parking at the side of the main road (B888) and walking along the lochside to the stone causeway that leads to the crannog. The causeway is often partly submerged and its rocks are slippery and sometimes loose so take great care! On the crannog are the remains of a medieval church and its ancillary buildings.

Glen Usinis

The most remote archaeological remains of South Uist are the Iron Age wheelhouse and souterrains in Glen Usinis on the west coast of the island. There is no short route to these well-preserved prehistoric ruins and visitors should allow for a whole day (or even two) to walk there and back. They can be approached over rough terrain either from Loch Ainort or from Loch Skiport. Sheep ticks and sprained ankles are hazards on this long walk so be properly dressed and equipped. Make sure that someone knows where you are going and for how long.

Cille Bhannain and Dun Mhor

Drive westwards through West Gerinish (Geirinis) and park on the roadside just before the entrance to the rocket range. Walk southwards to a promontory on Loch Cille Bhanain marked on the OS map as 'Dun (rems of)'. There is a ruined stone building which may be the site of the medieval church (although its north–south orientation perhaps indicates that it was a secular building). Look at its foundations and you will see that it sits on the wall of an Iron Age broch.

Further east, and visible from the main road (A865), is the small island on which sits Dun Mhor, an impressive Iron Age broch. Its causeway is on the north side but it is difficult to get to.

Dun Trossary (Dun Trosaraidh)

Park at the modern Catholic church at Trosaraidh (near Gearraidhnamonaidh [Garrynamonie]) and, on its north side, walk eastwards up the hill to the cairn known as Dun Trossary. There is a sheep wash and other disturbances on top of it but the large slab and other big stones are remains of the chambers of a Neolithic long cairn.

Airigh Mhuillin and the crannog in the mill loch south of the museum

Airigh Mhuillin, Flora Macdonald's birthplace, has a car park on the west side of the A865, just a kilometre south of Kildonan Museum. Walk up the low hill to the Flora Macdonald monument where an information board explains the history and layout of the blackhouses and their fields.

From the museum, walk 300m southwards along the road to the edge of the loch where a stone causeway leads to a crannog on which a rectangular or oval building once stood. It was probably built in the sixteenth or seventeenth centuries but little is known of this structure. Back at the museum, don't forget to look at the rebuilt Pictish cairn (rescued from the sea at Cille Pheadair) just inside the gateway, and also the stone outline of the Cill Donnain Iron Age wheelhouse (moved here from the machair) about 10m southeast of it on the other side of the fence.

Gortan and the cairns at Tobhta Mhor na Leaccaich

Park at South Glendale and walk eastwards along the coast until you come to a ruined house and a sandy cove. A Beaker-period settlement was excavated among the sands in the 1980s but nothing survives of it today. Continue eastwards for another kilometre, climbing up a small stream to the two monuments at Tobhta Mhor na Leaccaich marked as 'Cairn' on the OS map. The larger of these is a Neolithic or Early Bronze Age tomb and the smaller one, below it, is a rectangular Pictish cairn. Look for the remains of a blackhouse which was built within the larger cairn.

Reineval, the Frobost roundhouse and the island dun

At the Gearraidh Bhailteas (Milton) crossroads, turn east towards Mingearraidh (Mingarry) and take the south fork up the unmetalled track toward the Neolithic chambered cairn of Reineval. The cairn is easily visible as a huge pile of stones about 100m south of the track and has fine views westwards as far as St Kilda.

From the Milton crossroads, walk southwards to the north end of Loch Cnoc a' Buidhe which has a rectangular or oval island dun at the end of a promontory on its north side. An almost circular ring of stones at its base may be the foundations of this medieval or later building but could also be a prehistoric construction.

There is the basal wall of a roundhouse (marked on the OS map as a 'hut circle') on the higher ground above the loch's east side. It probably dates to the first millennium BC, perhaps to the Late Bronze Age.

Ormacleit Castle and the machair settlement mounds

You can drive to Ormacleit Castle and may be able to park on its west side, but do not inconvenience the work of the farm. The older part of the building is at its south end, which is roofless. This is private property and the roofless structure should not be entered.

If you walk west through the field gate and across the machair you will come to a high settlement mound (slightly north of due west) which lies close to the line of high coastal dunes which overlook the beach. This mound was a settlement during the Iron Age and six of the small mounds to its south were also ancient settlements occupied between the Late Bronze Age and the Viking period.

Howmore, Caisteal Bheagram and Dun Raouill

Howmore is one of the prettiest townships of South Uist and still has a number of thatched houses. Park off the road before you get to the modern church and walk northwards to the ruined medieval chapels, either across the rough ground or along the path that passes the youth hostel. A booklet which describes the history and architecture of Howmore is available at the museum.

You can walk from here northwards the best part of a kilometre to Loch an Eilean to the causeway which leads to Caisteal Bheagram, or approach it over a shorter distance from the main road (A865) to the north of Howmore. The causeway is generally submerged and, providing that it is not in use by anglers, a small boat can be rowed to the castle island. Further north, within Loch Druidibeg on the east side of the A865, there is another island dun. This is Dun Raouill, also a late medieval building constructed in three phases. Unless you can find a boat, there is no access to it other than by swimming!

The SEARCH project and beyond

When the Sheffield Environmental and Archaeological Research Campaign in the Hebrides (SEARCH) began, three of the authors were students at the University of Sheffield (JM, HS and AW) and the other three of us had not yet appeared on the scene. The South Uist arm of the project was at first directed by Andrew Fleming, John Moreland and Marek Zvelebil, all lecturers at Sheffield University. Working with them were a contingent of researchers and research students: Jean-Luc Schwenninger, Barbara Brayshay, Mark Dinnin and Eddie Moth, John Grattan, JM, HS and AW. The environmental research was co-ordinated by David Gilbertson with colleagues such as Kevin Edwards and Martin Kent from other universities.

The environmental arm of the project carried out a major study of environmental change in the last 14,000 years and provided background results that would later be of great importance for the excavations. Rather than try and survey the whole island, the team took the decision to select a cross-section east to west through the island. John Moreland and AW tackled the mountainous east coast around Loch Ainort, where John Moreland began an excavation at Kirkidale of a blackhouse and other structures, finishing work in 1993. Andrew Fleming led a team to survey the peatlands in the middle, in Cill Donnain and Milton townships. Marek Zvelebil embarked on three excavations on the machair of Cill Donnain, concentrating his efforts on digging a small wheelhouse between 1988 and 1991. Eddie Moth carried out rescue recording in the modern sand quarry at Cladh Hallan in 1988 and 1989 and another team undertook a coastal survey along the southern end of the island.

The project was due to end in 1993 and the three Sheffield staff stepped down at or before that date. The project would have ended then and there, except that it had gained a new lease of life. One of us (MPP) joined Sheffield University as a lecturer in 1990 and invited NS to come and work alongside. In the summer of 1990, AW and Jean-Luc Schwenninger noticed erosion at the broch of Dun Vulan and in 1991 we carried out a trial excavation. Results were very promising and a second and third season ensued, concentrating on the hitherto unknown buildings and deposits that lay outside the broch. From 1991 onwards we formed a project team (with JM and HS as environmental specialists) that has continued to work on the island. While digging at Dun Vulan MPP began a survey of the machair, finding over 200 new sites and identifying those most at risk from erosion, rabbit burrowing and quarrying.

In 1994 a series of new initiatives were taken. We began investigation of the large Viking and Norse settlement at Bornais, identified a smaller Norse settlement at Cille Pheadair which was about to be washed away (we excavated it in 1996-1998) and began excavations of the Bronze Age and Early Iron Age settlement in the sand quarry at Cladh Hallan. At the same time JS started planning the Flora Macdonald Project, investigating the site of her birthplace at Milton. After working as part of the student team on Cille Pheadair, in 2000 JR began trial excavations on several machair sites to search for the elusive settlements of the medieval period. Vicki Cummings and Cole Henley studied the Neolithic sites of the Uists; their results are summarized in chapter 3.

As well as carrying out these large excavations over many years, we have also conducted many more small evaluations and investigations through test trenching and geophysical survey. Andrew Chamberlain, Mike Hamilton and Bill Sellars have helped us with their various gadgets such as magnetometers, resistivity meters and ground-penetrating radar. Pete Marshall, Mark Brennand, Anna Badcock, Rowan May, Jayne Gidlow, Claire Ingrem, Rachel Jackson, Dave Wyatt, Jerry Bond, Suzie Reeve, Katinka Stentoft, Katherine Stronach, Sam Emmett, Jane Webster, Tessa Roper, James Ward, Andrew Reynolds and many others have helped in supervising the excavations. Scientific analyses have been carried out by a growing team of specialists but special mention should be given to Cathy Batt, Oliver Craig, Jean-Luc Schwenninger, Victoria Parsons and Siobhan Stevenson.

As team leaders gained university posts (NS at Cardiff; HS at Bournemouth; JM at Southampton, Oxford, Winchester and finally Cardiff; JS as director of Sheffield's consultancy unit, ARCUS; AW at Lampeter, Edinburgh and St Andrew's) so the Sheffield focus has been displaced, with the project becoming a collaborative venture between different universities. With teams of students from these different institutions, and with JS's team including Earthwatch volunteers from North America and Mary Beaudry and Stephen Brighton with a field school from Boston University, the project has tested the limits of the island's accommodation capacity in some years.

More than 1,000 archaeology students and volunteers have trained on the project, and many of them will become, or already are, the next generation of professional archaeologists. Angus John MacKinnon, the staff – and regulars – at the Polochar and the Borrodale have been unfailingly kind to this influx of young people every summer, and we thank them for their patience. We have also been joined by local volunteers (especially Jacqui MacMillan and Criag Allaker) and many others who are content not to get their knees dirty, perhaps, but to help in so many other ways. Paul Rae deserves special mention for the reconstruction of the walls of the Cladh Hallan roundhouse.

The late Gill MacLean and her late husband Donald were a mine of information on the history of South Uist. Bob Dodgshon's research into the region's history has also been an invaluable aid. The South Uist Historical Society has been a constant source of encouragement and support. In particular, Effie MacMillan, Neil MacMillan, Father John Galbraith, James MacDonald, Willeam MacDonald, Michael McInnes, Paul MacCallum and Bill Neil have all taken a supportive interest in our work, together with Dana MacPhee of Museum nan Eilean. Uist Builders, Laing Motors, Norman and Donald MacAskill, Audrey Kennedy, Delina and Andrew Laing and all the landladies – Mrs Morrison, Mrs MacKinnon, Mrs MacIsaac, Mrs MacKenzie, Mrs Fraser, Mrs MacPhee, Mrs Peteranna, Mrs Campbell, the MacMillans and the Masseys – have provided the infrastructure that is vital for the project's smooth running. Angus MacIntyre and family in Cille Pheadair and Neil MacMillan and family in Milton have provided space in their farmyards for essential work on the finds from the excavations, and Ruairidh MacKay spent hours doing the wettest and hardest of jobs. Ronald and Maggie MacDonald are thanked for access to the Flora MacDonald site. In Canada, Professors Steve Davis and Jack Bumsted collaborated on the project. Without the permissions of South Uist Estates (and the help of Tim Atkinson, the factor), the grazing committees and the individual crofters, none of this would have even begun.

Our funding has come from very many sources: the Royal Archaeological Institute, the Society of Antiquaries of Scotland, the Clan Donald Society, LEADER, NERC, the Earthwatch Volunteer Corps, the Katherine MacKichan Trust and above all Historic Scotland, whose staff – especially Patrick Ashmore, Sally Foster, Noel Fojut and Rod McCullagh – have been so supportive of the project. We have enjoyed every minute of working and living in South Uist and we owe a debt to the living as well as to the dead of the island.

Finally we thank Andrew Fleming for reading and commenting on an early draft of the manuscript, as well as for guiding our work on South Uist from its inception.

PICTURE CREDITS

Most of the black and white photographs were taken by MPP. NS took *1, 9, 10, 11, 14, 16, 20-22, 60, 63-66, 70, 71, 75-77, 88, 90* and *108*. JS took *97, 99, 101-103* and *107*. JR took *91, 92* and *95*. The remainder were taken by John Moreland (*2*), David Gilbertson (*8*), Kate Seddon (*7*), Victoria Parsons (*42*), Ian Dennis (*83*), Marek Zvelebil (*57*) and Stornoway Museum (*41*). The colour photographs (including the front cover picture) were all taken by MPP except for *2* and *15* (NS), *12-14* (Ian Dennis), *18* (JS), *3* (John Moreland), *11* (Patrick Foster) and *17* (Andrew Fleming).

The draughting team were Ian Dennis (*4, 15, 17, 18, 29, 62, 74* and *89*), Irene de Luis (*19, 26, 31, 78, 82, 96* and *112*), Mark Brennand (*12, 49, 56, 79, 81, 86*), Melanie Giles (*50* and *59*) and Adrian Chadwick (*113*). Other illustrations were produced by Anna Badcock (*98, 106*), Emma Graham (*34*), Mike Hamilton (*73*), Jo Mincher (*100* and *105*), JM (*58*) and HS (*33*). We are grateful to Andrew Fleming and AW, as well as the Society of Antiquaries of Scotland, for reproduction of *94*. We also thank David Lockwood of Dumfries Museum (*5*), the School of Scottish Studies, University of Edinburgh (*110*), Tim Neighbour, the Centre for Field Archaeology (Edinburgh) and Historic Scotland (*61*), Historic Scotland (*85*), the University of St Andrews (*104*), the Talbot Rice Gallery, University of Edinburgh (*111*), Crown copyright: RCAHMS (*72*), Crown copyright: HMSO (*93*) and Ian Armit (*114*). We were unable to trace any holders of copyright for Andrew Melrose Limited (*6*).

GLOSSARY OF SOUTH UIST PLACE NAMES

Aird a Mhachair	Ardivachar	Groigearraidh	Grogarry
Aisgernis	Askernish	Hellibost	Hellibost
Baghasdal	North Boisdale	Iochdar	Eochar
Baile Gharbhaidh	Balgarva	Leth Mheadhanach	South Boisdale
Bornais	Bornish	Lionacuidhe	Linique
Cill Amhlaidh	Kilaulay	Loch Ainort	Loch Eynort
Cill Donnain	Kildonan	Loch Baghasdal	Loch Boisdale
Cille Bhanain	Kilivanan	Loch Bee	Loch Bee
Cille Bhrighde	West Kilbride	Ormacleit	Ormiclate
Cille Pheadair	Kilpheder	Peighinn nan Aoireann	Peninerine
Dalabrog	Daliburgh	Pol a'Charra	Polochar
Dreumasadal	Drimsdale	Smercleit	Smerclate
Druim Mor	Drimore	Sniseabhal	Snishaval
Eiriosgaigh	Eriskay	Stadhlaigearraidh	Stilligarry
Frobost	Frobost	Staoinebrig	Stoneybridge
Gearraidh Bhailteas	Milton or Garryvaltos	Thoirnis	Hornish
		Tobhta Bheag	Howbeg
Gearraidh na Monadh	Garrynamonie	Tobhta Mhor	Howmore
Gearraidh Sheile	Garryheillie	Tobhtahur	Totahur
Geirinis	West Geirinish	Trosairaidh	Trossary

BIBLIOGRAPHY

CHAPTER 1

Our own project has generated a large number of publications and summaries can be found in *Current Archaeology*, number 152 (1997; vol.13) on pages 293-307 and in number 193 (2004). The main publications are:

Gilbertson, D., Kent, M. and Grattan, J. (eds) 1996, *The Outer Hebrides: the last 14,000 years*, Sheffield: Sheffield Academic Press.

Mulville, J. 2002, 'The role of cetacea in prehistoric and historic Atlantic Scotland', *International Journal of Osteoarchaeology*, 12: 34-48.

Parker Pearson, M. and Sharples, N.M. with Mulville, J. and Smith, H. 1999, *Between Land and Sea: excavations at Dun Vulan, South Uist*, SEARCH volume 4, Sheffield: Sheffield Academic Press.

Parker Pearson, M. and Smith, H. (eds), Forthcoming, *From Machair to Mountains: survey and excavation on South Uist*, Sheffield: Continuum.

Parker Pearson, M. and Smith, H. with Brennand, M. and Mulville, J. Forthcoming, *Cille Pheadair: a Norse period farmstead on South Uist,* Sheffield: Continuum.

Sharples, N.M. 2004, *Excavations at Bornais, South Uist. Volume 1: Mound 3*, Cardiff Studies in Archaeology, Oxford: Oxbow.

Sharples, N.M. Forthcoming, *Excavations at Bornais, South Uist, Volume 2: Mounds 1 and 2*, Cardiff Studies in Archaeology, Oxford: Oxbow.

Other useful reading for the chapter is:

Armit, I. 1996, *The Archaeology of Skye and the Western Isles*, Edinburgh: Edinburgh University Press.

Barber, J. 2002, *Bronze Age Farms and Iron Age Farm Mounds of the Outer Hebrides*, Edinburgh: Scottish Archaeological Internet Reports. http:/www.sair/sair4/

Branigan, K. and Foster, P. 2002, *Barra and the Bishop's Isles: living on the margin*, Stroud: Tempus.

Cohen, A. 1986, *Symbolising Boundaries: identity and diversity in British cultures*, Manchester: Manchester University Press.

Obeyesekere, G. 1992, *The Apotheosis of Captain Cook*, Princeton: Princeton University Press.

RCAHM(S). 1928, *The Outer Hebrides, Skye and the Small Isles*, Edinburgh: HMSO.

Russell, M.W. 1997, *A Poem of Remote Lives: the enigma of Werner Kissling 1895-1988*, Glasgow: Neil Wilson Publishing.

Russell, M.W. 2002, *A Different Country: the photographs of Werner Kissling*, Edinburgh: Birlinn.

Sahlins, M. 1985, *Islands of History*, Chicago: University of Chicago Press.

Sahlins, M. 1995, *How 'Natives' Think*, Chicago: University of Chicago Press.

Thomas, F.W.L. 1868, 'On the primitive dwellings and hypogea of the Outer Hebrides', *Proceedings of the Society of Antiquaries of Scotland*, 7: 153-95.

CHAPTER 2

Angus, S. 1997, *The Outer Hebrides: the shaping of the islands*, Cambridge: White Horse Press.

Boyd, J.M. and Boyd, I.L. 1996, *The Hebrides – a habitable land?*, Edinburgh: Birlinn.

Boyd, J.M. and Boyd, I.L. 1996, *The Hebrides – a mosaic of islands,* Edinburgh: Birlinn.

Boyd, J.M. and Boyd, I.L. 1996. *The Hebrides – a natural tapestry,* Edinburgh: Birlinn.

Edwards, K. 1996, 'A Mesolithic of the Western and Northern Isles of Scotland? Evidence from pollen and charcoal', in T. Pollard and A. Morrison (eds) *The Early Prehistory of Scotland*, 23-38, Edinburgh: Edinburgh University Press.

Edwards, K.J., Whittington, G. and Hirons, K.R. 1995, 'The relationship between fire and long-term wet heath development in South Uist, Outer Hebrides, Scotland', in D.B.A. Thompson, A.J. Hester and M.B. Usher (eds) *Heaths and Moorlands: cultural landscapes,* Edinburgh: HMSO.

Edwards, K. and Ralston, I. (eds) 1997, *Scotland: environment and archaeology 8000 BC–AD 1000*, Chichester: Wiley.

Ritchie, W. 1966, 'The post-glacial rise in sea level and coastal changes in the Uists', *Transactions of the Institute of British Geographers,* 39: 76-86.

Ritchie, W. 1967, 'The machair of South Uist', *Scottish Geographical Magazine,* 83: 161-73.

Ritchie, W. 1976, 'The meaning and definition of machair', *Transactions and Proceedings of the Botanical Society of Edinburgh*, 42: 431-40.

Ritchie, W. 1979, 'Machair development and chronology in the Uists and adjacent islands', *Proceedings of the Royal Society of Edinburgh,* 77B: 107-22.

Ritchie, W. 1985, 'Inter-tidal and sub-tidal organic deposits and sea level changes in the Uists, Outer Hebrides', *Scottish Journal of Geology*, 21: 161-76.

CHAPTER 3

Armit, I. 1992, 'The Hebridean Neolithic', in N. Sharples and A. Sheridan (eds) *Vessels for the Ancestors*, 307-21, Edinburgh: Edinburgh University Press.

Ashmore, P. 1996, *Neolithic and Bronze Age Scotland*, London: Batsford and Historic Scotland.

Henshall, A.S. 1972, *The Chambered Cairns of Scotland, Volume 2*, Edinburgh: Edinburgh University Press.

CHAPTER 4

Shepherd, I.A.G. 1976, 'Preliminary results from the Beaker settlement at Rosinish, Benbecula', in C. Burgess and R. Miket (eds) *Settlement and Economy in the Third and Second Millennia BC,* 209-19, Oxford: British Archaeological Reports (British Series) 33.

Shepherd, I.A.G. and Tuckwell, A. 1977, 'Traces of Beaker cultivation at Rosinish, Benbecula' *Proceedings of the Society of Antiquaries of Scotland*, 108: 108-13.

Simpson, D.D.A. 1976, 'The later Neolithic and Beaker settlement at Northton, Isle of Harris', in C. Burgess and R. Miket (eds) *Settlement and Economy in the Third and Second Millennia BC*, 221-31, Oxford: British Archaeological Reports (British Series) 33.

CHAPTER 5

Barber, J. 2002, *Bronze Age Farms and Iron Age Farm Mounds of the Outer Hebrides*, Edinburgh: Scottish Archaeological Internet Reports. http:/www.sair/sair4/

Barber, J., Halstead, P., James, H. and Lee, F. 1989, 'An unusual Iron Age burial at Hornish Point, South Uist', *Antiquity,* 63: 773-8.

Pitts, M. 2002, 'Cladh Hallan', *Current Archaeology,* 179: 455.

CHAPTER 6

Fairhurst, H. 1971, 'The wheelhouse site A'Cheardach Bheag on Drimore machair, South Uist', *Glasgow Archaeological Journal*, 2: 72-106.

Lethbridge, T.C. 1952, 'Excavations at Kilpheder, South Uist, and the problem of the brochs and wheel-houses', *Proceedings of the Prehistoric Society*, 18: 176-93.

Young, A. and Richardson, K.M. 1960, 'A'Cheardach Mhor, Drimore, South Uist', *Proceedings of the Society of Antiquaries of Scotland,* 93: 135-73.

CHAPTER 7

Armit, I. (ed.) 1990, *Beyond the Brochs: the Later Iron Age in Atlantic Scotland*, Edinburgh: Edinburgh University Press.

Foster, S.M. 1996, *Picts, Gaels and Scots*, Edinburgh: Historic Scotland.

Hingley, R. 1996, 'Ancestors and identity in the later prehistory of Atlantic Scotland: the reuse and reinvention of Neolithic monuments and material culture', *World Archaeology*, 28: 231-43.

Neighbour, T. and Burgess, C. 1996, 'Traigh Bostadh', *Discovery and Excavation in Scotland 1996*: 113-14.

CHAPTER 8

Crawford, B.E. 1987, *Scandinavian Scotland*, Leicester: Leicester University Press.

Doxtater, D. 1990, 'Socio-political change and symbolic space in Norwegian farm culture after the Reformation', in M. Turan (ed.) *Vernacular Architecture: paradigms of environmental response,* 183-218, Aldershot: Avebury.

Graham-Campbell, J. and Batey, C.E. 1998, *Vikings in Scotland: an archaeological survey*, Edinburgh: Edinburgh University Press.

Maclaren, A. 1974, 'A Norse house on Drimore machair, South Uist', *Glasgow Archaeological Journal,* 3: 9-18.

McDonald, R.A. 1997, *The Kingdom of the Isles: Scotland's western seaboard, c. 1100- c. 1336*, Edinburgh: Tuckwell Press.

Sharples, N.M. and Parker Pearson, M. 1999, 'Norse settlement in the Outer Hebrides', *Norwegian Archaeological Review*, 32: 41-62.

CHAPTER 9

Dodgshon, R.A. 1977, 'Changes in Scottish township organization during the medieval and Early Modern periods', *Geografiska Annaler*, 58B: 51-65.

Dodgshon, R.A. 1981, *Land and Society in Early Scotland*, Oxford: Clarendon.

Dodgshon, R.A. 1993, 'West Highland and Hebridean settlement prior to crofting and the Clearances: a study in stability or change?', *Proceedings of the Society of Antiquaries of Scotland*, 123: 419-38.

Dodgshon, R.A. 1998, *From Chiefs to Landlords*, Edinburgh: Edinburgh University Press.

Fleming, A. and Woolf, A. 1992, 'Cille Donnain: a Late Norse church in South Uist', *Proceedings of the Society of Antiquaries of Scotland*, 122: 329-50.

Fojut, N. 1997, 'Howmore: romancing the stone', *Current Archaeology*, 152: 308-10.

Maclean, G. 1994, 'Making of the landscape: South Uist. A historical and environmental survey', unpublished manuscript, available in Kildonan Museum.

Macleod, F. 1997, *The Chapels in the Western Isles*, Stornoway: Acair.

Rixson, D. 1998, *The West Highland Galley*, Edinburgh: Birlinn.

Williams, R. 1984, *The Lords of the Isles: the Clan Donald and the early Kingdom of the Scots*, London: Chatto & Windus.

CHAPTER 10

Caird, J.B. 1979, 'Land use in the Uists since 1800', *Proceedings of the Royal Society of Edinburgh*, 77B: 505-26.

Dodgshon, R.A. 1992, 'Farming practices in the western highlands and islands before crofting: a study in cultural inertia or opportunity costs?', *Rural History*, 3: 173-89.

Fenton, A. 1978, *The Island Blackhouse*, Edinburgh: Historic Scotland.

Kissling, W. 1944, 'House traditions in the Outer Hebrides. The black house and the beehive hut', *Man,* 44: 134-40.

Maclean, G. 1989, 'Locheynort, South Uist: appraisal of Uist documentary sources, *c*.1600-1980', unpublished manuscript, available in Kildonan Museum.

MacLellan, A. 1997, *Stories from South Uist*, translated from the Gaelic by J. Lorne Campbell, Edinburgh: Birlinn.

MacLellan, A. 1997, *The Furrow Behind Me: the autobiography of a Hebridean crofter*, translated from the Gaelic by J. Lorne Campbell, Edinburgh: Birlinn.

Symonds, J. 1999, 'Surveying the remains of a Highland myth: investigations of the birth-place of Flora MacDonald, Airigh-mhuillin, South Uist', in M. Harper and M.E. Vance (eds) *Myth, Migration and the Making of Memory: Scotia and Nova Scotia c.1700-1990*, 73-88, Halifax and Edinburgh: Fernwood Publishing and John Donald.

Symonds, J. 1999, 'Toiling in the vale of tears: everyday life and resistance in South Uist, Outer Hebrides, 1760-1860', *International Journal of Historical Archaeology*, 3: 101-22.

Symonds, J. 2000, 'The dark island revisited: an approach to the historical archaeology of Milton, South Uist', in J.A. Atkinson, I. Banks and G. MacGregor (eds) *Townships to Farmsteads: rural settlement studies in Scotland, England and Wales*, 197-210, Oxford: British Archaeological Reports (British Series) 293.

Symonds, J. 2003, 'An imperial people? Highland Scots, emigration and the British colonial world', in S. Lawrence (ed.) *Archaeologies of the British*, London: Routledge.

CHAPTER 11

Carmichael, A. 1994, *Carmina Gadelica: hymns and incantations*, Edinburgh: Floris Books.

Dodgshon, R.A. 1975, 'Scandinavian 'solskifte' and the sunwise division of land in eastern Scotland', *Scottish Studies,* 19: 1-14.

Dodgshon, R.A. 1985, 'Symbolic classification and the development of early Celtic landscape', in E. Lyle (ed.) *Duality*, 61-83, Edinburgh: Traditional Cosmology Society.

Dodgshon, R.A. 1988, 'The Scottish farming township as metaphor', in L. Leneman (ed.) *Perspectives in Scottish Social History: essays in honour of Rosalind Mitchison*, 69-82, Aberdeen: Aberdeen University Press.

MacDonald, A. 1958, *Gaelic Words and Expressions from South Uist and Eriskay*, edited by J. Lorne Campbell, Dublin.

Sahlins, M. 1985, *Islands of History*, Chicago: University of Chicago Press.

Shaw, M.F. 1986, *Folksongs and Folklore of South Uist*, third edition, Aberdeen: Aberdeen University Press.

Symonds, J. 1999, 'Songs remembered in exile? Integrating unsung archives of Highland life', in A. Gazin-Schwartz and C. Holtorf (eds) *Archaeology and Folklore*, 106-28. London: Routledge.

INDEX